How to Say It at Work

*Putting Yourself Across with
Power Words, Phrases, Body Language,
and Communication Secrets*

JACK GRIFFIN

PRENTICE HALL PRESS

Library of Congress Cataloging-in-Publication Data

Griffin, Jack.
    How to say it at work / by Jack Griffin.
        p. cm.
    Includes index.
    ISBN 0-13-242546-7 (hardcover). — ISBN 0-7352-0012-2 (pbk.).
    1. Business communication. 2. Communication in organizations.
    3. Oral communication I. Title.
    HF5718.G748 1998
    658.4'52—dc21   98-9748
                                                              CIP

Acquisitions Editor: *Tom Power*
Production Editor: *Eve Mossman*
Formatting/Interior Design: *Robyn Beckerman*

© *1998 by Prentice Hall*

All rights reserved. No part of this book may be reproduced in any form or by any means, without permission in writing from the publisher.

Printed in the United States of America

10

ISBN 0-7352-0012-2

ATTENTION: CORPORATIONS AND SCHOOLS

Prentice Hall books are available at quantity discounts with bulk purchase for educational, business, or sales promotional use. For information, please write to: Prentice Hall Special Sales, 240 Frisch Court, Paramus, New Jersey 07652. Please supply: title of book, ISBN, quantity, how the book will be used, date needed.

PRENTICE HALL PRESS
Paramus, NJ 07652

On the World Wide Web at http://www.phdirect.com

Why This Book Is for You

When you speak, speak as if your life depended on it. Because it does—at least when you're on the job. Maybe what you communicate will make the difference between being able to pay your rent this month and not. Maybe it will make the difference between paying rent and owning a house. Or perhaps it will be the difference between a job and a career: spending your time and drawing a check or turning time into self-fulfillment and satisfaction. In business, the way you put yourself across is always about getting something you need or something you want. It's about making a difference in your life and the lives of those who depend on you.

Putting yourself across. Nothing you do in business is more important. And you have to do it every day. Good thing you've gotten hold of this book: the *complete* guide to power words and phrases, body language, and communication secrets. With it, you can explore strategies and ready-to-use models of verbal and nonverbal communication designed to be effective for today's businessperson. *How to Say It at Work* is a contemporary guide to persuasion, offering a minimum of theoretical speculation and a maximum of practical tips, advice, and examples taken *from* the real world for use *in* the real world.

REAL COMMUNICATION TOOLS FOR THE REAL WORLD

This book provides the tools for successful real-world communication and the techniques for applying them. Along the way, you'll also find diagnostic self-tests designed to save you time by helping you pinpoint just what skills you need to hone to make you consistently more effective as a communicator. Let's go back to that phrase "real world" for just a moment. Tools and techniques are fine, but they're not much use until they are actually *used*. At every step of the way, this book shows you how to apply the tools you acquire to specific business situations. The emphasis here is on practice rather than on theory.

The tools and techniques you'll acquire are of two kinds: equipment to *prepare* for communication and equipment you need when the time actually comes to put yourself across. In Part I you will find a special test to help you determine how effective your current verbal—and, just as important, your nonverbal—communications skills are. This book will introduce you to a core set of the words and phrases that should be a part of every business vocabulary.

SECRETS OF NONVERBAL COMMUNICATION

Effective communication is a lot more than a gift for gab. One of the paradoxes of our technically and culturally advanced civilization is that, as we have become more sophisticated, we have increasingly come to recognize how much in our highly mechanized, apparently abstract, and hyper-intellectualized daily lives is dependent on "primitive," "primal," or "unconscious" motives, forces, and signals. Of course, all of us learn at an early age that people sometimes say one thing while meaning another. Sometimes, when they do this, they actually believe they're telling the truth. Sometimes they're deliberately lying. And at other times still, we can just *look* at a person, and we know—we're convinced—he or she believes passionately and every word he or she utters. The person "looks convincing," we say, and maybe we wish *we* could always be assured of looking that way when we have something important to communicate. For it is a fact: The most effective, moving, and persuasive communication occurs when verbal and nonverbal signals are in perfect sync. The result is communication synergy. For this reason, Part I of *How to Say It at Work* includes a special set of tools to help you build not only your verbal, but your *nonverbal* vocabulary, the looks and gestures by which we often telegraph our "real" message.

Part I concludes with a checklist for effective communication. Use it to assist you to define your objectives, clarify your goals, and illuminate your options *before* you open your mouth to speak. Complete it, and you're about ready to start talking. Go on to Part II.

HOW TO HANDLE SPECIFIC SITUATIONS AND PEOPLE

Part II—the rest of the book—shows you how to put yourself across in every major business situation and to all the key players in business: supervisors, colleagues, subordinates, clients and customers, vendors and suppliers, and creditors and investors. Included are full chapters devoted on getting a great job for yourself and to hiring a great employee for your firm. Each chapter begins with a brief and highly revealing opportunity to "Self-Test Your Savvy," so that you'll know where you are before you begin. Then, instead of making you slog through theory and speculation—you don't have the time for that—you get lists of power words and phrases that are specific to the person or situation covered in the chapter. Next come the words and phrases to *avoid*, the pitfalls that can sabotage any negotiation, deal, or critical conversation. Two concise discussions follow: "Body Language Strategy" and "Body Language to Avoid." As with the power words and phrases lists, both of these are carefully geared to the specific situations and persons treated in the chapter.

After covering these essentials, each chapter launches into an in-depth consideration of the most effective steps and strategies in a given situation. The emphasis is always on examples and ready-to-use models for communication. Wherever possible, brief scripts are included to help you do what great communicators have always done: prepare to be spontaneous.

Finally, because *How to Say It at Work* is written for the real world, we confront the tough issues, ranging from overcoming indifference to handling hostility to dealing with inappropriate, unfair, even abusive behavior.

MASTERING THE MAGIC OF COMMUNICATION

Think of *How to Say It at Work* as a manual of magic. Successful communication transforms your thoughts, will, and desires into action. It moves people. It transforms the thoughts, will, and desires of others. What better word for this process than *magic*?

But, as with most magic, there is really nothing supernatural about it. The apparent miracles of communication are worked by means of tools skillfully handled. And nearly anyone can acquire the tools and become proficient in the techniques of using them. It's a matter of knowing how to think through goals and objectives, then practicing how to become conscious of the combined effect of the words and the nonverbal signals we receive and broadcast every day. This book will guide you—quickly and practically—through that process of self-awareness. What I can promise you is that learning to put yourself across will be both personally and professionally profitable.

Contents

PART I

Setting the Stage for Communication Success

P A R T   I I

P A R T   I I

How to Handle Specific Situations and People

Chapter 5
Putting Yourself Across . . . to Colleagues—147

Chapter 6
Putting Yourself Across . . . to Subordinates—173

Chapter 7
Putting Yourself Across . . . to Prospective Clients and Customers—221

Chapter 8
Putting Yourself Across . . . to Current Clients and Customers—245

Chapter 9
Putting Yourself Across . . . When Handling Credit, Collection, and Customer Complaints—279

Chapter 10
Putting Yourself Across . . . to Vendors and Suppliers—323

Chapter 11
Putting Yourself Across . . . to Lenders and Investors—355

Index—383

Setting the Stage for Communication Success

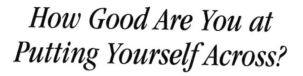

CHAPTER 1

How Good Are You at Putting Yourself Across?

SELF-TEST: GAUGING YOUR COMMUNICATION EFFECTIVENESS

The following is a simple diagnostic test. Its purpose is not to test your knowledge of communication theory or techniques, but to help you gauge how effectively you communicate in a day-to-day business context. For the most part, you will find it easy to guess the "right" answer. But getting the "right" answer is not the point of the test. Respond honestly, even if you feel that your response is not the best one possible. This is *not* a contest. The object is solely self-inventory.

SECTION ONE

1.	I communicate effectively.	T/F	___
2.	People really listen to me.	T/F	___
3.	People enjoy talking to me.	T/F	___
4.	I usually get my way.	T/F	___
5.	People believe what I say.	T/F	___
6.	People value my opinion.	T/F	___
7.	I speak with confidence.	T/F	___
8.	I feel good when I speak.	T/F	___
9.	I like the sound of my voice.	T/F	___
10.	I have no trouble saying what I mean.	T/F	___

11. I am persuasive.   T/F ____

12. I have a good vocabulary.   T/F ____

13. I look you in the eye when I speak.   T/F ____

14 I have a warm handshake.   T/F ____

15. I enjoy talking to new people.   T/F ____

16. I enjoy making small talk.   T/F ____

17. I look relaxed when I speak.   T/F ____

18. I feel relaxed when I speak.   T/F ____

19. I'm a good negotiator.   T/F ____

20. I enjoy talking about money.   T/F ____

21. I enjoy "haggling."   T/F ____

22. I enjoy friendly "haggling."   T/F ____

23. I usually get a good deal.   T/F ____

24. I usually get a fair deal.   T/F ____

Score 1 for each "True" response, 0 for "False":

TOTAL 1-24   ____

25. My voice is too high.   T/F ____

26. My voice is too soft.   T/F ____

27. I feel nervous when I speak.   T/F ____

28. I fidget when I speak.   T/F ____

29. I find it difficult to make eye contact.   T/F ____

30. I don't like shaking hands.   T/F ____

31. Sometimes I put my hand to my mouth when I speak.   T/F ____

32. Sometimes I touch my hair when I speak.   T/F ____

33. Sometimes I rub the back of my neck when I speak.   T/F ____

34. Sometimes I fold my arms across my chest when I speak. T/F ____

35. Sometimes I speak with my hands on my hips.	T/F	____
36. Sometimes I gesture with clenched fists.	T/F	____
37. I get angry easily.	T/F	____
38. I take arguments personally.	T/F	____
39. I have an angry voice.	T/F	____
40. I bite my lip when I get nervous.	T/F	____

Score 1 for each "True" response, 0 for "False":

TOTAL **25-40** ____

SECTION ONE TOTAL (SUBTRACT TOTAL **25-40** FROM TOTAL **1-24**) ____

SECTION TWO

The following are my favorite business words (True or False):

41. analysis	T/F	____
42. answer	T/F	____
43. brainstorm	T/F	____
44. collaborate	T/F	____
45. collaborative	T/F	____
46. confer	T/F	____
47. control	T/F	____
48. cooperate	T/F	____
49. cooperative	T/F	____
50. good listener	T/F	____
51. guide	T/F	____
52. hear	T/F	____
53. helpful	T/F	____
54. huddle	T/F	____

55. idea   T/F ____

56. learn   T/F ____

57. listen   T/F ____

58. manage   T/F ____

59. offer   T/F ____

60. open mind   T/F ____

61. productive   T/F ____

62. solve   T/F ____

63. synergy   T/F ____

64. team   T/F ____

65. team player   T/F ____

66. team up   T/F ____

67. thanks   T/F ____

68. together   T/F ____

69. work together   T/F ____

70. cost-effective   T/F ____

71. effective   T/F ____

72. emerge   T/F ____

73. evaluate   T/F ____

74. expedite   T/F ____

75. experience   T/F ____

75. feasible   T/F ____

76. improve   T/F ____

77. increase   T/F ____

78. productive   T/F ____

79. profitable   T/F ____

80. reduce   T/F ____

81. smart	T/F	____
82. successful	T/F	____
83. valuable	T/F	____
84. value	T/F	____
85. vigorous	T/F	____

Score 1 for each "True" response, 0 for "False":

TOTAL **41–85**   ____

The following words are part of my regular business vocabulary (True or False):

86. mine	T/F	____
87. you	T/F	____
88. yours	T/F	____
89. afraid	T/F	____
90. bad luck	T/F	____
91. blame	T/F	____
92. cannot	T/F	____
93. cheated	T/F	____
94. circumstances	T/F	____
95. cornered	T/F	____
96. crisis	T/F	____
97. delay	T/F	____
98. delinquent	T/F	____
99. demand	T/F	____
100. disaster	T/F	____
101. excuse	T/F	____
102. experiment	T/F	____
103. fail	T/F	____

104. fault   T/F ____

105. fear   T/F ____

106. final   T/F ____

107. forgot   T/F ____

108. frustrating   T/F ____

109. guess   T/F ____

110. hopeless   T/F ____

111. impossible   T/F ____

112. impractical   T/F ____

113. inadequate   T/F ____

114. insist   T/F ____

115. loser   T/F ____

116. loss   T/F ____

117. lost   T/F ____

118. make do   T/F ____

119. must   T/F ____

120. nervous   T/F ____

121. no   T/F ____

122. non-negotiable   T/F ____

123. one-time offer   T/F ____

124. overloaded   T/F ____

125. panic   T/F ____

126. relax   T/F ____

127. slipped   T/F ____

128. sorry   T/F ____

129. stupid   T/F ____

130. tired   T/F ____

131. unaware	T/F	____
132. unfair	T/F	____
133. unreasonable	T/F	____
134. wasted	T/F	____

Score 1 for each "True" response, 0 for "False":

TOTAL **86-134** ____

SECTION TWO TOTAL (SUBTRACT TOTAL **86-134** FROM TOTAL **41-85**) ____

GRAND TOTAL (ADD SECTION ONE TOTAL AND SECTION TWO TOTAL) ____

(Note: A *negative* score is possible.)

WHAT IT MEANS TO YOU

This test is a quick-and-dirty diagnostic tool. Look at your Grand Total score. If it is

Higher than +50: You are probably a highly effective business communicator.

+35 to +49: You are probably often effective as a business communicator.

+20 to +34: You are probably sometimes effective as a business communicator.

+10 to +19: You are probably only occasionally effective as a business communicator.

+1 to +9: You are probably often ineffective as a business communicator.

Negative numbers: You are probably rarely effective as a business communicator.

I like to think that anyone can benefit from reading this book. Those who are likely to benefit most, however, are businesspersons who have scored below +50 points on this diagnostic test. Throughout this book, you will find additional diagnostic tests designed to help you gauge your effectiveness in specific areas of business communication.

CHAPTER 2

Building Your Basic Verbal and Nonverbal Communication Vocabulary

We could begin with the various theories of communication and persuasion. There are a great many of these—no end, it would seem. We could begin by discussing such issues as the credibility of the communicator, the role of self-interest and fear in creating persuasive appeals, the importance of organizing your arguments, the effect of group membership and identification on the success or failure of your appeal, the effect of personality on susceptibility to persuasion, and the effect of the passage of time on opinion formation and retention. All of these things are important—if you have the time for them.

But that is a very big *if*. Whom are we kidding? It's no *if* at all. You *don't* have the time, certainly not enough time to approach business communication by a tortuous theoretical route. Let's not even start with strategy. Instead, we begin with the building blocks of communication: the words.

THE 50 WORDS EVERY BUSINESSPERSON SHOULD KNOW AND USE

The first three are ridiculously easy words:

we

us

our

Or are they so easy?

Communication is essentially an exchange between an *I* and a *you*. Even as communication attempts to bridge the gap separating the *I* from the *you*, it continually defines and reiterates that gap. *I* want this, and *you* want that. The most basic step you can take to begin effective communication is to translate the *I* and the *you* into a *we*. Wherever possible and however possible, begin communication by defining areas of common interest, concern, and benefit. It doesn't take a rocket scientist to tell you that the person you are talking to is more interested in what he or she needs and what he or she wants than in what you need and want. One way to appeal to this other person is to forsake and forget your needs and wants and devote your communication to the person. This, of course, is not always desirable or even possible. A more realistic goal is to find common ground, the places where *I* and *you* can become *we*, where interests, needs, and wants can be seen as mutual. This is a powerful basis for all communication, especially in business, which is rooted in the exchange of value for value.

As you go through this book, in situation after situation, in putting yourself across to person after person, you will find that *we*, *us*, and *our* are among the most powerful words you can use.

- To the degree that you are able to translate *I* and *you* into *we*, you will become persuasive and your point of view will become compelling to the other person.

- To the degree that you are unable to effect this feat of translation, you and the other or others will remain separated by a gulf of differing concerns and needs.

From *we*, *us*, and *our*, let's go to the next essential word:

rapport

You may or may not have occasion actually to use the word in everyday business communication, but you should know it and consider it. *Rapport* is a relationship of mutual trust or emotional affinity. Typically, rapport develops over a long period of time between friends, between spouses, between business partners, between teachers and students. The more rapport you build in this way, the better. However, many—probably most—business relationships don't develop over years or even months. Many are brief exchanges defined by the length of a single conversation. Usually, then, you don't have the luxury of time over which to develop rapport. You have to move quickly.

The quickest way to create rapport is to use *we, us,* and *our* instead of *I, me,* and *you.* Here's an example. Let's say you are speaking to a sales prospect:

You: What do you see as your greatest need in the such-and-such area?

Prospect: Definitely fulfillment—getting the orders out on time.

You: I understand. Working together, *we* could solve *that* problem. I did X, Y, and Z for Acme Widget, and I believe *we* could apply some of those solutions here.

The rapport-building approach used here can be studied by looking at the word *we* in this brief exchange. Quickly, you move from *I* and *you* to *we.* You avoid telling the prospect, *"You've* got a real problem here." Instead, you take a share in ownership of that problem by using *we.* Notice that the problem becomes *"that* problem" rather than *"your* problem." It is something objective, which both you and the prospect will deal with. The prospect is no longer alone with the problem. It has, in fact, become the cornerstone on which your rapport will be built.

We, us, and *our* are words of inclusion, cooperation, coordination, and alliance—the very essence of rapport. Other words that cultivate rapport and that are, therefore, essential to your basic business vocabulary are:

analysis	idea
answer	learn
brainstorm	listen
collaborate	manage
collaborative	offer
confer	open mind
control	productive
cooperate	solve
cooperative	synergy
good listener	team
guide	team player
hear	team up
helpful	thanks
huddle	together
	work together

All these words convey the power, benefit, and value of working together, of taking joint ownership of problems, of in effect, translating *I* and *you* into *we*. Beyond these words, which emphasize the collaborative and cooperative aspects of the business relationship, are the words that focus on the exchange of value that is another key positive element in the productive business relationship. These words include:

cost-effective	productive
effective	profitable
emerge	reduce
evaluate	smart
expedite	successful
experience	valuable
feasible	value
improve	vigorous
increase	

Before we look more closely at some of these words, we'd better ask: Are these the only fifty words you need in business? Of course they aren't. But they are words you *should* use, because they build positive relationships, which are the bases for productive subsequent communication.

The words of the group beginning with *analysis* and ending with *work together* all convey the benefits of collaboration. Words such as *analysis, answer, control, guide, huddle, manage,* and *solve* emphasize control and management, the power of shared responsibility. Other words stress joint invention and cooperative creativity: *brainstorm, collaborate, collaborative, confer, idea, learn, productive, synergy, together,* and *work together.* A few more words are vital—*good listener, hear, helpful, listen, team, team player,* and *thanks.* These are necessary to demonstrate that, while you are eager to translate *I* and *you* into *we,* you are not about to forget that the "other" person is *another* person. You want to convey that you will listen to that person with gratitude and that you see the relationship not as one of dominance and submission, but as a relation between one team member and another.

The words of the next group, beginning with *cost-effective* and ending with *vigorous,* shift the communication to the bottom-line products of effective collaboration. These words emphasize cost-effectiveness, cost savings, productivity, and profitability. Notice that *price* and *cost* (except as part of the compound *cost-effective*) are not among these basic words. Why? Effective bottom-line communication guides the conversation away from mere price and cost to the far more relevant concept of *value*. Whatever your business, it is *value* that you are selling, not cost and not price. It is *value* that elevates a business transaction into a business relationship.

Before we go on to the 50 words the businessperson should avoid, let's consider for a moment the difference between business based on transactions and business based on relationships. Here's a question with at least one obvious answer: *What is a good salesperson?* The obvious answer is *A good salesperson makes sales*. And it's a good answer, as far as it goes. The trouble is that it doesn't go very far. While it is true that a good salesperson makes sales, a *great* salesperson makes customers. What is a sale, after all? An event that is soon over and done with, a transaction. What is a customer? A human being who may produce sale after sale and then tell others about you, thereby producing even more sales. This is a relationship. Obviously, then, it is beneficial to communicate in order to create relationships, not merely to generate transactions.

- The language of collaboration is all about creating relationships.

THE 50 WORDS TO AVOID—AND WHY

You probably don't need the list that I'm about to give you. I can tell you what words to avoid, even without listing them. Steer clear of negative words, of words that deny, of words that refuse, of words that turn away from, of words that close doors instead of opening them. Steer clear of limiting words.

This does not mean that you should avoid facing problems or use language that sugarcoats and covers up difficulties. On the contrary, the successful businessperson welcomes problems.

- She calls them challenges.
- She calls them opportunities.

What you should avoid is language that describes problems not as challenges and opportunities, but as causes of inevitable loss and limitation.

If *we*, *us*, and *our* are the words of choice, it might logically follow that *I*, *mine*, *you*, and *yours* should top the list of words to be avoided. Logical or not, and like it or not, it is obvious that you will have occasion to use these words; however, you should avoid them in all cases where *we*, *us*, and *our* can be made to work. So, yes, wherever possible avoid:

I

mine

you

yours

Avoid all language that divides and limits, that defines a winner and a loser, that pits an *I* against a *you*. This includes:

afraid	impractical
bad luck	inadequate
blame	insist
cannot	loser
cheated	loss
circumstances	lost
cornered	make do
crisis	must
delay	nervous
delinquent	no
demand	non-negotiable
disaster	one-time offer
excuse	overloaded
experiment	panic
fail	relax
fault	slipped
fear	sorry
final	stupid
forgot	tired
frustrating	unaware

guess	unfair
hopeless	unreasonable
impossible	wasted

The object is not to avoid reality, even unpleasant reality, nor to distort reality by disguising problems.

- The purpose of avoiding a vocabulary of limitation is to build business relationships.

"What's in a name?" Shakespeare asked. While most people call a problem or crisis or glitch an *obstacle*, you should think of it as an *opportunity*. Difficulties are opportunities to demonstrate problem-solving skills and to build business relationships, to forge teamwork, and to create a sense of partnership.

- Approach difficulties with language that defines them as opportunities, not as dead ends.

THE 12 ESSENTIALS OF NONVERBAL COMMUNICATION

In a famous 1971 study, psychologist Albert Mehrabian found that when listeners judge the emotional content of a speech, they give the most weight to the speaker's facial expressions and body movement: his or her "body language." Just how much weight? Fifty-five percent. This means that 55 percent of the speech's power of persuasion—its effectiveness—depends on visual, not on verbal, cues.

So only 45 percent of the effectiveness of a speech comes from the words?

No.

The next most important factor, according to Mehrabian's test audiences, were "vocal qualities"—not words, but tone of voice, voice pitch, and the pace of delivery. These accounted for 38 percent of the speech's effectiveness.

Now, add 55 and 38 percent. This gives you 93 percent. According to Mehrabian's study, 93 percent of the effectiveness of a speech—ostensibly a *verbal* presentation—has nothing to do with the meaning of the words used. The words themselves accounted for a mere 7 percent of the effectiveness of a speech.

The lesson of Meharabian's study applies to everyday communication as well as to formal speech: The business communicator ignores body language and quality of voice at his or her peril.

- Movement, expression, and tone speak volumes, regardless of the words that are used or not used.

Here are a dozen basic rules to help you think about, develop, and hone your nonverbal "vocabulary":

1. Make an Effective Entrance

"That woman sure knows how to make an entrance!"

How many times have you heard a comment like that? Too often, I suspect. It's become such a cliché that we don't think about what it really means. Too bad, because it means a lot. How you enter a room makes a powerful statement about who you are and who you think you are. For some, making a powerful positive first impression comes naturally and is easy. For others, awkward and uncomfortable practice is required. But even if making a positive entrance and effective first impression is difficult, it's a lot easier to put in the effort to make such an impression than it is to attempt to undo a bad first impression. In many situations, you may never have the opportunity even to try.

2. Walk Tall (Even if You're Short)

Nonverbal communication begins before a single word is uttered. When you make your entrance or approach the person or persons with whom you want to communicate, begin by walking tall. If you're on the short side, you won't like to hear that tall people tend to command greater authority than short people. This isn't fair, of course, and it is even disheartening that people attach so much value to something so arbitrary and superficial as physical stature. But it's the way things are.

Are men under six feet tall and women under, say, five-nine doomed to fail as effective communicators? Of course not. But they do approach the task with a disadvantage.

Must these folks then take their first steps toward effective communication in elevator shoes? Not necessarily, but it wouldn't hurt for shorter men to wear shoes with built-up heels and for shorter women to favor high heels. Moreover, it is a good idea for short men and women generally to dress in ways that appear to make them taller.

- Avoid boxy-looking tailoring.
- Avoid horizontally striped patterns.
- Shorter men should avoid baggy, loosely cut pants, and shorter women should favor longer hemlines.

3. Enter with a Purpose

Far more important than dressing to accent stature, however, is to practice walking tall. This means never entering a room or approaching another person in a cringing, stooped, or slouching manner. Concentrate on maintaining an erect posture as you make your entrance, and forthrightly, without hesitation, and with a purposeful stride.

How do you acquire a "purposeful stride"? Have a purpose, and know where you are going.

- Try always to approach any communication situation having already formulated the purpose and the objective of the communication.
- If you have to do your thinking as you make your entrance, chances are that you'll appear hesitant or absentminded. Work out your thinking as much as you can beforehand.
- The initial message you want to deliver is nonverbal, but it *can* be put into words: *I know how to carry myself.*

4. Smile

Close your eyes for a moment and summon an image of someone who walks tall. Maybe you know somebody personally. Maybe you already walk tall. Or maybe, just maybe, your mind's eye focuses on John Wayne. This movie star was—and remains—an American icon, a tall man who knew how to walk like a tall man.

Too bad that's not the way *you* should walk tall. Think of John Wayne, and you may think about walking tall. but you also think about a tight-lipped, unsmiling, taciturn presence: the so-called "strong, silent type" that Hollywood has long favored as the ideal of American manhood. Such a look works wonders on the screen, but in everyday business contexts, coming on strong and silent is usually perceived as hostile, threatening, and unsympathetic. It sets up barriers to communication rather than creating bridges.

- Walk tall, but walk in smiling.

A grim, closed-mouth negotiator can expect little success, a frowning salesperson probably won't make the sale, and the last public speaker to win over an audience without cracking a smile was Sir Winston Churchill. (But he was a great world leader, and there was a very nasty war on.)

A smile is an invitation. Anything less than a smile sends the message that you intend to offer little or nothing and that you are receptive to little or nothing. If you come on like a tough nut to crack, many of the people you approach will decide that you just aren't worth dealing with.

To some people, a smile comes naturally. Others must make a conscious effort to put one on. Everyone whose facial muscles and nerves are healthy can manage a smile, of course, but a phony smile is usually transparently fake and will turn people off. If you're not naturally a smiler, what can you do to acquire a *genuinely* genial and pleasant facial expression?

- Begin by relaxing. Before you make your entrance, glance downward, move your jaw around, then move your tongue around the inside of your mouth. Inhale deeply, hold it, then let out your breath forcefully. Repeat these exercises a few times.
- When your facial muscles feel relaxed, think about something or someone or some place you enjoy. Imagine pleasurable times, people, and places. Chances are that the combination of facial relaxation and a pleasant frame of mind will bring the easy, welcoming smile that is a tremendous communication facilitator.

5. Make Eye Contact

As soon as you walk into a client's, associate's, or boss's office or approach anyone you need to communicate with, look him or her in the eyes. This accomplishes two things. First, it is an unfailing token of openness and honesty. ("Look me in the eye and say that.") Second, eye contact instantly transmits energy. We've all heard people speak about the "sparkle" in someone's eye, as if that sparkle were an unusual thing, a thing that made the person in question seem special. Actually, *all* of us have a sparkle in our eyes, but it is rarely noticed because most people do not make full eye contact when they meet or speak, and full eye contact is required to make that sparkle visible. To exploit the sparkle in your eyes, to convey honesty and transmit energy, make eye contact—immediately, before the first words are spoken.

6. Give a Great Handshake

There was a time when all good fathers took their sons aside—back in the days when little boys, not little girls, were expected to enter the world of commerce—and solemnly explained the vital importance of a good, solid handshake. The right handshake was a key to commercial success, a kind of universal, all-purpose *open sesame*. A hearty handshake was regarded almost as a mystical thing. ("Son, *this* is important!")

Such a rite of passage may seem corny or at least quaint to us nowadays. We enjoy seeing ourselves as too "sophisticated" to put much stock in a ritual like shaking hands: *I'll shake your hand, but just cut to the chase and show me the bottom line.* The fact is that, try as we might to assert our "civilized," "intellectual," and "verbal" selves, physical touch and physical warmth continue to make a powerful *human* impression on us all—even in so-called professional or business contexts. If you want to test this proposition, think of a memorable handshake in your life. You'll soon discover this isn't as silly as it sounds. Most of us remember the handshake of some individual we have met, remember it because it was exceptionally warm and powerful or, perhaps, colder and deader than any cold, dead fish. Either way, it made an impression. We remember touch—contact—as much as we do words, and maybe even more.

Fortunately, it is not difficult to deliver a hearty handshake that conveys straightforward warmth, openness, and a willingness to communicate.

STEP 1: Try to deliver a dry-palm handshake. It's a good idea to carry a handkerchief with you and use it to wipe your hands before you go into a meeting or conference that involves handshakes.

STEP 2: Grasp the other person's hand fully, at the palm rather than at the fingers.

STEP 3:   Deliver a *moderately* tight grip. A firm handshake does not require a bone-crushing grip, but you should not offer a passive dead fish, either.

STEP 4:   Hold the other person's hand a few fractions of a second longer than you are naturally inclined to do. This conveys additional sincerity and quite literally "holds" the other person's attention while greetings are exchanged.

STEP 5:   While giving the handshake, do not look down at the clasped hands but, rather, into the other person's eyes.

STEP 6:   Start talking *before* you let go: "It's great to meet you" or "Glad to be here."

7. *Think Before You Sit*

Making an entrance often concludes with seating oneself in an office or at a conference table. Just how you do this tells those present something about your attitude and approach to business. Be aware that the people already in the room cannot help but watch you sit. Perhaps it's a throwback to our common mammalian heritage: we look intently at anyone who enters "our" territory. Whatever the reason, *you* tend to be the focus of attention when you enter the room and take a seat.

Don't rush to that seat. Doing so will make you appear anxious. More important, if others in the room are already seated, your standing will give you a few moments to be looked up to—literally. By standing in a room in which the others are seated, you take on an aura of authority, however temporary.

Give some thought, too, to where you sit. If you have a choice, choose a firm chair rather than a sofa or a very soft chair. You want a chair that keeps you upright and that allows you to maintain an erect posture, not a chair that swallows you whole.

If you are to be seated at a table, it is not appropriate for you to usurp the seat at the head of the table—unless, of course, you are running the meeting. Beyond this, be aware that there is a psychological power geography at work around any conference table.

- The greatest power position is, of course, at the head of the table.
- The second most dominant position is at the other end of the table.

- Perhaps surprisingly, the seats to either side of the head of the table are the weakest positions at the table and should be avoided, if possible.

8. Convey Relaxed Energy

Energy is a positive quality that is conveyed largely through nonverbal signals. But you don't want to give the impression of restlessness or nervousness. The ideal energy to convey is relaxed energy, a combination of enthusiasm and confidence that may be summed up in the word *poise*.

Relaxed energy—poise—begins with breathing. Now, we all have breathing patterns that are natural and comfortable for us. This is our normal state, a state in which breathing is thoroughly automatic, so that we are largely or entirely unaware of it. When you become upset, nervous, or scared, however, breathing typically becomes shallower, shorter, and faster. You often become conscious of the change in breathing pattern. More important, such changes are noticeable not only to you but, most likely, to any other astute observer.

There is no advantage to being perceived as short of breath and anxious, but, fortunately, it is possible to train yourself to breathe slowly and deeply, even when you are nervous. This requires some thought, but it can be done, and doing so will benefit you in two ways.

- Not only will learning to control your breathing keep your nervousness from being communicated, it will also actually cause you to feel less nervous.

Anxiety is a devilish thing. We feel scared, which creates certain physical sensations and symptoms; then, as we become aware of these sensations and symptoms, we become even more anxious, which, in turn, intensifies the sensations and symptoms. A vicious cycle is born.

9. Use Your Head (and Face)

Nothing "speaks" body language more eloquently than the head and face. Think about the messages you are delivering.

- The head tilted to one side indicates interest and close listening. This is a desirable gesture. Just make certain to vary it. No body language gesture is positive if it is held statically.

- A *slightly* out-thrust chin conveys confidence, but don't go overboard. Boldly thrust out your chin, and you will probably be perceived as arrogant.
- Nodding up and down conveys agreement, while shaking the head from side to side conveys disagreement. This should come as news to no one; however, it is all too easy to fall into the trap of sending mixed signals. We've all talked with people who *say* yes even as they—ever so slightly—shake their head *no*. Become conscious of your body language in order to prevent such garbled "transmissions."

10. Use Your Hands

Next to the head and face, the hands are the most fluent conveyors of body language. Many people worry about "what to do with" their hands. Why worry? You can use them consciously to help harness or drain off nervous energy. Feel free to gesture with your hands in order to help drive home your verbal points.

- Open hands, palms up, suggest honesty and openness.
- Rubbing the hands together communicates positive expectancy.
- Putting the fingertips together steeple-fashion conveys confidence.

11. Stick to the Basics When Speaking in Public

Most of the body-language basics that apply in everyday communications are also useful in more formal public speaking situations.

- In a formal speaking situation, maintain eye contact with your audience. This is not always easy when you have to look down at your typescript; therefore, rehearse the speech and practice looking up frequently. Each time you look up from your typescript, try to make contact with a specific person in the audience. Don't stare out blankly. Vary the targets of your gaze, but do pick a specific target each time.
- Smile as often as possible—unless the content of the speech makes this clearly inappropriate.
- Use hand gestures to underscore key points. Choreograph and practice useful, expressive gestures as required.

- Adopt a firm, upright, but comfortable stance at the podium. Soldiers required to stand at attention for extended periods quickly learn to appear rigid without actually standing rigidly. Do not lock your knees, but, instead, flex them slightly. This will have the effect of relaxing you without leading to a slouch position.

12. Communicate with Clothes

Another aspect of nonverbal communication is dress. The general rule is to make an effort to identify the prevailing "dress code" of the individual or group with whom you'll be communicating. Dress appropriately for that context. A casual look may be appropriate in one context, but inappropriate, even self-destructive, in another.

Many sales professionals make it a practice to dress "a notch above" their customers. This is a safe, conservative rule of thumb for nonverbal communication.

13. Learn to Use Your Voice

Just as tall people tend to command more authority than shorter folk, people with deep voices are generally perceived as more persuasive than those whose voices are relatively high pitched. This is true of women as well as men. If your voice is pitched in the higher registers, consider consciously trying to speak in a lower pitch. Practice until you are comfortable.

- Pitching your voice lower has the added benefit of producing a more pleasing tone. It also has the effect of slowing you down, thereby encouraging the more precise articulation of each word.

- Lowering pitch also tends to minimize any nasal vocal quality, which many listeners find annoying. (If you suffer from persistent allergies or chronic breathing problems, the state of your health as well as the effectiveness of your communication may benefit from a visit to the doctor.)

- In formal speaking situations, be sure to speak loudly enough. Don't strain, but be aware that a speaker can do absolutely nothing more annoying than fail to make himself or herself heard. How loud is loud enough? You should consciously enjoy the full, resonant sound of your own voice. When you have reached that point, you are probably speaking loudly enough.

- Whether in conversation or in a formal speaking situation, most speakers can benefit from making a deliberate effort to slow down. For public speakers, the rule of thumb is not to exceed 150 words per minute, which means that it should take you a full two minutes to read a double-spaced, typewritten page of text. The 150 WPM rule is too slow for most casual conversation, which usually proceeds at about 200 words per minute.

BEWARE OF THESE 25 NONVERBAL PITFALLS

If body language can help you communicate effectively, it can, unfortunately, also sabotage and undermine your intended message. Trouble often begins before a single word is spoken.

Hesitancy and Evasiveness

1. Avoid the tentative, hesitant, "aw shucks" entrance. When you decide to enter a room, a meeting, a conference, or even simply to approach someone with whom you want to speak, carry the action through smoothly and forthrightly. Know what you want and make an effort to move as if you know what you want.

2. Do not fail to establish eye contact quickly. Avoidance of eye contact will be interpreted as fear, indecisiveness, weakness, dishonesty, or any number of other negative things.

Handshake Problems

3. The limp, dead-fish handshake is never welcome and always a disappointment. There is an anticipated pleasure in a warm, firm grip. Fail to deliver this, and you will initiate communications with a failure of expectation.

4. The only thing more offensive than the dead-fish grip is the bone crusher. Give up the painfully childish idea of trying to dominate the other person with a display of your manual strength.

5. Many men automatically offer women a loose, overly delicate handshake. In a business context, an excessively soft handshake is likely to be perceived as patronizing or chauvinistic. Men should use the same *moderately* firm grip they would deliver to another man.

Nervous Energy and Anxiety

6. A feeling of energy is valuable in any communication; however, avoid displaying what is generally called "nervous energy." Learn to overcome and discard such activities as tapping feet, darting eyes, drumming fingers, and fingers that fiddle with necktie, jewelry, or hair.

7. If you are subject to anxiety in meetings and interviews, practice breathing deeply and regularly. The rapid, shallow breathing associated with anxiety will not only increase your anxiety—thereby creating a vicious cycle that will tend to make your breathing even more rapid and shallow—but will communicate your anxiety, fear, and uncertainty. It will make you that much less persuasive.

8. Avoid sighing. It will be interpreted either as a sign of distress or of boredom.

Dangerous Distractions

9. Avoid yawning. The reasons are obvious.

10. Scratching your head indicates confusion or disbelief.

11. Biting your lip signals anxiety.

12. Rubbing the back of your head or neck suggests frustration, impatience.

13. A lowered chin conveys defensiveness or insecurity.

14. Narrowing of the eyes communicates disagreement, resentment, anger, or disapproval. Marked narrowing may suggest puzzlement.

15. Avoiding eye contact conveys insincerity, fear, evasiveness, or, at the very least, lack of interest in what's being discussed.

16. Eye contact is great, but a steady stare suggests an arrogant need to control, intimidate, and dominate. At its worst, vacant staring seems weird and will alienate the person or persons with whom you are speaking.

17. Raising the eyebrows indicates surprise. Nothing wrong with that, if you want to communicate surprise. In some contexts, raised eyebrows suggests disbelief. You may inadvertently offend the speaker.

18. Peering over the top of your eyeglasses suggests doubt and disbelief.

19. Crossing your arms in front of your chest communicates defiance, defensiveness, resistance, aggressiveness, or a closed mind.

20. Using the hands to rub eyes, ears, or the side of the nose conveys doubt. This can really sabotage your verbal message.

21. Hand wringing is a strong sign of anxiety verging on terror. Avoid it.

22. Avoid holding head position and facial expressions for a long time or repeating any single gesture over and over. The idea is to look alive and lively!

Bad Habits

23. Learn to recognize and deal with tics and nervous habits. Here's what to watch for and avoid: continuous hand motions, rubbing your face, putting your hands anywhere near your mouth, repeatedly shrugging your shoulders.

24. In formal speaking situations, beware of nervously shifting your weight from side to side. This is highly distracting to your listeners.

25. Avoid ending declarative sentences on a rising note. This is a verbal habit more common to women than men. It makes a statement sound tentative, even doubtful, as if the speaker were continually seeking approval.

PART TWO

How to Handle Specific Situations and People

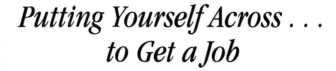

CHAPTER 3

Putting Yourself Across . . . to Get a Job

SELF-TEST YOUR INTERVIEWING SAVVY

The following is a simple diagnostic test. A smaller and more selective version of the self-test in Chapter 1, its purpose is not to test your knowledge of communication theory or techniques, but to help you gauge how effectively you communicate when interviewing for a job. For the most part, you will find it easy to guess the "right" answer. But getting the "right" answer is not the point of the test. Respond honestly, even if you feel that your response is not the best one possible. This is *not* a contest. The object is solely self-inventory.

1. I'm afraid I won't be able to answer the interviewer's questions.   T/F ____

2. I almost never have questions to ask at an interview.   T/F ____

3. I am prepared to answer the ten most commonly asked interview questions.   T/F ____

4. I am a good listener.   T/F ____

5. I come to the interview prepared with questions to ask .   T/F ____

6. I communicate high energy and vitality.   T/F ____

7. I dress to express myself. That's the most important thing. T/F ____

8. I face interviews with dread.   T/F ____

9. I feel that the interviewer wants to trip me up.   T/F ____

10. I feel good about my interview wardrobe.   T/F ____

11. I feel I have little to offer an employer.   T/F ____

12. I feel confident that I can answer any question the interviewer asks.   T/F ____

13. I formulate objectives *before* going into a job interview.   T/F ____

14. I get bad "stage fright" at job interviews.   T/F ____

15. My greatest concern in the interview is salary.   T/F ____

16. I handle interview anxiety well.   T/F ____

17. I have nothing to say at job interviews.   T/F ____

18. I have prepared a list of accomplishments.   T/F ____

19. When I go into an interview, I know how much salary to expect.   T/F ____

20. During job interviews, I talk about *accomplishments*, not *experience*.   T/F ____

21. I know how to send the message that *I will fit in.*   T/F ____

22. I know how to send the message that *I can do the job.*   T/F ____

23. I know how to *help* the interviewer interview me.   T/F ____

24. I know how to do effective research on a prospective employer.   T/F ____

25. I know how to send the message that *I will deliver.*   T/F ____

26. I know how much salary I want/need.   T/F ____

27. I look at a job interview as a sales situation.   T/F ____

28. I perform well in a job interview.   T/F ____

29. I prefer "winging it" to preparing for job interviews.   T/F ____

30. I prepare effectively for interviews.   T/F ____

31. I present myself as a problem solver.   T/F ____

32. I want to get to the salary discussion as quickly as possible.   T/F ____

Total: ____

Score 1 point for each "True" response and 0 for each "False" response, EXCEPT for questions 1, 2, 7, 8, 9, 11, 14, 15, 17, 29, and 32. For *these questions only*, SUBTRACT 1 point for each "True" response. Record your total. A score below +20 indicates that you would benefit from practicing the communication techniques discussed in this chapter. (Note: It is possible to have a negative score.)

WORDS TO USE DURING INTERVIEWS

accomplishments

advise

anticipate

awake

aware

built

consult

coordinate

coordinator

corporate

created

earned

efficient

energetic

evaluation

goal

improved

information

initiated

motivated

profit

reevaluated

responsive

revamped

revised

revitalized

seek

self-starter

sensitive

started

success

successfully

team

teamwork

PHRASES TO USE DURING INTERVIEWS

accept criticism

corporate image

eager to take on additional responsibility

extra effort

eyes open
for the first time
goal-oriented
head on
in touch
make use of criticism
management team
nothing stops me
take direction
take charge
team effort
walk through walls for this job

WORDS TO AVOID DURING INTERVIEWS

bad
bored
depressed
frustrated
hard

incompetent
slow
tired
trouble

PHRASES TO AVOID DURING INTERVIEWS

dead end
didn't see eye to eye
disagreed with my boss
get away with
no future
terrible boss
too difficult
too easy
too many hours
too much work

BODY-LANGUAGE STRATEGY FOR JOB INTERVIEWS

The employment interview is a veritable showcase for body language. You are under intense scrutiny. While it is true that few interviewers are psychologists, amateur or professional, and therefore do not deliberately set out to "read" your body language, the average interviewers are far more sensitive to nonverbal signals than they realize. They may not consciously articulate how they admired the confidence, honesty, and energy communicated by steady eye contact, nor is it likely that they will report to a colleague that they couldn't trust you because you repeatedly rubbed the back of your neck when you spoke; nevertheless, such signals broadcast volumes, especially in an interview. Let's put the situation in its crudest, crassest terms. Manufacturers and retailers know the importance of creating appealing packaging to sell a product. The package is the consumer's first contact with the merchandise. Is packaging superficial? Yes, of course. By definition, packaging is superficial: external, on the outside. And it is important precisely because it is, in this sense, superficial. Body language and other aspects of nonverbal communication are likewise superficial. They are the equivalent of packaging and are vital to "selling" the "merchandise."

In a job interview, communication begins before a single word is spoken. How you enter the employer's shop, office, or conference room makes a powerful nonverbal statement about who you are and, even more important, who you think you are.

You can greatly increase the effectiveness of your communication if you begin by establishing objectives and *then* plan your strategy. The more you know about what the prospective employer is looking for, the more effectively and persuasively you will be able to communicate. "Preparing for the Interview: Plan to Be Spontaneous," later in this chapter, will help you learn about the target employers need and want *before* the interview begins. But there is one thing *every* employer needs and wants, and it doesn't take inside information or research to discover what that is. *Every employer wants an employee who can do the job.*

Simple? Not just simple; it's self-evident. And even novice job hunters understand that their chief task at the interview is to persuade the employer that they can do the job. Most job hunters—novices as well as those with more experience—think that this is a matter of having an impressive work history and an ability to present it impressively. Certainly, these things help. However, the persuasion begins before a word is spoken. The chief objective toward which you should direct your body language strategy is to send a nonverbal message that *you can do the job.*

Begin by making yourself as impressive a physical presence as possible. This includes your grooming and dress, which we'll discuss later in the chapter, but it also depends greatly on how you carry yourself. As was observed in Chapter 2, those lucky enough to have inherited "tall" genes have the edge on those of us who are on the middling to short side. Tall people are more readily perceived as leaders and self-starters. This isn't fair, this isn't good, and this isn't even rational. But it's the way things are.

- If you are tall, do nothing to compromise your physical stature.
- Practice good habits of posture. Do what your mother told you to do: Stand up straight.

> **TIP**
>
> Many tall women, in particular, grow up self-conscious of their height. As a result, some tend to slump or stoop in an unconscious effort to minimize their stature. Well, in the world of business, tall women have an advantage over shorter women, just as tall men enjoy an edge over short men. Like their male counterparts, tall women should exploit, not compromise, their stature.

Is it impossible for shorter men and women to become powerful executives? Of course not. And you don't have to wear elevator shoes, either. However, both men and women should dress in ways that enhance height.

- This means emphasizing the vertical dimension rather than the horizontal.
- Avoid boxy tailoring.
- Shoes? Shorter men can benefit from thicker soles and a somewhat built-up heel, and women might favor a reasonably high heel. (Moderation is the rule here, though, and we'll discuss this matter further in "Dressing for the Interview," later in the chapter.)
- Tall or short, you'll benefit from a display of erect posture. It broadcasts the message that you *know how to carry yourself, that you are self-confident, that you feel good about yourself,* that you take pride in yourself, that, in short, you are a competent, capable person.

Walking tall does not mean that you should present a stiff, humorless, unfriendly, disdainful, and aloof image. Nor should you come across with an equally humorless arrogance and swagger. There is no anatomical or physiological reason that you should be unable to maintain impressive posture and smile at the same time.

- A key part of your body-language strategy should be a smile.

If all employers want employees who can do the job, they also want to hire people who will fit in. After all, for at least 40 hours out of most weeks in the year, you will be living with your boss, colleagues, and subordinates. Make it clear, before a word is exchanged, that you are friendly, approachable, courteous, and considerate. All of this is conveyed in a smile. To be sure, an interview is a stressful situation, and a smile may not come naturally at the moment. Don't wait for your feelings to change (they probably won't); just smile. You'll probably receive smiles in return, and that in itself will help ease the tension. Moreover, your own smile should make you feel at least a little better. While it is true that happy feelings produce a smile, it is also the case that the act of smiling can induce some semblance of happy feelings: *I can't be all that scared. I'm smiling!*

What else can you count on an employer to look for?

- Someone who can do the job.
- Someone who's approachable, pleasant, and courteous.
- Someone who is honest, straightforward, and vital.

As with the other basic requirements, you can begin to communicate, nonverbally and from the outset, your ability to deliver. The key here is to establish and maintain eye contact. In fact, as soon as you walk into the room, target the principal interviewer (if there is more than one in the room) and look him or her in the eyes. The result will be an instant transmission of energy: an impression of vitality, openness, and honesty.

Start with a Strong Handshake

You've now made your entrance. Only a few seconds have elapsed since you appeared in the room. Those few seconds, however, have proven rich with messages and, more important, rich with the potential for powerful, positive, and persuasive messages. Yet not a word has been spoken. The culmination of these first few critical, but nonverbal, seconds of the interview comes with the handshake.

There once was a time when businessmen—and, back then, the world of business was almost exclusively male—gave a good deal of thought and even devoted considerable conversation to the subject of the handshake. A firm, warm grip was considered absolutely essential to success in commerce. These days, we hear little talk about the handshake. The subject seems quaint at best, corny at worst. True enough, it *is* possible to regard the handshake as a meaningless social ritual. But you can also rethink it, reflecting on the handshake as a powerful form of nonverbal communication. It is, after all, one of the few intimate acts our society endorses between strangers. Through the handshake may be transmitted strength and warmth, of course, but beyond this, a sense of confidence and openness as well. A weak or indifferent handshake, in contrast, transmits indecisiveness and coolness. It tends to create doubt in the other person.

Fortunately, it is not difficult to give a hearty handshake.

STEP 1:   Begin with dry palms. Taking into one's grip the cold, clammy hand of another is not a pleasant sensation. Moreover, it tells the other person that you are anxious, nervous, scared. Carry a handkerchief and use it to wipe your hands before you enter the interview room.

STEP 2:   Within a few paces of the interviewer, take the initiative and extend your hand as you walk toward him or her.

STEP 3:   Deliver a full, *moderately* tight grip.

STEP 4:   So far, nothing out of the ordinary. But here is a tactic that will elevate your handshake a cut above an ordinary greeting. Be certain to hold the other person's hand a few fractions of a second longer than you are naturally inclined to do. Then, while holding the other person's hand, look him or her in the eye.

STEP 5:   Before you let go, start talking: "It's great to meet you" or "Glad to be here."

Don't Rush to Sit Down

Interviews are not conducted standing up. However, when you enter the interviewer's office, do not rush to a vacant seat. Stand as you exchange greetings. You may then be *invited* to sit. If you are not asked to sit, do so after a few seconds. Just remember that, as long as you are standing, the interviewer or interviewers will see you at your full height. If they sit down first, there will be a moment or two in which you will be looked up to—literally. Standing in a room in which the others are seated is a powerful gesture. It imbues you with an aura of strength and authority. Temporary though this is, it makes a favorable nonverbal impression.

Convey Relaxed Energy

During the course of the interview, it is to your advantage to communicate a sense of relaxed energy, as discussed in Chapter 2. The elements of relaxed energy include:

- Measured breathing. Breathing patterns are a remarkably accurate barometer of the emotions. Anxiety disrupts our normal breathing patterns, typically rendering them short, rapid, and shallow. The result of this pattern is increased anxiety. Moreover, any careful observer will readily pick up on your short, shallow breaths and conclude that you are anxious. You can—and should—consciously slow down and deepen your breathing. You'll not only feel better for it, you will also communicate confidence rather than insecurity.

- Eye contact. Maintaining eye contact can be a challenge. To begin with, don't turn the valuable notion of eye contact into a blank staring contest. It is perfectly all right to look aside from time to time or to look downward for a moment as you compose an answer to a question. Do, however, focus on the other's eyes as often as possible, especially when you are making an important point. Continued eye contact helps maintain the energy level of the interview.

- Sit—relatively—still. This does not mean sitting rigidly or stiff as a board. We'll talk in a moment about what specific movements to avoid, but, in general, sit upright—don't slump—but do relax.

- Seated, your energy and acuteness of attention should be expressed chiefly through facial expression, the angle of the head, and the use of the hands.

- Smile as much as possible.

- Open your eyes wide to express heightened interest.

- Nod—gently—to communicate understanding and assent.
- Lean forward to express intensity of interest.
- Gesture with open hands, palms upward. This suggests openness, honesty, and acceptance.
- Steepling your hands—putting the fingertips of the left and right hands together in the manner of a church steeple—is a powerful gesture that suggests thought, confidence, and active, ongoing appraisal of what is being said.

BODY LANGUAGE TO AVOID DURING JOB INTERVIEWS

Body language that is self-destructive in an interview generally is of two kinds: gestures that communicate anxiety and gestures that communicate a closedness or failure to connect.

Watch Out for Signals of Fear

Let's begin with the body language that signals fear, but let's pause a moment to consider the nature of fear.

What's so bad about it? Surely, any sensitive, humane interviewer will forgive a certain amount of anxiety. It's only natural, after all.

Consciously, most interviewers are indeed charitable and decent. But the power of nonverbal communication lies in its appeal to the layer beneath conscious thought. Even the most forgiving interviewer will, at some level, react negatively to messages of anxiety. Remember, every employer wants to feel that he or she is hiring a person who can do the job. That feeling depends, in part, on the feelings *you* project. Anxiety is contagious. If your body language conveys fear, the interviewer will soon be "infected" as well—only his or her anxiety will be more narrowly and specifically focused: *I just don't feel as if this guy can do the job. I am afraid to hire him.*

Here are some of the "fear broadcasters" to recognize and avoid:

- You may dismiss swinging legs, tapping a foot, or pumping your leg like a piston—poising your foot on its toes and pumping your leg up and down—as mere "nervous energy." Well, that's bad enough. In any conversation, such fidgeting is annoying. However, it's worse than that. Leg or foot movement sends a strong message of anxiety. It communicates an urgent desire to get up and leave, indeed, to run away.

- Twirling the hair—a gesture more common to women than to men—not only suggests acute anxiety, it effectively transmits that anxiety to others. Nobody likes to feel anxious, and the last thing you want to do in an interview is make the interviewer feel bad.

- Aimless hand gestures. Many interviewees worry needlessly about their hands, having heard somewhere that it is a bad thing to "talk with your hands." This isn't true at all. Meaningful gestures, gestures that underscore important points or add needed emphasis, aid effective communication. Nor should you worry, as some do, that "talking with your hands" is overly "ethnic." As long as hand gestures add to the meaning of your words, they are valid and unobtrusive adjuncts to communication. However, avoid constant or meaningless use of the hands, gestures accompanying virtually each and every word. These suggest nothing more or less than sustained anxiety.

- Few gestures communicate more intense distress than hand wringing. This is a fatal signal to send an interviewer.

- Anxiety tends to dry out the mouth and lips. Repeated lip licking strongly signals fear. Like hair twirling, it is also a gesture that makes others uncomfortable.

- Touching the mouth or nose or, indeed, bringing the hands near the face suggests anxiety or dishonesty, as if you have something to hide. Many otherwise intelligent people make themselves look dumb by covering their mouths when they speak.

- Finger or nail biting sends an anxiety message that is fatal in an interview. This is not a subtle piece of body language. It screams: *Steer clear of me!*

It is worth devoting time and effort to eliminating the kinds of body language that broadcast anxiety, not only because these gestures send negative signals to the interviewer, but also because your own awareness of such movements, especially on a less than fully conscious level, fans the flames of fear. Anxiety produces the actions, but the actions confirm and reinforce the anxiety. Break the cycle, and you will feel better as well as perform more effectively.

Don't Convey a Failure to Connect

Anxiety is not the only negative message body language can transmit to an interviewer. If you consistently fail to make eye contact or if you go out of your way to avoid eye contact, you may be perceived as awkwardly shy and not self-confident. Even worse, you may be seen as evasive or dishonest, as if you were hiding something.

- Beware of bringing your hands near your face. Some gestures of this kind suggest anxiety. Others suggest deception, lack of trust, disbelief, or confusion.
- Stroking the chin suggests deception or disbelief.
- Running the fingers through the hair or rubbing the back of the neck suggests confusion.
- Touching the nose suggests disbelief.
- Crossing the arms across the chest suggests defiance, disbelief, or resistance to an idea or suggestion.

As important as positive body language is when you make your entrance, negative body language can undermine everything that follows. Here are a few *don'ts*:

- Don't avoid eye contact quickly. The idea is to demonstrate that you "belong" in this new "territory," and immediate eye contact is an effective way of staking your claim.
- Don't offer a limp, dead-fish handshake.
- Men, don't patronize a woman interviewer by offering her a gentle handshake. Use the same *moderately* firm grip you deliver to another man. In a business context, an excessively soft handshake is likely to be perceived as chauvinistic and offensive.
- Don't rush to take a seat. If there are other people in the room who have not yet taken seats, avoid the embarrassing slapstick of musical chairs by remaining on your feet until the others sit.
- If you have a choice, don't sit on sofas or soft, overstuffed chairs. The ideal interview chair is slightly uncomfortable, prompting you to sit straight up at all times. You do not want to occupy a chair that swallows you up and makes you feel (and perhaps look) immature or even foolish.

PREPARING FOR AN INTERVIEW: PLAN TO BE SPONTANEOUS

In many ways, the prospect of an interview is exciting, a challenge that is filled with opportunity. For many job hunters, however, it is a challenge they would just as soon forgo, if that were possible. If you are among those who face interviews with dread, you are not alone. But it is not only many candidates who cringe at the thought of an interview; employers—probably most of them—hate interviewing. Far from seeing the interview as an ego-boosting opportunity to play God with the fate of the interviewee, most employers see interviewing job candidates as an unwelcome intrusion into their daily routine. Other matters always seems more urgent, and they tend to resent having to put their day on hold to talk to a job candidate, no matter how badly they need the new employee. Beyond this, most supervisors and executives are simply uncomfortable with the interview process. They should be. Many—perhaps most—enter the interview unprepared or, at least, poorly prepared, having been too busy to review their needs thoroughly, let alone the details of the candidate's background and qualifications.

If you want to score interview points, prepare yourself with questions, comments, and issues *you* can raise during the interview, so that the interviewer doesn't have to do all the work. The easier you make it on the anxious and beleaguered interviewer, the more positive the impression you'll create.

- Forty-seven out of every one hundred job interviews lead to a job.

Too many job candidates confuse lying awake nights fretting about the upcoming interview with constructively preparing for it. Use the days or weeks before an interview to perform the following 12 tasks:

1. Learn about the organization to which you are applying.
2. Learn about the role of your target position (the job for which you are applying) within the organization.
3. Try to find out about the organization's special needs, goals, and problems.
4. Formulate some ideas about how you can fulfill the needs, help achieve the goals, and solve the problems you learn about.

5. Prepare a concise list of your accomplishments. Limit the list to specific accomplishments that are *relevant* to the target position.

Before we go on to the next seven items, let's pause a moment to look at the word *accomplishments*. Most job candidates believe that the employer is interested in their *experience*. In fact, much more compelling than experience are accomplishments.

- Experience is passive—"I had this job and that job and that job"—whereas *accomplishments* are active, creative, and individual: "I achieved this, I did that, I accomplished this."
- Prepare for the interview by making a list of your *accomplishments*—successes you "achieved"—rather than jobs you "held."

6. Formulate your salary needs. We'll discuss this in "Money Talk," later in the chapter.
7. Read "To Give the Right Answers, Get the Right Questions," later in this chapter. It will help you prepare answers for the ten most frequently asked interview questions and will suggest ten questions *you* should ask.
8. Create an Interview Kit, which we discuss in the next section.
9. Ensure that you have appropriate attire for the interview. This is discussed later in the chapter, in "Dressing for the Interview."
10. Be sure that you have accurate information covering all of the interview logistics, including the exact time and place of the interview.
11. Make certain that you know how to get to the interview and how long it will take to get there. If you need directions, ask.
12. Obtain and carry with you all necessary names and contact numbers. These include the names and numbers of everyone you may have spoken to on the telephone in connection with the interview. If your interview invitation came by letter, be certain to bring that letter along.

ASSEMBLING A STRONG INTERVIEW KIT

Make the interview most effective by bringing along something besides yourself. The Interview Kit is a kind of scrapbook, which may contain such items as the following:

- An additional three copies of your résumé
- An "executive briefing" summarizing your résumé in a single narrative paragraph
- Letters of commendation
- Awards
- Copies of (nonproprietary and nonclassified) business presentations you have made
- Photos of equipment you have worked with
- Other specific, graphic evidence of your accomplishments

You keep control of the Interview Kit. You may give the interviewer one of the copies of your résumé, if he or she asks for it, but the Interview Kit itself stays in your hands. Share it with the interviewer, but always convey the idea that the work it contains is yours, that it is of value, and that it is not up for grabs.

Think of the Interview Kit as a "conversation piece": something to spark and focus discussion. It will not only help you illustrate how your accomplishments can be applied to your prospective employer's needs, goals, and problems, it will also take some of the burden of the interview off the shoulders of the interviewer. The prop helps you, and it helps the interviewer. The beauty of this is that it allows you to come into the interview armed with precisely the solution to the employer's currently most pressing problem: how to get through the interview. And it is much more convincing to *demonstrate* your prowess as a problem solver than it is merely to *tell* the interviewer that is what you are.

DOING PREINTERVIEW RESEARCH

Before you walk into any meaningful communication, arm yourself with a clear understanding of your objectives. In no case is this more true than in the employment interview. Most job candidates concentrate on figuring out how much salary to ask for. To be sure, this is important, and "Talking Money During the Interview," later in this chapter, gives you some guidelines not only for deciding how much to ask for—as well as when *and when not to ask*—but also advises you on how to figure out, *before* the interview, how much salary you need. But salary is not the only objective you need to define before the interview. There are issues both broader and more profound, including:

- Career goals
- Fit with background and education
- Lifestyle considerations: hours required, type of tasks, travel requirements, and so on
- Opportunities for growth on the job
- Location

Do not go into the interview without having heeded the advice of the Oracle at Delphi, to "Know thyself." Set clear—perhaps flexible, but clear—employment objectives *before* you step across the interviewer's threshold.

Know thyself, yes, by all means. But, so far as the interviewer or interviewers are concerned, it is even more important to show that you know *them.* Many candidates manage to do a clear and convincing job of presenting their qualifications and their needs, only to fail to secure an offer. Why?

- The employer is interested in your accomplishments, qualifications, and needs, but he or she is *far more* interested in his or her own needs and requirements; therefore, it is critically important that you take the time to learn about the target organization, with particular emphasis on what issues and needs are likely to be of most concern to the interviewers.

At the least, demonstrating a thorough knowledge of the target company conveys to the interviewers the intensity of your interest and the high level of your initiative. Gratifyingly, it suggests that yours will be a smooth, low, and easy learning curve. You are likely to hit the ground running, proving yourself an immediate asset to the operation.

Great! What a great idea! Who *wouldn't* like to go into an interview loaded with inside information? But how do you come across it?

Getting Inside Information

Getting on the inside from the outside is less difficult than you might think. Let's say XYZ Corp calls you for an interview. Great! But don't sit back and put your feet up on the desk. Get to work, checking out the following:

- XYZ's annual report
- XYZ's catalogs, brochures, ads, and other published material
- Material supplied by XYZ's Public Relations and/or Customer Service departments
- Journals and newsletter articles covering XYZ
- Up-to-date books (often available in the public library) that mention XYZ or that discuss the industry of which XYZ is a part
- Online sources, including the Internet and commercial online providers, such as America Online, Csi (Compuserve), Prodigy, and others. It is even possible that XYZ maintains its own online BBS (electronic bulletin board service). You can usually find this out by first searching for an XYZ Web site on the Internet.

As determining a clear set of objectives should precede an interview, so a decision as to just what kinds of information to look for should be made before you plunge into researching the target company. You'll want to learn something about:

- The business of the company: What does it do or make?
- The scope of the company: How large? Where does it do business?
- The target company's competition: Who are they, and what is the target company's standing among them?

Before you venture too far afield—or even down to the local public library—to obtain information in these areas, be certain to try to get a formal job description from the target company itself. Some employers are sufficiently on the ball to send you one without having been asked. Such firms are in the minority, however. Always ask for a full job description when a company calls to schedule an interview.

This does not necessarily mean that you'll get one, for many organizations fail to prepare this very basic document. If this is the case, you'll have to take even more initiative by doing your best to assemble a description.

- Tactfully pump the employer for information. You are called for an interview. You ask for a job description and are told: "We don't have one." Don't let this end the conversation. Respond: "Well, I certainly understand what a widget analyst does in most organizations, but is there anything special and specific I should know about the position at XYZ? The information will help me prepare for the interview, so that I can give you a better idea of just who I am and how I can meet your needs."

Pause here a moment to take note of how the request for information is framed, not merely as something that will help the job candidate, but as a way that will help the job candidate perform more efficiently and productively at the interview *for the benefit of the employer.*

You might also go beyond the employer.

- Tap sources available in the public library.
- Contact people who do the job in question—but *not* anyone who works for the target company. If you are applying for the position of widget analyst, call friends and friends of friends who already are widget analysts. If you don't know any, call a widget company and ask to speak to a widget analyst. Introduce yourself, explain your situation, and ask for help. Why should this stranger help you? The surprising fact is that most people welcome the opportunity to be helpful.

DRESSING FOR THE INTERVIEW

No one can prescribe a foolproof interview outfit, but it is possible to establish at least one enduring principle: Dress in a way that makes you comfortable and expresses how you feel about yourself, but that is also appropriate to the field or industry in which you are seeking employment.

It is easy to overrate the concept of "dressing for success." If you think that finding the right combination of clothes will get you a job, you are almost certainly mistaken. However, it is also easy to *underrate* the concept. If you dress in way that *fails* to convey the message that you've been able to get yourself together in a professional manner, you will turn off potential employer after potential employer.

But "getting yourself together" may not be quite enough. A great many career fields and professions have unspoken dress codes. To the degree that you succeed in demonstrating an understanding of the code, you are likely to shine in the estimation of the interviewer, even before a word is exchanged. Whether or not you are hired depends in large part on the employer's perception that you can do the job. It is also based, in no small part, on his or her perception that you will "fit in." Approach the organization *looking* as if you are already a part of it, and you will begin the interview with a significant head start.

But how do you crack a particular company's dress code? Begin by recognizing that this is one code that is hardly kept secret. On the contrary, it's on exhibit every day. If possible, pay a casual visit to the target company and observe. Or, if the firm publishes a newsletter or other literature illustrated with photographs, look at these.

The "code" is important, but it is not the foundation of effective interview dress.

- Begin by ensuring that whatever you wear is sharp and clean. Suits, for men and women, should be dry-cleaned immediately before the interview, and shirts and blouses should be freshly laundered. You don't have to go out and buy a brand-new interview wardrobe, but make certain that whatever you wear is in impeccable repair.

- Take care to attend to personal hygiene as well. Shower or bathe, of course, and be certain to use deodorant, but avoid excessive use of perfume, cologne, or after-shave.

Some interviewers find sitting in a small office with a scent-soaked job candidate more than a little annoying. Some may even be mildly or severely allergic to perfume. But more important than this, if you use perfume, cologne, or after-shave liberally, you risk sending the psychological message that you are trying to "cover up" something. Olfactory sensation reaches far below the conscious, rational level and can provoke a strong, irrational response. Don't avoid scent; if you have a favorite perfume, cologne, or after-shave that makes you feel good about yourself, use it—sparingly. The scent should be *barely* perceptible.

- Another highly charged grooming issue is hair length, especially for men. This was an explosive issue in the 1960s, and although long hair for men or very short hair for women is no longer shocking, very long hair on men is still perceived in many quarters as a token of rebellion or, at least, unacceptable sloppiness, and some employers may find "mannish" female hairdos intimidating.

TIP

Even extremely short hair on men may raise employer doubts, evoking extremist images of the world of the "skinhead."

To be sure, certain "creative" industries—fashion, the arts, magazine work, and so on—invite and welcome a liberal array of hair fashions for men as well as women, but more traditional and conservative industries favor cuts that are strictly middle of the road.

- While it is true that, by federal law, no employer may discriminate in hiring on the basis of age, gender, or race, legislation cannot thoroughly regulate unthinking prejudice. Generally, the trend in business has been toward wider acceptance and even active development of ethnic and cultural diversity in the workplace; nevertheless, you may want to avoid "ethnic" hairstyles that represent significant departures from what is generally perceived as the cultural mainstream.

- The same applies to deciding whether to dye or tint hair to disguise gray. It is against the law for employers to discriminate on the basis of age, but many employers place a premium on youth and the appearance of youth. On the other hand, you may find that gray hair is an advantage, suggesting an image of seasoned wisdom.

If you find the preceding observations culturally obnoxious, well, the prejudices that make such observations necessary *are* indeed obscene, let alone obnoxious. The point is that, generally speaking, the "best" interview look is the safest. If you err, err on the side of conservatism and traditionalism.

- Dress appropriately for the position you seek, not for the position you currently have.

If you are an office assistant accustomed to wearing a sports jacket, shirt and tie, and jeans, invest in the best conservatively cut suit you can afford when you interview for the position of assistant account executive. Remember that fashion is communication, so set clear objectives for what you want to communicate to the interviewer. Let those objectives guide your fashion choices.

How to Say It with Clothes

The following is a brief "vocabulary" of general clothing choices and the messages they convey.

FOR MEN:

1. Dark colors convey authority, and dark blue conveys the greatest degree of authority.

2. If you do opt for dark colors, avoid black, which suggests mourning and death—hardly positive interview messages.

3. Choose natural fabrics. They look better than synthetics and do not retain body odors as readily. Even more important, natural fibers project an image of honesty—advocacy of the "real thing"—as opposed to synthetics, which might be perceived as suggesting phoniness.

4. Solids and subtle patterns are best for most suits. Muted, narrow pinstripes ("banker stripes") are appropriate to conservative finance and politics.

5. Loud-checked patterns suggest questionable taste and, as some see it, questionable ethics (summoning up images of sleazy old-timey salesmen).

6. Choose a suit cut to your build. Slender European cuts are fine if you have a slender build; otherwise, go with a fuller—and more conservative—American cut.

7. Wear only a long-sleeved shirt.

8. Choose solid white or solid pale blue for the shirt color. No patterns or stripes.

9. Avoid monograms. Many interviewers see monograms as pompous. It is even more important to avoid *designer* monograms, which convey insecurity about your own taste—as if you need the designer's seal of approval on what you choose to wear.

10. Choose a cotton shirt. Avoid synthetics.

11. The interview shirt should be professionally laundered, with medium-crisp starch.

12. Some experts say that, of all articles of clothing, the necktie makes the strongest initial impression.

13. For the tie, choose 100 percent silk.

14. The tie should complement the suit, but not match it.

15. Tie widths vary with changing fashion, but a safe rule of thumb is that the width of the tie should approximate the width of the suit lapels.

16. Choose a traditional pattern, such as a solid, foulard, stripe, or muted paisley. Avoid polka dots, pictures (animals, the heads of hunting dogs, and so forth), and sporting images (golf clubs, polo mallets). Also avoid designer logos, which suggest fundamental insecurity about your own taste.

17. It is important to tie the tie carefully and neatly. For some years now, fashion has favored a small, tight knot. The tied necktie should not extend below your trouser belt.

18. Don't wear a bow tie.

19. Shoes should be of black or brown leather only.

20. Europeans marvel at the American businessman's obsession with highly polished shoes. Better make certain yours are polished.

21. Heels should be even and relatively unworn.

22. Managers tend toward lace-up wing-tip styles, while accountant types seem to favor tasseled slip-on dress shoes. Only those interviewing for "creative" positions—such as advertising art director—should wear premium loafer styles.

23. The color of the socks should complement the suit; usually, this means a choice of blue, black, dark gray, or dark brown.

24. A simple and slim attaché is the best choice. Avoid anything that suggests a salesman's clunky sample case.

25. Carry a plain white cotton or linen handkerchief.

26. A leather belt should match or complement the shoes, and the buckle should be simple, small, and entirely unobtrusive.

27. Suspenders (or "braces") are less popular than they were in the 1980s; some interviewers find them pretentious.

28. Simple cuff links and a wedding band (if you're married) are safe jewelry choices for men. Everything else—neck chains, stickpins, bracelets, and pinky rings—should be avoided.

TIP

Some interviewers may find French cuffs, with their attendant cuff links, a bit pretentious. You may wish to play it safe with plain buttoned barrel cuffs.

29. Avoid wearing a topcoat, if possible—it gets in the way—but don't freeze yourself in cold weather, either. A wool camel hair or cashmere topcoat is most attractive and impressive.

Women do not have to be as conservative as men are in dressing appropriately for the employment interview; however, they are also under greater economic pressure to invest in current fashions. Whereas a man can get away with a two- or three-year-old suit, a woman cannot. Is this fair? Absolutely not. But it's the way it is.

FOR WOMEN, THEN:

1. In most interview situations, a suit is appropriate.
2. A woman's suit need not be an imitation of a man's suit in cut or color; but do note that a charcoal-gray suit with a white blouse is the safest interview combination.
3. Solids, pinstripes, and muted plaids in a variety of colors are all acceptable for women's suits.
4. For women's suits, natural-synthetic fabric blends are ideal. Given the styling of women's suits, all-natural fabrics tend to wrinkle.
5. Skirt length varies from season to season, but you and the interviewer will be most comfortable if you choose a more conservative length than what you might wear on a social occasion or even in an *everyday* business situation.
6. Choose a long-sleeve blouse. Completely avoid sleeveless blouses.
7. The blouse should be in a natural fabric, preferably cotton or silk.
8. Blouses in a wide range of colors are acceptable, but white, pale blue, or pearl gray are universally accepted in the business world.
9. Keep the blouse simple.
10. A beautiful scarf can add a dramatic accent to the interview wardrobe. Don't match the scarf with the blouse and avoid large polka-dot patterns; small polka dots are acceptable.
11. Wear simple, elegant shoes. A closed-toe pump with a one-and-a-half-inch heel is a safe choice.
12. Avoid very high heels, especially if you are not accustomed to them.
13. The color of the shoes should complement your suit and accessories.

14. Hosiery should be unobtrusive; neutral or skin tones are best.

15. Take along an extra pair of pantyhose or stockings in your briefcase or purse.

16. Briefcase or purse? You can't carry both. A briefcase projects more authority than a purse and creates a stronger image of professionalism. Why not put the essential contents of your purse in a small clutch bag, which you stow in the briefcase?

17. The belt should complement the shoes.

> **TIP**
>
> Think twice before you choose a belt made of unusual or exotic animal skin—snakeskin, alligator, lizard, and the like—that may offend an interviewer who happens to be sensitive to environmental issues. Plain leather is best.

18. With jewelry, less is more. It is best to limit the number of rings you wear. Thumb rings are out.

19. Wear small, discreet earrings, if you like.

20. Avoid all long, dangling jewelry, which may jangle irritatingly or catch on clothing.

21. Avoid gaudy jewelry.

22. Simple necklaces and bracelets are fine, but never wear an anklet to an interview. Avoid charm bracelets, which create a juvenile image, and avoid jewelry that bears your initials.

23. As with jewelry, the rule for makeup is simple: Less is more. The idea is to look natural, so if you are comfortable without lipstick, avoid it or apply a subdued shade only—and that sparingly.

TO GIVE THE RIGHT ANSWERS, GET THE RIGHT QUESTIONS

What makes most job candidates most nervous about the prospect of an interview are the questions. Many candidates fear that the interviewer has carefully stockpiled a list of questions designed to trip them up.

- The fact is that few interviewers go out of their way to concoct difficult questions. Nor do they have any desire to watch you squirm.

But if most interviewers don't *mean* to ask you hard questions, they may end up asking vague and poorly prepared questions that are open to so many possibilities that you may be overwhelmed if you do not prepare for them in advance.

- It's a good idea simply to assume that the interviewer won't be very well prepared for the interview. That's true more often than not.

Unfortunately, an interview conducted by an unprepared interviewer is a disappointment. What the interviewer will recall, as he or she evaluates your candidacy, is that the interview was unimpressive, which must mean that *you* are unimpressive. (You can bet that the interviewer won't blame himself or herself!)

It's up to you to help the interviewer make your interview an impressive event. Here's how:

1. Prepare. Learn as much possible beforehand about the company and the job, then come to the interview armed with topics of conversation related to currently hot issues, leading trends, major challenges faced by the company or the industry, and so on.

2. Based on your preinterview research, anticipate questions and prepare answers that will play to your strengths. The object is to direct the interviewer to subjects you know well and that will give you an opportunity to demonstrate your abilities, talents, accomplishments, and qualifications.

3. Again based on your research, prepare specific questions about the job and about the industry. These questions should demonstrate that you have given the job and the industry careful and creative thought.

TIP

If you take the time and effort to prepare, you will most likely create a more stimulating and persuasive interview, and you will earn the gratitude of the interviewer for taking much of the burden from his or her shoulders.

Ten Basic Questions Interviewers Ask

Comb the shelves of your local bookstore and you'll find any number of volumes that offer interview questions and answers. The truth is that no book can give you a really useful set of "canned" Q and A, because employer needs and wants vary greatly in detail. However, there are certain basic questions that almost all employers get around to asking sooner or later. Of the following ten questions, expect to be asked at least five in the course of an interview:

1. **What can you tell me about yourself?** This is as basic as it gets. But if you don't prepare for it, this apparently simple question will start the interview out with a grinding halt. Maybe you'll be able to pull yourself together sufficiently to ramble on with a drawn-out autobiography, but that's *not* what the interviewer wants to hear.

The secret to answering this question is twofold.

First, come to the interview armed with a *memorized* answer that fits the following formula:

- My name is _____.
- I've worked for *X* years as a [job title].
- Currently, I'm a [job title] at [company].
- Before that, I was [job title] at [company].
- I love the challenge of my work, especially the major strengths I offer, including [A, B, and C].

Simple? Yes. And that's the point. The danger of this question is that, by opening up so many possibilities and directions, it will overwhelm you, in effect swamping your thought process.

You can really turn this question into an opportunity for persuasion by taking a second step. After delivering the formula answer, *help* the interviewer by focusing the question: "But what about me would be most relevant to you and what this company needs?" This will help you focus your answer and will ensure that you give the interviewer the information he or she really wants.

2. **Why do you want to leave your current job?** Beware of questions that invite negative responses: "I don't get along very well with my boss," or "My supervisor is an uncreative slug who won't let me try out new ideas," and so on. Turn such questions into opportunities for positive response. Instead of letting the question focus your answer on why you want to *leave* your present company, explain why you want to *move to* the target compa-

ny: "I am eager to take on more challenges, and I believe I will find them at Acme, Inc." The less negativity you project, the more positive the impression you will create.

If you have difficulty coming up with positive reasons for moving from one job to another, try the CLAMPS formula. It's an acronym that stands for

*C*hallenge

*L*ocation

*A*dvancement

*M*oney

*P*ride (or *P*restige)

*S*ecurity

Positive responses embodying any of these motivating factors should persuade the interviewer that you have a sound, intelligent, thoughtful reason for wanting to leave your current position.

3. What do you know about us?   This often comes at the beginning of an interview as an "icebreaker." There is no formulaic answer to this question, no substitute for having learned as much as you can about the target company before going to the interview.

4. How much experience do you have?   Here's another chance for preinterview research to pay off. Try to identify the target company's special needs and concerns, then marshal the experience you have that is relevant to these areas. But "experience" is really the wrong word. Translate "experience" into *accomplishments*—specific achievements, which will be much more persuasive in an interview. The more specific you can be the better.

Let's pause a moment to talk about being specific. The most specific you can get is to talk numbers, which is the very language of business.

- If at all possible, express your achievements in terms of money: money earned for your current or past employer, money saved, production increased, efficiency achieved—whatever. Try to quantify your accomplishments. Money, as the saying goes, talks.

But what if your research has failed to reveal any clear-cut areas of concern to the target company? Don't despair. Answer the question with a question in order to get the interviewer to define the areas of most concern to him or her:

- "Are you looking for overall experience or experience in some specific area of special interest to you?"

The interviewer's response should allow you to frame your answer in a way that will directly address the target company's needs.

5. What do you most like and most dislike about your current job?   Don't fall into the trap of emphasizing the negative. Even if you are very specific and honest in listing what you don't like about your current job, the interviewer will probably forget the details and remember only the negativity. The result: an *overall* impression of negativity, and that is not the impression you want to create. Even more important, while dissatisfaction with your current position may seem to *you* a very good reason to change jobs, it does not address the needs of the target *employer*. And while your needs are obviously important to you, it is the employer's needs that are most important in an interview. Your answers should always address those needs.

Your safest answer to this question? Pass up the negative part and just answer that you "like everything about my current position." Then go on to list the skills, abilities, and qualifications that your current or last position has given you or allowed you to hone these qualifications that you now offer the prospective employer. Conclude your answer with, "I'm now ready for a new set of challenges and an opportunity for greater advancement and greater responsibility."

6. How many hours a week do you need to get your job done?   This can be a difficult question to answer in a winning way. If you reply with something like 40 hours, you risk labeling yourself as a clock watcher, yet if you say 60, you may be implying that you're slow, inefficient, and easily overwhelmed. Your best course is not to reply with a specific number, but to deliver a more flexible and creative answer:

- "I try to plan my time efficiently. Usually, this works well. However, as you know, this business has crunch periods, and when that happens, I put in as many hours as necessary to get the job done."

7. How much are you making now and how much do you want? A bit later in the chapter, we'll talk about negotiating salary, but the important principle to note now is that, in a salary negotiation, the first person who talks money is at a disadvantage. You have two objectives in responding to this question:

- First, *divorce* the first part from the second part. Don't let your current salary define or limit a salary offer.

- Then, for the second part of the question, you should do everything you reasonably can to avoid responding with a specific figure. If you ask for too much—or too little—you could disqualify yourself as a candidate for the job. And, certainly, you don't want to saddle yourself with a low figure and start a new job feeling disappointed.

Go ahead and answer the first part of the question, but don't allow the reply much significance: "I'm earning $28,000, but I'm not certain that helps you evaluate my 'worth,' since the two jobs differ significantly in their responsibilities."

> **TIP**
>
> How honest should you be about stating your current or most recent salary? The answer: very honest. Why? You might get caught if you lie. This said, however, make certain that the compensation figure you mention includes all benefits: insurance, profit-sharing, bonuses, commissions, and so on. Furnish the maximum figure you can honestly report.

Moving to the second part of the question, *avoid* stating a figure. Instead, reply by itemizing the skills, talents, abilities, and responsibilities the target position entails:

- "If I understand the full scope of the position, my responsibilities would include . . . Have I overlooked anything?" Then come to your eminently logical conclusion: "Given all of this, what figure did you have in mind for someone with my qualifications in a position as important as this?"

Here is another reply that sidesteps a figure:

- "I expect a salary appropriate to my qualifications and demonstrated abilities. What figure did you have in mind?"

> **TIP**
>
> "Talking Money During the Interview," later in the chapter, includes advice on what to do if the interviewer insists on obtaining a figure from you.

8. What's the most difficult situation you ever faced on the job? This is a good question, and it invites an effective answer; however, avoid responding with a description of a situation so difficult that it resulted in personal failure or general disaster.

- Prepare in advance by thinking of a story of difficulty overcome, a tale with a happy ending—happy not only for you, but for your current or most recent employer.

- Under no circumstances should you answer this question with a discussion of personal or family difficulties.

- Also avoid discussing unresolved problems you've had with supervisors, peers, or subordinates.

> **TIP**
>
> Discussing a difficult situation involving a subordinate is fine, however, provided that the issues were resolved inventively and productively.

9. What are you looking for in this job?

- Remember: Regardless of how this question is phrased, the employer really is less interested in what *you* are looking for than in how hiring you can benefit *him or her*.

You may be "looking for" more money, more prestige, a nicer office—whatever. Mention none of these things. Instead, reply in a way that shows that you are looking for opportunities to serve the interests of the employer. Use such words as *contribute, enhance,* and *improve* in your response.

- "At XYZ, Inc., I discovered just how much one person could contribute to a company. As production supervisor, I increased efficiency an average of 16 percent, which meant a quarterly bottom-line increase of $29,000 in net revenue for our department. I'm looking to do even more for ABC Industries. *That's* what I'm looking for. *That's* what will give me satisfaction in this job."

10. Why should I hire you?   This little blockbuster is a favorite employer question. Whatever its tone, don't let it put you on the defensive. Treat it instead as the employer's request for help: "Help me to hire you."

- Keep your response brief.
- Recap any job requirements the interviewer may have enumerated earlier in the interview, then, point by point, match your skills, abilities, and qualifications to those items. The logic of such a reply is inescapable.

INAPPROPRIATE QUESTIONS (AND HOW TO ANSWER THEM)

Employers are forbidden by law to ask any questions bearing on your marital status, your sexual orientation, your age, your ethnic or national origins. Does this mean that you call the cops if you are asked one of these forbidden questions?

Well . . . not if you want the job.

Issues of discrimination are serious, but they are beyond the scope of this book. If you believe that you have been discriminated against, seek legal advice. Just be aware that discrimination cases are difficult, expensive, and time-consuming to prosecute. Right now, presumably, your objective is to secure employment, not to fight a legal battle. What follows, then, are suggestions for coping with inappropriate—even illegal—questions in ways that keep your candidacy alive.

- Obviously, if the employer's questions are truly outrageous or offensive, you should think very carefully before accepting an offer, if one is forthcoming.

1. Are you married? The usual purpose of this illegal question is to determine if your family duties will interfere with your job. It may also be an attempt to assess your sexual orientation. If you are married, reply with something like this:

- "Yes, I am. My wife/husband and I are both professionals who have spent X years very happily keeping our professional lives separate from our family lives."

If you are not married, a simple no is sufficient.

2. Do you plan to have children? Men are rarely asked this one. The employer most likely wants assurance that the woman he or she is interviewing will not quit soon after she is hired—and after the employer has spent time and money training and developing her—to raise a family. The question is inappropriate and at least verging on being illegal; however, the easiest course is simply to answer:

- "No, I don't currently have plans to raise a family."

If you do intend to have children, and you feel strongly inclined to answer frankly, you can still turn the question to your advantage:

- "Yes, eventually, I plan to raise a family. But these plans are directly dependent on the success of my career."

3. What is your sexual orientation? There's no graceful way to respond to this illegal question. Politely ask the interviewer to "explain the relevance of the issue to the position" or just reply that you "don't think the question is appropriate."

4. How old are you? Age discrimination is prohibited by law, and this illegal question exposes the employer to civil as well as criminal liability. But, again, do you really want to spend your time litigating, or do you want to find a job? If you want the job, find a way to answer the question positively:

- "Now that I'm in my forties, I've had more than a quarter century of experience in the widget industry."

Translate age into experience and youth into energy and flexibility.

5. Do you believe in God? What is your religious background?   If you *want* to answer, it is best to keep specifics to a minimum.

- "I worship regularly, but I make it a practice not to involve any of my personal beliefs in my work."

If your religious activity involves charitable work, you should discuss that work here, especially if it involves organization, leadership, and administration on your part.

If you have no religious beliefs, don't make an issue of the fact.

- "My personal spiritual beliefs are very important to me, but I don't let them get involved with my professional life, and I make it a practice not to discuss them."

This response is also appropriate if you simply do not wish to discuss your spiritual beliefs.

6. Were you born in the United States?   It is illegal to ask this question in the context of an employment interview, but if you were born in the United States, just say so. If not, but you are a citizen, reply:

- "No, but I became a citizen by very proud choice in [year]."

If you are not a citizen, you might want to reply:

- "No. I'm currently working toward becoming naturalized as a citizen."

TEN QUESTIONS YOU SHOULD ASK AT THE INTERVIEW

Perhaps the most self-destructive mistake you can make in an employment interview is to reply with a *no* to this question: "Do you have any questions?"

- Failure to ask questions at the interview tells the employer that you just don't care very much about the job or that you aren't very bright and are accustomed to accepting whatever anybody hands you. None of this bodes well for your chances of securing a job offer.

- Be certain to come to the interview prepared with relevant questions.

The key word is *relevant.* Do not ask off-the-wall questions or, even worse, questions to which you should already have the answer: "What does the telephone company do, anyway?"

Your interview questions should serve two purposes:

- To gather information that will help you evaluate a job offer
- To demonstrate—further—your qualifications, skills, and accomplishments

Here are some suggestions:

1. Have you had a chance to review my résumé?   Ask this early in the interview, and, please, phrase it in just this way. A great many interviewers fail to read your résumé before the interview or give it a glance so cursory that they might as well not have read it. Few interviewers, of course, will admit to this. Expect a response like this: "I haven't had the chance to review it as thoroughly as I'd like to."

Don't be offended or discouraged. Seize the opportunity to highlight your accomplishments: "Well, then, perhaps you'll find it helpful for me to hit the highlights of my qualifications."

2. Is there anything else I can tell you about my qualifications?   This is a good follow-up to the first question, or it may be asked as a stand-alone question toward the *end* of the interview. Not only does this question give you an opportunity to present yourself in the best possible light, it also requires the target employer to invest more time in you. The more time the interviewer invests, the more valuable you come to seem.

3. How would you describe the duties of this job?   Isn't this one of those obvious "questions to which you should already know the answer"? No. Even if you've received and read a job description, the question is still valuable. It asks the *interviewer* to describe the duties, to give you his or her take on the job, which, you may discover, is a far cry from what's in the official job description. Additionally, by asking the interviewer to describe the duties, you can get a better handle on which functions are perceived as most important and, therefore, really *are* the most important. This information will help you as you ponder an offer, and it will also furnish a spring-board for launching a description of your particular skills and qualifications.

- "I'm glad to hear that you consider client contact so important in this position. For me, client contact means building a business, each and every day, one client at a time."

4. What are the principal problems facing your staff right now? To begin with, understanding the target employer's problems gives you an opportunity to present yourself as a solution to them. Second, the question may reveal some situation that might make you think twice about taking the job. This could avert a bad career move.

5. What results would you like me to produce? This would be a valuable question if it accomplished nothing more than to demonstrate your intention to *do* a job rather than *take* a job. It focuses on what most concerns the employer: *his or her* needs and *his or her* problems. Your object is to respond point by point to whatever list of requirements, tasks, or criteria the question elicits.

6. What do you consider ideal background and experience for this position? The chief purpose of this question is to get the interviewer to paint an outline into which you—verbally—can step. Try to show just how you fit in, as if the job were created with you in mind.

7. How would you describe the climate in this company? Stormy? This question may catch the interviewer slightly off guard and reveal problems or it may elicit a description to which you can respond, showing how you'll fit right into the work environment:

- "I like high-pressure situations. To me, nothing's more energizing."

8. Was the person who held this job before me promoted? This is a lot better than saying, "What happened to the last guy who had this job?" Phrased positively, this question aims to find out why the job in question is vacant. The question should also give you an opportunity to assess the prospects for advancement at this company and from this position.

9. Could I meet with the person who held this job before me?   This request shows thoughtfulness and prudence, and your conversation with this person may provide valuable insight into the position.

Of course, it is possible that your request will not be honored. Perhaps the employee is no longer with the company. If the incumbent is still present, however, you may have reason to be suspicious of a negative response. Ask what the objections are.

10. Based on what I've told you, don't you think I could deliver all that you need in this position?   This is what sales professionals would call a "closer." It invites—though certainly does not guarantee—a positive response.

FIVE STEPS TO GETTING A JOB OFFER

Question number ten should not be asked until you have reached the final stage of the interview. But what is the final stage of the interview? It is the point at which you believe you have made the "sale," the point at which you believe the interviewer is eager—is ready—to make an offer. It's the have-to-have point. There are five steps to getting there:

Step 1: *Listen*. During the early part of the interview, listen as much as possible. Listen to what the interviewer says about his or her company, its needs, its goals, its problems. Listen to what the interviewer says he or she needs. Formulate a response based on what you've heard. Soon, you will begin transforming yourself from a stranger looking for a job to a potential employee and colleague committed to the success of the enterprise.

Listening should not be an entirely passive activity. Provide feedback that tells the interviewer that you are listening. At intervals, underscore the interviewer's most important points by repeating and rephrasing them: "What I hear you saying is . . ." or "If I'm understanding you correctly . . ."

Step 2: *Arouse attention*. Remind the interviewer of why *he* or *she* called *you* in for an interview. Here's what you say: "I'm really excited to be here, since it seemed to me that my qualifications so closely coincided with what you need." Or: "I'm thrilled to be here. What I have to offer seems to me a perfect match for this company." The reason you were called for an interview is that you are the right person for the job. *Now* you have the interviewer's attention.

Step 3: *Transform attention into interest.* Develop the interviewer's interest in you as a prospective employee by demonstrating your value as a member of the employer's team. This is done by making an effort to turn everything you say into an expression of accomplishment, achievement, or qualification.

- Don't just heap praise on yourself. Be specific: "I specialize in handling the details and anticipating needs, so that you can be more efficient."

Step 4: *Transform interest into involvement.* At this point, be on the lookout for "buy signals." These may be obvious. The interviewer says:

- "That interests me," or
- "I like that," or
- "Great!"

More frequently, the buy signals are subtler, more neutral:

- "Tell me more about . . ." or
- "Can you be more specific about . . ."

It doesn't matter. A buy signal is a buy signal, an indication that you've pressed the right button. Once you detect a buy signal, focus on the point or issue that triggered the positive response. Develop that point further. Get specific—not so much about yourself, but about what you can do for the target employer.

TIP

Nothing develops the interviewer's involvement more strongly than money: money you will bring into the company and money you will save for the company. Money is the language of business. Whenever possible, speak this language. Quantify your accomplishments in dollars.

Step 5: *Push for action.* This is the moment to pose question number ten or its equivalent:

- "Based on what I've told you, don't you think I could give you all that you need in this position?"

However, if your sense is that you haven't quite connected with the interviewer—haven't reach the have-to-have point—try this alternative:

- "I've enjoyed talking with you, and I believe I can bring much of value to this company. Tell me, please, is there anything I haven't addressed to your satisfaction? What could I tell you that would prompt you to make an offer?"

If you've gone through the first four phases of the interview, the object is to push toward closure, toward action. The best outcome is a job offer. But action may be deferred. Perhaps you will be told that time is required for review, or the matter must be discussed by the "committee." Respond with thanks and ask when you should expect a decision:

- "Thank you very much. This has been a pleasure. When should I expect your decision?"

Closure—a push toward action—conveys a necessary urgency, creating an impression of your value. You cannot—and will not—wait indefinitely for a decision.

TALKING MONEY DURING THE INTERVIEW

Just as you need to prepare for the interview by learning as much as you can about the target company and industry, you should also establish your salary requirements and expectations. Two steps are involved:

Step 1: Establish your minimum cash requirements. "Minimum" means the least you need to feel reasonably secure and comfortable—not merely to subsist.

This is a very personal matter, but if you are looking for a starting point, total all your monthly obligations, add 3 percent, which is what you should save each month, and then add another 10 percent for emergencies. Experts advise a minimum of a three-month cash reserve on hand to ensure that you are never a paycheck or two from financial collapse.

Step 2: Once you have determined your comfortable minimum requirements, try to ascertain the going price of your qualifications and skills on the current market.

This may have emerged clearly as a result of homework you've already done. If not, consult the following:

- Obtain a copy of the latest report of the Bureau of Labor Statistics from the local office of the U.S. Department of Labor.
- Log on to the Internet and access the BLS at **http://www.bls.gov** or at **umslvma.umsl.edu**. (for *The Occupational Outlook Handbook*).
- Consult Les Krantz's *Jobs Rated Almanac* (New York: Wiley, 1995).
- Consult professional and trade journals in your field or industry; many of these periodically publish salary surveys.
- Pick up the *National Business Employment Weekly*, which runs salary surveys. Back issues are available through the publisher, or you might check your local library.

Before the interview, then, you should have two figures: the minimum salary you need and the average salary associated with your target position. Using these two figures, formulate a third: a reasonable salary requirement, which meets your requirements and falls within industry guidelines.

- What do you do if your requirements are far distant from industry standards? The answer is either to alter your lifestyle in order to change your requirements, or find a better-paying career.

Armed as you are with a salary figure, you may walk into the interview tempted to "cut to the chase" and commence a discussion of salary. This would be a mistake, since the first person to mention a figure is always in the weaker negotiating position. Indeed, try to delay discussion of salary until the final phase of the interview, by which time, if all has gone well, you have brought the interviewer to the stage at which he or she is eager to make an offer.

For a discussion of delaying tactics, review question number 7 in "To Give the Right Answers, Get the Right Questions," earlier in this chapter.

- Do not alienate the interviewer by being overly evasive. If he or she insists on your naming a figure, respond—not with a single target, however, but with a salary range. You can calculate it this way: Let's say you've decided that you need a minimum of $36,000. Your research suggests that the salary range for the target position is $33,000 to $41,000. You tell the prospective employer your range bracket so that it interlocks with the upper range of what you might expect as an industry standard and exceeds your own minimum requirement. In this case, a good range would be $38,000 to $43,000.
- Make certain that your low figure is still above your "real" minimum. You can always negotiate downward, but once you have established a floor, you cannot raise it.

Once you are ready to discuss salary—when you feel the interviewer has reached the have-to-have point—respond to the salary question by attempting to discover the ballpark:

- "This is the first time we've really broached the subject. Could you tell me what the authorized range is for someone with my qualifications?"

It is critically important that you maintain a poker face. Avoid looking disappointed or elated in response to the figure or range that emerges.

- Don't grimace.
- Don't smile.
- Don't look down.
- Don't squint or shut your eyes.
- Don't look up at the ceiling or roll your eyes.
- Don't cross your arms (it indicates defiance).
- Don't bring your hand to your face or mouth (it indicates insecurity).
- Just maintain neutral eye contact through the negotiation.

Once a salary range is on the table, you may:

1. Accept the range. Say: "The upper end of this range is in the ballpark."

2. Counteroffer with your own range, which overlaps the top end of the target employer's.

3. Respond with polite neutrality, thanking the interviewer for the information and asking for time to consider the figure. Be certain to agree on a specific time by which you will respond.

4. Reject the range.

The first alternative is the easiest, and there is nothing wrong with choosing it, if you are pleased with the offer. But you should know that most employers don't open with their best offer. They usually leave some negotiating room above the top end of the range. Assuming the employer is within your ballpark, it is probably worth the extra effort to respond with the second option. This may open up a somewhat higher range.

Now, don't expect the employer to give you what you want just because you asked for it. You'll have to work. Quickly hit the highlights of your qualifications; remind the employer of why you are worth top dollar. Add to this a demonstration of your knowledge of industry standards:

- "Based on my research into industry salary surveys, my range is reasonable. Since we're agreed that I have the qualifications that will more than satisfy your needs, I can say with confidence that I'll be up, running, and producing for you within a week. This is why I feel that compensation above your upper range is appropriate and fair—fair for me and, certainly, a fair value for you."

Hardball negotiation is what the fourth option represents. Backing the employer against the wall may get you the offer you want, but, more likely, playing hardball will get you thrown out of the game. The negotiation will end. Once you flatly reject an offer, it is difficult or impossible to reverse yourself. Therefore, the better alternative, if the offer is substantially below your range, is to ask for time to think over the offer. Set a specific time when you will call with your response—usually 24 to 48 hours hence—and use that time to evaluate, without pressure, the pros and cons of the job. Equally important, the employer will also have time to think and ponder that he or she is in danger of losing you.

You can get some idea of how much negotiating room you have by considering the position and salary level.

- At the lower levels, salaries are usually firmly fixed and least negotiable.

- As you go up in compensation, salary ranges increase in flexibility.
- At the highest ranges—above $60,000—there is often quite substantial room for negotiation.

Consider:

- Entry-level position—under $20,000 a year: fixed salary level
- Middle-level position—$20,000-$60,000 a year: may negotiate as much as 15 percent above the initial offer
- Upper-level position—$60,000+: substantial increases possible

Don't expect a smooth road in negotiation. Objections to your salary requirements are almost always variations on one of four themes:

1. "Your figure exceeds the range authorized for the position."
2. "Your figure is outside our budget."
3. "Others similarly qualified within the company don't make that kind of money."
4. "Your salary history doesn't warrant what you are asking for."

In entry-level positions, there may be little or nothing you can do to overcome the first objection. Characteristically, the specific salaries authorized for entry-level jobs are essentially carved in stone. Rather than offer you more money, the employer will simply go on to the next candidate. In all cases and at all salary levels, the other three objections tend to be less inflexible.

The key feature of these objections is that the most common of them focus on *cost*. It is your task to refocus the employer on *cost* versus *benefit*; that is, *value*. Your special qualifications, talents, and abilities are an investment in greater profitability. Perhaps you "cost" a little more than the employer had planned to pay, but the value you give is much greater:

- "I understand that you budgeted under $38,000 for this position, but I think that we're both agreed that I bring to the table special qualifications and skills, as well as a deep commitment to performance. Those things represent value for you and amply justify the $40,000 figure I'm asking for."

If you're told that others currently employed don't make the salary you're asking for, redirect the issue to your own performance. What the employer pays others is a matter between the employer and the others. What he or she pays you concerns only the employer and you:

- "I understand your concern, but, based on our conversation so far, I understood that my salary would be based on *my* performance and *my* qualifications and that it is not capped by what others in the organization earn."

From here, you can launch an even more aggressive negotiating maneuver:

- "In fact, this brings up another issue that I'd like clarification on. How will I be rewarded for performance? Are raises based primarily on a cost-of-living formula, or are they tied to performance?"

Your toughest obstacle may not be what others earn, but what you have earned in the past. The objective of negotiation in this case is to divorce the issue of prospective compensation from the record of what you earned in the past:

- "I don't understand what bearing my past salary has on the work I will do for you. I see performance—performance and my qualifications—as relevant to salary. I think that we're both agreed that I offer great value to the company. Wouldn't you also agree that a combination of the qualifications I offer and industry standards is a fair way of arriving at an appropriate salary figure?"

Negotiate the base money issues first, but be aware that straight salary is not the whole compensation package. Where employers may be unwilling or unable to budge on salary, you may be able to get improvements in such areas as:

- Performance-based bonuses
- Longer paid vacation
- Flex time
- Profit sharing

- Day-care services
- Professional membership dues
- Relocation expenses (including such items as moving, temporary housing, guaranteed purchase of your former residence)

Don't fail to negotiate, but do be aware that limits and brick walls exist. If you find that you and the employer are simply too far apart, either offer thanks, take your leave, and continue your job search elsewhere, or work on negotiating the *future.* Accept the employer's best offer now, but accept it with the proviso that your salary will be reviewed in six months in light of your performance.

WHAT IF YOU'RE ASKED TO TAKE A DRUG TEST?

These days, it is not uncommon to be asked to take a drug test as part of an employment-screening process. This issue has been tested in the courts, and, as of this writing, the courts have upheld an employer's right to require drug testing. Today, about half of the *Fortune* 500 companies include some form of drug testing, either during or after the hiring process. Of course, no employer can force you to take a drug test, but if you decline the test, you will almost certainly be found guilty without benefit of a trial. You won't get an offer. If, on the other hand, you indicate your willingness to submit to a test, the chances are good that no test will actually be administered. Only about half the candidates who agree to take a test are actually given one.

If you do submit to a drug test, make certain that the testing company fully explains the test and provides you with a complete list of foods, over-the-counter medications, and prescription drug items that may cause *false positive* results.

- The fact is that at least 5 percent of drug tests yield false positives due to the presence of perfectly innocuous, perfectly legal substances. (One authority places the false-positive figure at a staggering 14 percent!)

If you are the victim of a false positive, insist on being given a back-up test of a *different* type. Document your request in writing.

CHAPTER 4

Putting Yourself Across . . . to Supervisors

SELF-TEST YOUR SAVVY IN COMMUNICATING WITH YOUR BOSS

The following is a simple diagnostic test. A smaller and more selective version of the self-test in Chapter 1, its purpose is not to test your knowledge of communication theory or techniques, but to help you gauge how effectively you communicate with supervisors in a day-to-day business context. For the most part, you will find it easy to guess the "right" answer. But getting the "right" answer is not the point of the test. Respond honestly, even if you feel that your response is not the best one possible. This is *not* a contest. The object is solely self-inventory.

1. I accept praise and compliments easily. I like getting them.   T/F ____

2. I'm afraid to talk to my boss.   T/F ____

3. I allow my boss to motivate me.   T/F ____

4. I always assume the boss is right.   T/F ____

5. I am the victim of a slave-driving boss.   T/F ____

6. I am depressed when my boss criticizes me.   T/F ____

7. I am creative.   T/F ____

8. My boss respects me.   T/F ____

9. My boss is easy to talk to.   T/F ____

10. My boss isn't easy to talk to, but we manage to communicate.   T/F ____

11. My boss makes me feel guilty.   T/F _____

12. My boss is an idiot.   T/F _____

13. My boss welcomes my ideas.   T/F _____

14. My boss is bigger than life.   T/F _____

15. My boss makes me angry.   T/F _____

16. I can't talk to my boss.   T/F _____

17. I'm easily discouraged.   T/F _____

18. I effectively convey my ideas to my boss.   T/F _____

19. I feel threatened by my boss.   T/F _____

20. I focus on facts rather than on personalities.   T/F _____

21. I focus on responsibility rather than on blame.   T/F _____

22. I frequently ask my boss for advice.   T/F _____

23. I hate talking to my boss.   T/F _____

24. I hate to apologize.   T/F _____

25. I have a good relationship with my boss.   T/F _____

26. There is nothing I can do to change my boss.   T/F _____

27. I keep my ideas to myself.   T/F _____

28. I know how to appeal to my boss's self-interest.   T/F _____

29. I know how to do the necessary research to back up
    my request for a raise.   T/F _____

30. I know how to decline assignments gracefully.   T/F _____

31. I know how to "handle" my boss.   T/F _____

32. I learn from criticism.   T/F _____

33. I like to confront my boss.   T/F _____

34. I look my boss in the eye when I speak to him/her.   T/F _____

35. I look for the opportunities in crisis.   T/F _____

36. My motto: *Take this job and shove it!*   T/F _____

37. I never run away from a good fight.   T/F ____

38. I'm not afraid to fail—once in a while.   T/F ____

39. I respect my boss.   T/F ____

40. I see criticism as opportunity.   T/F ____

41. I take ownership of problems, not blame.   T/F ____

42. I think of my boss as a human being.   T/F ____

43. I've told my boss, "I deserve a raise."   T/F ____

44. I try to withhold immediate judgment of my boss's ideas. T/F ____

Total: ____

Score 1 point for each "True" response and 0 for each "False" response, EXCEPT for questions 2, 4, 5, 6, 11, 12, 14, 15, 16, 17, 19, 23, 24, 26, 27, 33, 36, 37, and 43. For *these questions only*, SUBTRACT 1 point for each "True" response. Record your total. A score below +23 indicates that you would benefit from practicing the communication techniques discussed in this chapter. (Note: It is possible to have a negative score.)

WORDS TO USE WITH YOUR BOSS

able	appropriate	careful
accept	approve	caution
accomplished	armed	change
achieved	asset	circumstances
acknowledge	aware	commitment
advice	balance	committed
advise	best	confidence
agree	better	confident
alter	can	consider
alternatives	capable	continue
amazed	care	contributed
appreciate	career	convert

WORDS TO USE WITH YOUR BOSS, *cont'd*

correct	faith	judgment
create	family	kind
creativity	feasible	knowledge
dedicated	firm	learned
delay	flabbergasted	loyal
delighted	formulated	manage
deserved	future	management
different	generosity	memories
difficulties	generous	methodically
discuss	goals	motivation
do	goodwill	negotiate
duties	grateful	new
effective	gratified	objectives
efficient	great	obstacles
encourage	happy	offer
encouraging	help	opportunity
enjoyed	helpful	performance
enthusiastic	helps	perspective
equipped	hope	plan
established	hurdles	planning
evaluate	idea	pleasant
excited	ideas	pleased
exciting	if	pleasure
expand	imagination	pointers
expedite	imaginative	positive
experience	improve	possibility
experienced	innovate	possible
expertise	innovative	potential
extend	input	prepared
fair	investigate	pride

WORDS TO USE WITH YOUR BOSS, *cont'd*

priorities	responsibility	suspend
problems	responsible	talent
productive	revamp	temporary
profitable	review	tested
propose	revise	thank
proud	revitalize	thankful
prudent	reward	thanks
qualified	rewarding	think
questions	rework	thrilled
reasonable	right	time
recognition	service	transition
reconsider	shocked	unstinting
record	skill fairness	untiring
redo	snags	valuable
reevaluate	solve	value
regret	source	weigh
reschedule	special	willing
resolve	strategy	wisdom
resource	strength	wonderful
resourceful	studied	workable
resources	stunned	
responsibilities	support	

PHRASES TO USE WITH YOUR BOSS

able to make decisions

achieved goals

adjust our priorities

apportion our resources

approval from someone I respect

PHRASES TO USE WITH YOUR BOSS, *cont'd*

best use of resources

best for the company

best for the team

best job possible

best for the project

better suited

big picture

both sides of the desk

break new ground

by all means

by the book

can we negotiate

can count on me

commitment to productivity

command decisions

commitment to the company

commitment to this department

consider the alternatives

cost in resources

cost in time

cover ourselves thoroughly

cut costs

delightful memories

difficulties to work out

do a creditable job

do it right

do a more thorough job

expanded territory

from bottom to top

from now on

PHRASES TO USE WITH YOUR BOSS, *cont'd*

gained experience

get your input

give full credit to

give me a day to review the assignment

give this a trial

given a great deal of thought to

good point

greatest admiration

happy to try it your way

helps me see

I appreciate

I look forward to working on this

I look forward to working with you

I know you'll be pleased with the result

I need your advice

I need your take on

I think you'll find

I'll be back to you with some questions

I'll get on it immediately

I'm going to enjoy this

I'm pleased

I've been preparing for this

improve the bottom line

increased market

increased productivity

in the future

invaluable experience

it would help me be more effective

know I'll have questions

make better use of

PHRASES TO USE WITH YOUR BOSS, *cont'd*

management team
minimum risk
more efficient
more flexibility
move forward
opens up possibilities
our company
our department
our mission
play to my strengths
problems to resolve
questions to answer
reaction has been good
really run with
reevaluate priorities
room to maneuver
run all the numbers
serious considerations
sink my teeth into
sink our teeth into
stronger in this area
take the ball and run with it
take time to weigh
take the upside
team player
thank you for this opportunity
thank you for asking me
the intelligent way to
think this through
this is great

PHRASES TO USE WITH YOUR BOSS, *cont'd*

this is helpful

this will be fun

time to review

time to evaluate

trial period

try something new

user-friendly

very excited about this

well-founded

win-win situation

with great pleasure

without risk

you have a good point

you will appreciate

you can count on me

you can rely on me

your advice is welcome

WORDS TO AVOID WITH YOUR BOSS

afraid	can't	disaster
ask	cannot	doubt
backward	catastrophe	dull
bad	cheap	dumb
beg	cheated	embarrassed
better	confining	experiment
blame	crisis	exploded
bored	delay	fail
boss	demand	fault
brass	destroyed	fear

WORDS TO AVOID WITH YOUR BOSS, *cont'd*

final	mistaken	stuck
forgot	nervous	tedious
foul-up	non-negotiable	tired
frightened	overburdened	unappreciated
hopeless	overloaded	underpaid
impossible	panic	undeserved
inadequate	quit	unfair
incapable	refuse	unqualified
late	reject	unworkable
luck	ridiculous	unworthy
mess	risk	waste
misjudged	silly	wasted
mismanagement	snafu	won't
mistake	stodgy	worthless

PHRASES TO AVOID WITH YOUR BOSS

afraid to do it

back burner

bad pay

before you know it

beyond me

beyond repair

big mistake

big trouble

bit the big one

blew it

bombed out

can do better than this dead-end job

can't ask me to do something like this

PHRASES TO AVOID WITH YOUR BOSS, *cont'd*

can't be done

can't be fixed

can't do it

can't imagine how I could do it

cannot do it

doesn't thrill me

don't blame me

don't want to do it

doubt it will work

fatal error

get off my case

give me a break

give it a shot

have too many doubts

haven't got the experience

huge problem

I can't afford

I demand

I forgot

I can't

I insist

I need

I can't do any more

I can't do anything about it

I really don't deserve this

I was just lucky

I'll do the best I can

I'll have to quit

I'm fed up

I'm late

PHRASES TO AVOID WITH YOUR BOSS, *cont'd*

I'm only human
I'm overworked
I've had it
incapable of
it got by me
it was easy
it was a piece of cake
it was nothing
it slipped past me
just can't seem to get along
just don't have the qualifications
just one of those things
low wages
might work
my fault
no future
no opportunity
not my fault
not my problem
out of the question
quick and dirty
risk-adverse
save your compliments
screw up
set in our ways
struck out
take a risk for a change
take a chance
take a flier
that's my final word on the subject

PHRASES TO AVOID WITH YOUR BOSS, *cont'd*

there was nothing to it

think nothing of it

this is not negotiable

this is unfair

time flies

unavoidable error

unreasonable demand on me

waste of time

what can go wrong

what the hell

won't work that way

won't try it

worn out

wrong way

wrongheaded

you don't appreciate me

you expect too much

you have no choice

you have to

you must

BODY-LANGUAGE STRATEGY FOR COMMUNICATING WITH YOUR BOSS

Ask any number of people, and you will find many who confess to having a hard time "talking to the boss." No earth-shaking revelation here, but the fact is that *talking* is the wrong word. The trouble is not just talking to the boss, it's *communicating* with him or her. The difficulties actually begin before any words are spoken. Your attitude toward—your relationship with—your supervisor is typically telegraphed by your body language.

Before we look at the kinds of body language to avoid, which, alas, is the body language most people adopt in the presence of their bosses, let's look at the way things *should* be:

- Approach the supervisor politely, but as an equal.
- Knock on the door. When admitted, walk all the way in. Do not poke your head in the door. Do not linger on the threshold.
- Establish immediate eye contact.
- Maintain periodic eye contact, but do not stare.
- Shift eye contact to the forehead; that is, periodically focus your gaze just above the supervisor's eyes. This sends a subtle signal of domination.
- Do not rush to be seated. It is preferable to linger a moment or two standing in front of the supervisor's desk. He or she should look up to you. This puts you in a position of power.
- When seated, keep your hands fully visible. Use them to make gestures underscoring important points.
- Sit upright.
- Keep your hands away from your face, neck, hair, and mouth.
- Gesture frequently with an open, slightly upturned palm.

BODY LANGUAGE TO AVOID WITH YOUR BOSS

The basic desirable body-language strategy conveys both firmness and openness. Avoid stances and gestures that suggest the opposite:

- Avoid cringing. This includes poking your head in the doorway of the boss's office.
- Avoid looking down.
- Avoid looking to the side.
- Avoid rushing to be seated.
- Avoid slumping or slouching in the chair.
- Avoid leg movement when seated.
- Avoid bringing your hands anywhere near your face, mouth, neck, or hair. This suggests anxiety and evasion.

- Avoid crossing your arms in front of your chest. This suggests defiance.
- Avoid putting your hands in your pockets.
- Avoid aggressive gestures, including pointing, stabbing gestures, making a fist, pounding the desk.

SECRETS OF COMMUNICATING WITH EMOTIONALLY STUNTED SUPERVISORS

Communicating with a really competent supervisor is far easier than getting through to one who just doesn't have it all together. A supervisor's competence is in very large measure a function of his or her ability to facilitate communication. Unfortunately, most supervisors allow some particular aspect of their personality to dominate and control their interaction with subordinates. There are five major personality types among bosses.

- In the worst cases, the particular personality type completely takes over. There are, for example, plenty of supervisors who always act like a tyrant and are therefore tyrants, period.
- In most cases, the negative personality type emerges under pressure—such as the pressure of an unwelcome communication from a subordinate—and it can be said that the boss responds in the style of (for example) a tyrant.
- The object of communicating with the difficult supervisor is to identify what personality style is operative and respond to it. With luck, your response will get beyond the narrow personality style that has been adopted and will get through to the more fully rounded human being that lies behind it.

Type I: The Tyrant

Who is the tyrant? Well, he *thinks* he is your parent. This "parent" is not to be confused with your father or mother, who shows you love and concern, but with authority incarnate, absolute, commanding obedience and compliance, and never to be questioned. The tyrant's objective is to make you feel like a child in the narrowest and most negative sense: a *little* person wholly dependent on the parent and incapable of making decisions. To maintain this role, the tyrant relies on monologue and does what he can to avoid dialogue—though he may pepper you with lots of questions. The tyrant is interested in keeping you uneasy and unconfident. He wants you to feel that you are never doing an adequate job.

The tyrannical boss enjoys sitting behind a big desk, and his chair is always higher than yours, like that of a judge. He may have learned the trick of fixing his gaze not on your eyes, but on your forehead, which is a gesture of dominance. If he wears glasses, he may regard you by gazing over the top of his eyewear—another withering article of body language.

The tyrant boss is not subtle. He thrives on threats. That does not mean that he warns you daily about your performance or that he practices origami with a pink slip while he's talking to you. Expect to hear threatening phrases such as:

You'd better

Get a handle on

Get on top of

Get on the ball

Get on the stick

If, listening to the cliché-ridden speech of a tyrant boss, you get the feeling that he's speaking from a script, in a sense he *is*. The tyrant acts out of a hard-and-fast image of himself. He does not see *you*. Instead, he plays a role, and he expects you to respond by playing your role as well. If his role is that of the man in charge, yours is the obedient drone, the dependent, the victim.

- The most tyrannical bosses tend not to be those who really are in charge, such as owners of small businesses, but those with limited authority, who occupy a niche midway up the corporate food chain. While these bosses have power to wield, they also have pressure to bear, and the combination can bring out the worst in them. If the tyrant's boss knocks him, he's liable to pound you.

If all this sounds depressing, the good news is that the tyrant can be dealt with effectively, and you need not be his inevitable victim. Here's the most effective communication strategy:

STEP 1: Cut the boss down to size. This most emphatically does *not* involve anything you say or do *to* him. Focus on some failing or foible that pierces the tyrant's image and pretension—the grosser and sillier the better: Perhaps he picks his nose when he thinks others aren't looking. Maybe he probes his ear? Perhaps his voice is high, or his grammar is bad. Or just imagine what he looks like in silly pajamas. We are all imperfect. Faced with a tyrannical boss, start by visualizing in your mind's eye all the flaws.

STEP 2: If you can't find flaws, look harder.

STEP 3: If you still can't find them, make them up.

STEP 4: Practice these negative visualizations before you talk to your tyrant boss.

STEP 5: Now, here comes the maneuver that gives you the most power. While you are still visualizing the boss's foibles, find something to compliment him on. Make your boss feel good about something relatively neutral—his choice of necktie, the color of his jacket—even while you are imagining how that necktie or that jacket will look when your boss spills his lunchtime marinara sauce all over it.

Why do all this? The object is to put you in control of the encounter. You are accustomed to thinking of yourself as the victim of a tyrant. Now turn the tables by allowing your imagination, your power of fantasy, to tyrannize over your boss, but, at the same time, remain in conscious control of the situation by deliberately playing the hypocrite, paying compliments and expressing your admiration.

STEP 6: We're not through yet. Once you have imaginatively humbled your boss—in fact, fantasizing him as powerless—take steps to empower him *in his own eyes*. Do this by seeking his advice or asking his opinion. Show him that you value his thoughts. Suggest that you consider him someone from whom you have much to learn. This addresses his insecurity in a positive way. Instead of reinforcing the victimizer-victim relationship, it substitutes a more beneficent teacher-student relationship.

Your script: communicating with the tyrant

Here's an example of how a typical exchange with a tyrant might proceed:

Boss: I'm disappointed in you. I don't like what I see in your sales report for the northwest territory. I want my people selling out there.

You: I'm disappointed, too. Sales are not what I had projected. But I'm on top of it. I'm calling a meeting of the sales reps because I think it's time we took more control. I was about to come to you to seek your advice on the situation, which I'm sure is something you've handled plenty of times. Of course, I'd also like to get you in on the meeting, and I'd like to talk to you before the meeting so that you can help me clarify the issues and lay out the most effective approach. I want to expedite this. Can I see you at the end of the week and get your take on what I plan to do about the situation?

Note that the tyrant speaks like a parent: "I'm disappointed in you." He also verges on the vocabulary of a tin-horn dictator: "my people." These are his self-conceived roles. Don't reinforce his reality.

- Quietly and calmly decline to act the part of a naughty child or a downtrodden peasant.

- At the same time, however, as you dodge the tyrant's personal attack, address the *substance* of the issues he raised. If he's "disappointed," so are you.

- Conclude by showing that, although you are taking charge of the situation, you can do so far more effectively with the boss's advice and guidance.

Use caution. Be certain that, in empowering your boss, you don't give him the impression that you are not doing or cannot do your job. You are eager to present *your* plan and get *his* "take" on it. Empower your boss without relinquishing your own strength.

Negative responses to anticipate from the tyrant

1. Are you asking me to do your job for you?

Reply with:

No, I am not. But I *am* asking for your advice so that I can do my job more effectively.

2. This talk is all fine, but I'm just not sure you are motivated.

Reply with:

You don't have to worry about that. I promise you that I am motivated. I like to win, and I like to be on a winning team. That's why I want to take advantage of your experience.

3. Do you think you can get your people out there selling?

Reply with:

I know I can—especially with your help. We'll turn this situation around.

Type II: The Guilt Monger

The guilt monger boss gets you to do not just your work, but the work of two or three others. She is the mirror image of the tyrant boss. She makes no attempt to tower over you; instead, she shows you how you are tearing her down by your "unwillingness" to go "that extra mile."

- She will not threaten to fire you, but she will tell you (perhaps indirectly) that, unless "extra effort" is made, the company will collapse and you and everyone else will be out of work.
- She will not *tell* you to put in overtime, but she *will* look up from her desk at 5:30 and say something like, "Oh, no, don't stay late. You have more important things to do, like have dinner with your family. My family has gotten used to my working late by now."
- She'll use phrases like, "Somebody's got to do it—but don't you worry about it." Or: "I don't know where we're going to find the bodies to do this job, but we'll have to manage—somehow."

The guilt-mongering boss typically has a *passive-aggressive* personality, made evident through some of her favorite phrases:

Don't trouble yourself.

Think nothing of it.

No. We'll manage without you.

Oh—your *family* . . .

I can't remember the last time I had dinner at home on a weekday.

We'll find somebody to do it.

Well, if you're not available, you're not available.

I guess we'll manage.

I suppose you don't owe me any overtime.

The most effective strategy for dealing with the guilt monger is always to separate your commitment to your job from your relationship with your boss. Depending on how you feel about your work and what you realistically need to accomplish in order to do your job, you may have little choice about putting in overtime or pushing extra hard to meet a deadline. The crucial step is separating the unavoidable demands that come with the job from the emotional demands that come from a manipulative guilt monger. Then, once *you* have successfully distinguished between emotion and necessity, you need to help your boss do the same. There are two ways to accomplish this:

- If an unreasonable demand is made on your time and you have a legitimate excuse, use it: "Normally, I could work overtime, but today's our anniversary." Or: "I wish I could change my day off, but I have a medical appointment that would take months to reschedule." The problem with relying on such excuses is that, since the guilt-mongering boss is by definition chronic with her demands, you will soon run out of legitimate excuses.

- The second response to the guilt monger, then, is to administer a perspective-restoring dose of reality. Your boss says: "I suppose I'll just stay here and work on this report myself." You reply: "Do you think that's necessary? You know, I'll be completely available to you tomorrow. I could rough out a draft, and you could review it." Or: "Do you think it's a good idea to do something this important in such a hurry? Why don't we review it together first thing in the morning?" Provide real alternatives.

Your script: communicating with the guilt monger. The following is a typical exchange with the guilt-mongering boss:

Boss: I suppose we can manage—somehow—if we don't get this report out tomorrow. I'll make some excuse or other, I suppose.

You: I agree. It seems to me a lot better to take the time to do this thing right than to try to rush it through tonight. Tomorrow, I can give you all day. I'll rough out a draft, and we can go over it together. We need time to do a good job.

Note the two major elements of strategy here. First, the guilt monger works on emotion and expects you to respond emotionally. Choose not to. Instead, respond to the issues. The boss is insincere when she says "We'll manage," but you should take this at its face value and show her how, indeed, you *will* manage. Second, the pronoun *we* demonstrates that you are not deserting your boss. You are a member of the team, and committed to it.

NEGATIVE RESPONSES TO ANTICIPATE FROM THE GUILT MONGER

1. Well, I guess I'll just sit down and do what I can myself.

Reply with:

Why do that when I can give you all the help you want tomorrow? You deserve the night off.

2. It makes me nervous to work so close to a deadline.

Reply with:

That's why we need to approach this methodically, allowing ourselves time.

3. I guess it is unfair to ask you to do so much extra work.

Reply with:

It's not a question of fairness, but of making the most productive use of my time.

4. It would help if you could reschedule your appointments this evening.

Reply with:

I wish I could, but it's impossible on such short notice.

Type III: The Merchant of Blame

Some bosses take responsibility for their decisions and actions. Some do not. Some correctly, accurately, and fairly determine responsibility for problems and mistakes, and they make corrections appropriately; some do not. Some bosses deliberately dodge responsibility, while others just can't help responding with blame when a situation goes sour.

Effective strategy for communicating with the blamer

Let's pause a moment. Before we discuss strategies for verbally coping with the blamer, we must distinguish between those times when you are at fault and those times when you are not. If you have made a mistake, own up to it, confront it, deal with it, and repair it. Beyond this, distinguish between the boss who, on rare occasions, wrongly assigns blame and the habitual blamer, for whom blaming is an integral part of management style. The first case requires correction of a mistaken perception, the second is an issue of personality and style.

- Confronting the occasional accusation from an otherwise substantially stable boss calls for you to begin by getting the facts. Do not deny anything before you have the full story; that will just make you seem defensive.
- Collecting the facts will accomplish two things. First, it will calm your boss down by shifting his focus from personalities to events. Second, it will give you the opportunity not only to demonstrate your blamelessness, but might even lead to the resolution of the problem in question.

If you have the misfortune of working for a habitual blamer, begin the same way:

STEP 1: Focus calmly on the facts. Confront the events rather than the boss's accusation.

Now, getting to the facts is not always easy when you are dealing with a habitual blamer. The blamer's object is to shift responsibility from himself to you. Actually, the last thing he is interested in is facts that may prevent him from accomplishing this shift. You do have a secret weapon, however:

STEP 2: Offer a willingness to accept responsibility, not blame. Communicate that, while the snafu is not your fault, you are prepared to accept it as your problem and work to resolve it.

The blamer boss may resist your challenging him, but it is not likely that he will turn down your offer to take on the task of correcting a problem. While you have blocked the boss's attempt to fix blame on you, you have allowed him to feel as if he has won, because you have agreed to take on responsibility for resolving the problem.

Your script: communicating with the blamer

Boss: Well, you've really done it this time. I turn my back for five minutes and everything goes to hell. The warehouse says it has no record of any of these orders. How do you think we make money? We take orders, transmit orders, and ship orders. How could you have screwed up so badly?

You: Mrs. Smith, this is the first I've heard of a problem. Please give me the details so that we can get to the bottom of it and arrive at a solution quickly.

Boss: How can this be the first you've heard about it? Where have you been all this time?

You: I've been right here, but you've been stuck with fielding this complaint. Tell me the details so that I can help get us back on track. After I get the whole story, I will do whatever is necessary to fix the problem.

Boss: I'm not confident that you can "fix" anything.

You: Mrs. Smith, it's true I can't if I don't know what went wrong. Let's go over this situation together

The blamer does not see *you*. He sees only a target. Begin bringing him back to reality by deliberately using his name; yet, even while you establish personal contact, avoid responding to any personal attacks. Focus—or refocus—the exchange on the facts of the situation in question. Get the story. Don't draw conclusions until you've collected the facts. But do, from the beginning, volunteer to find a solution.

1. Don't try to wiggle out of this.

Reply with:

That's the last thing I want to do. What I want is to get into this problem and start fixing it.

2. You have to take responsibility for this.

Reply with:

That is exactly what I want to do. Let me work with you to fix the problem. Let's begin by going over the facts, so that we can agree on a solution.

3. You'd better do it yourself and do it right now.

Reply with:

I'll give it top priority. It will save us both time if we begin by going over the facts now.

4. I'm too angry to go into details now.

Reply with:

I'll do what I can now, but I'm going to have to discuss this with you later. I'll drop by in an hour.

Type IV: The Dreamer

Some bosses are self-confident, some not. Working for an insecure boss is difficult, while working for one who has healthy self-confidence can be gratifying and rewarding—unless that self-confidence is without basis. The dreamer is the boss who is convinced that her every passing idea bears the seeds of greatness. The dreamer will call you into her office and declare: "While I was driving in this morning I hit a pothole. I thought, 'Why can't R & D come up with a sensor that will alert the driver to a pothole in time to avoid it?' We've got the technology, and we've got the marketing muscle. I want you to start working on this right away."

Suddenly you are swept away in your boss's stream of consciousness, the victim of an idea that happened to drift by. Now, by no means should you dodge every idea your boss comes up with. After all, it *is* possible that she might come up with something good, profitable, even brilliant. Nor can I tell you how to distinguish a good idea from an unworkable one. There are no general rules for determining this in all fields. And, alas, you may have no choice other than to act on whatever assignment your boss hands out. Depending on your position and the hierarchy of your company, it may not be your place to offer an opinion. Nevertheless, strategies are available to help you respond to the dreamer without getting sidetracked— or derailed.

We've all seen the ancient Hollywood movie cliché in which someone becomes hysterical, drifts off into his or her own world, and is brought back to reality with a sharp slap on the face. Some experts advise administering the verbal equivalent of the sharp slap in the case of ideas that seem doomed to fail. The problem with this approach is that it rarely pays for a subordinate to respond to a boss in this way, and, even if you do feel sufficiently secure in your job to deliver a harsh truth, the result is likely to be defensiveness and resistance. There is a more effective strategy available.

STEP 1: Do not pass immediate judgment on the idea.

STEP 2: Respond to the mechanics of your boss's request or direction: "What kind of priority do you want me to give this?" Or: "Should I put the XYZ account on the back burner to handle this?"

Emphasizing mechanics and logistics will help focus your boss on day-to-day reality, suggesting that certain business will have to be rescheduled, delayed, or sacrificed. This will put the idea in perspective and perhaps even take some of the wind out of the Dreamer's sails and some of the pressure off you. At the same time, it will convey the message that you are taking the idea seriously enough to concern yourself with scheduling action on it.

STEP 3: Never say directly that you don't have time to act on the dreamer's idea. That dismisses both the idea and the person behind it.

STEP 4: Buy time. Reply to the dreamer with, "This is very interesting. Give me some time to think about this. I imagine I'll have lots of questions for you."

STEP 5:   Take advantage of whatever bureaucracy your company has in place for dealing with new ideas, concepts, and programs. If you must fill out forms or write up a report, get your boss involved in this: "Okay. The first step will be a preliminary P and L. I'll get the paperwork started and bring it in tomorrow."

Remember, your object is not to avoid work but to avoid as much *unnecessary and wasteful* work as possible. It is also to head off the development of an unworkable idea that may soon become your responsibility and, ultimately, your failure. But your other, equally important, objective is to avoid alienating your boss.

YOUR SCRIPT: COMMUNICATING WITH THE DREAMER

Boss: I was watching television last night, and I got an idea. We should do our Annual Report as a music video. I mean it. Set those dry facts to music. It would get us publicity and stir up the investors. I want you to get this started.

You: I've got the XYZ project in stage four, and I'm pitching the ABC account. Do you want me to turn these over to someone else to clear the decks for the video? Or how should I juggle that? We're talking about a good deal of business there.

Boss: No. You'd better see those through.

You: Okay. Then I'll schedule the video project accordingly, but first let me think about it and rough out a list of questions and issues for you before we move ahead.

Don't address the unworkability of the proposed project. Instead, focus on the impact it will have on present reality. In effect, this will relieve you from the responsibility of shaking the boss back into reality. *Show* her the reality, and she will shake *herself*.

NEGATIVE RESPONSES TO ANTICIPATE FROM THE DREAMER

1. I want you to give it your full attention.

Reply with:

Okay. But I'd better begin by giving you a report on my current projects, so that we can reschedule and reassign.

2. I don't want this to disappear into limbo. I want follow-through.

Reply with:

I need some time to review the idea, and then I'll prepare a list of questions and issues for you. I also need to discuss my current assignments, so that we can reschedule and reassign. I'm pretty heavily committed, and this is going to shake things up around here.

3. What do you think about this?

Reply with:

It is worth thinking seriously about. Let me give it some consideration and discuss it with you.

4. This is something we really need to be doing, and we need to move fast.

Reply with:

I'll start sketching out some ideas of the kind of resource commitment the project's likely to involve, and I'll get back to you with any questions.

Type V: The Volcano

Then there's the boss who just plain explodes. There's yelling, invective, ranting, finger jabbing, and fist pounding.

The emotional volcano is, by definition, a poor manager. While it is true that fear of the boss is a great motivator, what it motivates is passivity, the suppression of creativity, and the avoidance of communication. Perhaps most of all, it motivates a search for alternative employment. And, depending on many other factors associated with the job, that search may be your *best* alternative.

However, if you are stuck with an emotional volcano, you do have a variety of verbal strategies for dealing with him.

STEP 1:   Begin by understanding the basis of your boss's tendency to act on his feelings, and then think through your own response to those feelings. In most cases, the emotional volcano is driven by fear. What does your boss have to be afraid of? Plenty. If he has bosses to answer to, he suffers the same anxieties and pressures you do. If he owns the company, the consequences of failure, the sense that work is slipping, that profits are dwindling, that the business is leaking, triggers terrible emotions. In the anxiety-afflicted, insecure boss, any reversal—a late report, a lost sale—seems like the first step down the slippery slope not to a bad day, a poor month, or even a weak quarter, but to doom.

STEP 2:   Understand your own fear. The eruption of the emotional volcano creates two kinds of fear in you. One is the simple fear of losing your job: the thought that, in his rage, your boss will summarily fire you. Now, is this realistic? Well, people do get fired, but it is seldom an act of anger. Most employees are let go because of relatively long-term economic reasons, not as the immediate result of an emotional exchange.

- Another source of fear is the prospect of actual violence. Of course, you may know in your head that the one thing your boss will *not* do is strike you, and the one thing you will *not* do is lash out at him. But at some level of consciousness you imagine an exchange between Neanderthals. Verbal violence is always a symbol of physical threat. Your boss represents power and authority. In a heated exchange, your imagination gives concrete shape to those abstractions. Your boss, you feel, has the power and authority to crush you. Equally anxiety provoking is the feeling you may have of wanting to fight back, perhaps even launch a preemptive strike. You *know* that none of this will happen, but you *feel* the associated emotions nonetheless.

STEP 3:   Fear is a primitive emotion. You can neither avoid nor escape it, but you don't have to be governed by it. Once the volcano erupts, it is best to let the lava flow around you. Force yourself to listen to the tirade—while standing, if possible, with your arms at your sides. Force yourself to look into your boss's eyes, as if you were having a regular conversation. At some natural pause—a lull in the storm—inject calm.

STEP 4: Inject calm, but avoid telling your boss to "calm down." Never *tell* an angry person to do anything. It will only make him angrier. Nor should you tell him how to feel ("There's no reason for you to be so upset"), since meddling with another's emotions is also likely to elicit nothing but additional rage. Instead, acknowledge the other person's anger: "I can see that you are mad as hell, and I can't blame you, but . . ." The *but* is the point at which you introduce alternatives to the tirade: ". . . but I need to talk this through with you. Would it be better for me to come back and discuss this, or do you want to sit down and go over it now?"

STEP 5: Rage narrows vision, preventing consideration of alternatives. Your objective in confronting the emotional volcano is to make the alternatives visible:

A. *We can discuss this.*

B. *We can resolve this.*

C. *We can sit down together.*

D. *We can do it now.*

E. *We can do it later.*

TIP

Give your boss choices, alternatives. Compel him, in this way, to *think* for a moment rather than to *feel*.

STEP 6: As for yourself, while you should not roll over to abuse, neither should you yield to the temptation to jump into a shouting match. Once *both* of you are yelling, *neither* of you is in charge. The emotion—anger—is in control. You won't win the struggle, and neither will your boss. Rage triumphs. Instead, listen unmoved. Let him vent. Then provide some choices and alternatives.

This strategy may work, but it is not foolproof. If your boss is on a roll, the tirade may not only continue, but intensify. At this point, the most effective move you can make is out. Separate yourself from your boss. Don't run, and certainly don't storm out of the office. Just excuse yourself as calmly and politely as possible: "Excuse me, Mrs. Smith. I understand how angry you are, and, because of that, I think it would be best if I went down to my office for a while. Why don't you buzz me downstairs when we can sit down and talk about this problem without yelling at one another."

YOUR SCRIPT: COMMUNICATING WITH THE VOLCANO

Here's what you might expect:

Boss: I'm tired of things going wrong around here. I'm tired of nothing getting followed up on. You and your department better shape up, because I'm getting tired of all of you. This is a tough, push, push, push business. And if you stop pushing, you don't survive. Well, let me tell you something right now. You're going down before I do, and that's a promise. I'm tired of being jerked around like this!

You: I understand that you're upset about sales this quarter. Well, so am I, but this is something we need to talk through. We can sit down now over this, or, if you like, I'll come back at a better time, when we can hammer out a strategy. It's up to you.

Take whatever verbal action is required to transform the situation from *me*-against-*you* to *us*-against-the-*problem*. Suggest postponing discussion until emotions have cooled.

NEGATIVE RESPONSES TO ANTICIPATE FROM THE VOLCANO

1. I don't want to waste my time talking to you.

Reply with:

Then I'll go back down to my office. You can give me a buzz if you do decide to discuss this further.

2. I'm not finished with you yet.

Reply with:

I'm sure there's a lot more to say, but I'd prefer to come back at a better time. However, I'm willing to continue talking if we can conduct this as a conversation and not as a shouting match.

3. We have to hash all of this out right now!

Reply with:

Then I suggest that we sit down, calmly lay out the issues, and act on them accordingly. When we both have a clear idea of everything that's involved in this problem, I'm sure we can formulate a solution.

4. I don't want to hear any excuses.

Reply with:

And I don't have any excuses to give you. What I'd like is some time to review the problems you have brought up and come back to you with some suggestions for solving them.

5. You can't get away with sloppy work. I can't stand sloppy work.

Reply with:

I'm sorry that I've given you the feeling that I'm trying to get away with anything. Can we sit down and go over whatever problem areas you see? If I can get specifics, I can work with you on them one by one. Should I come back at a better time?

NEGOTIATING A RAISE

Here's a phrase not only to avoid saying, but one that you should expunge from your mind: *I deserve a raise.*

Your boss doesn't care. More important, you should not go into this negotiation thinking about what you deserve or don't deserve. Most of us are brought up with a false sense of modesty, which, at some level of consciousness, causes us to question whether we deserve anything good at all. Better not open that Freudian can of worms.

Well, then, what *do* you need a raise for? A new car? A new house? To make the payments on the house you've got? To send your kid through college?

Maybe your boss takes an interest in your needs. Maybe not. Personally, she may care about you very much. Personally, she may not. Whatever her feelings, if she's being at all professional about the matter, she will deliberately exclude your needs from her consideration of your salary. For one thing, a dozen other people in the company want a new car or new house or have a tough nut to make each month.

So, let's see. We've eliminated just deserts as a persuasive argument for getting a raise, and we've ditched personal needs as well. What's left?

- Answer: Your performance on the job. Period.

Now, this actually makes your task a lot easier, at least as far as your emotions are concerned. If it's hard enough to make a persuasive case for a raise based on your performance at work, think how much harder it would be if you had to justify the pitch on the basis of your whole life. (You see, your boss would be thinking, "Why does *he* need a new car? *I* don't have a new car. I can't afford a new car.")

Here's how to proceed. The first ten steps are preparation—don't stint on these—the rest is execution.

STEP 1: Focus on how you meet—and exceed—the demands of your job.

Let's work on getting that focus razor sharp. Most novice communicators make the mistake of thinking that eloquence is a matter of commanding a range of beautifully descriptive adjectives. They incorrectly assume that punchy adjectives most effectively evoke emotion. The truth is that *people, things, events,* and *deeds* evoke far more emotion than words and that nouns and verbs—the kinds of words most directly connected to people, things, events, and deeds—therefore evoke more emotion than adjectives and adverbs, which are related to the real world less directly. The firmest foundation of eloquence is constructed of simple nouns and verbs, not flowery adjectives and sonorous adverbs. How can you make your focus razor sharp? Talk about people, things, events, and deeds.

Instead of trying to convince your boss that you're a "great" sales manager who has created a "dynamic" department, prove your case with the people, things, events, and deeds that make such adjectives as *great* and *dynamic* superfluous. For example:

> Last year at this time, when I took over, we were doing a volume of $75,000 in X, $55,000 in Y, and $45,000 in Z. Today, the numbers are $125,000, $78,000, and $55,000. I've also directed what looks like a great launch for product A—$35,000 in first-quarter sales alone—and I'm developing the staff not only to maintain but to better these numbers. Joe Blow, whom I brought on board in December, has made it his business to penetrate our traditionally weakest territories. In Chicago, for example, he's increased sales by 43 percent. . . .

The American poet William Carlos Williams told would-be writers that there are "no ideas but in things." He may have thought he was issuing a prescription for good literature, but what he was really doing was providing a formula for highly effective persuasion.

TIP

Show. Don't *tell.*

STEP 2:   Make a list of highlights of your accomplishments during the preceding year or other period. Don't count on your boss's having dutifully kept score. In fact, you shouldn't even assume that she is on intimate terms with your job description. Make a list of your duties and responsibilities.

STEP 3:   Research what others—in similar positions, with similar duties, and in similar companies—get paid. If the average is significantly higher than what you are getting, add the information to your arsenal. If you fall within the average, don't use the information; however, be prepared to emphasize the ways in which you outperform the average, just in case your boss brings up the subject of "industry standards of compensation." Finally, if you discover that you are getting paid substantially more than the average, you should either count yourself fortunate (and learn to live within your present budget for the time being) or think in terms of a promotion rather than a raise.

Just ahead, in the next section, we will discuss strategies for putting yourself across to secure a promotion. But pause a moment to think about that now. If your research does reveal that you are being "overpaid" in your current position, consider this bold approach:

> I want to level with you. I was planning on meeting with you to negotiate a raise. But I've done some research, and I've given the matter a good deal of thought. The fact is, you're paying me too much. The average sales manager in our industry takes home X dollars in straight salary. I'm getting Y. Now, before you think I've lost my mind, let me propose something that will be good for our division, the company—and, of course, good for me. Instead of paying Y dollars for a sales manager, why don't you pay Z dollars for a director of sales. I'm already doing A,

B, and *C*—all director's responsibilities—and I'm really ready for the move. The hike from salary *Y* to *Z* makes a lot more sense than maintaining me in a lesser position at *Y.*

STEP 4: Edit and digest your research. Go over it. Memorize the highlights—especially be able to tick off your stellar accomplishments. Carry to the meeting a neatly typed summary of the information, but don't read from it, and don't trot it out unless your boss asks to *see* facts and figures. Rehearse and memorize instead.

STEP 5: Do supplementary research to hold in reserve. You should be aware of how well (or how poorly) your company and department performed during the past year. If your company issues an annual report, read it. Supplement your research on industry standards of compensation for your position by determining if you are a professional in short supply or if the market for your position is well stocked or even glutted. Again: don't volunteer this information at the interview, but hold it in reserve, in case you meet resistance.

TIP

Taking the time to acquire the facts will not only directly help you make your case, it will also give you a depth of knowledge that will increase your self-confidence and will prepare you to answer questions and overcome resistance. Don't pummel your boss with the lock, stock, and barrel of your research, but be assured that having the facts on hand will suggest that you have depth and that you are committed to the company, to the industry, and to your career.

TIP

Where do you find the facts? Within most larger companies, salary information (except for company officers in publicly held corporations) is usually a closely guarded secret. In many firms, employees are even barred from discussing their salaries with others. You should not, therefore, base your research on what friends and associates tell you. That, after all, is gossip. Find cold, hard, dispassionate *published* sources. The best sources of industry-wide salary information are the compensation surveys published by trade organizations within your field.

STEP 6:   Once you have found and digested the facts, take a few moments to "get your mind right." This means laying aside any self-doubt or questions about *Do I deserve a raise?* What you deserve or don't deserve should have no bearing on the task at hand. Nor should you let emotional—or financial—hunger take command. Focus on job performance. Period.

STEP 7:   Formulate a target salary level. Based on your research, decide on what you can reasonably expect. However, as in any negotiation, you should not start by disclosing the figure. The best tactic is to elicit an offer from your boss and, depending on how that figure jives with what your research and desires tell you is appropriate, accept the offer or use it as the basis for further negotiation. The potential problem of laying all your cards on the table is not that the dollar amount you ask for will be too high, but that it will be too low.

STEP 8:   Resolve not to *ask* for a raise. Psychologists who practice so-called "transactional analysis" say that each of us carries within our emotional selves a "parent," an "adult," and a "child." Ideally, two adults will relate to each other from the perspective of their "adult" selves. In actuality, many relations between adults involve the "child" in one relating to the "child" or the "parent" in the other. No matter how sophisticated we may believe ourselves to be, when we go to a supervisor to ask for a raise, we tend to cast ourselves in the role of the "child" and the supervisor in the role of the "adult." This emotional dynamic is more likely to result in resistance than in a raise. Avoid this counterproductive dynamic by *negotiating* for a raise, rather than *asking* for one.

What's the difference? It begins with attitude. You are not a charity case, out to get something for nothing. You are coming to the bargaining table with valuable skills and experience, for which you are trying to get the best price. Resolve to make this meeting a negotiation, a transaction, a bargaining session—not a hat-in-hand plea.

STEP 9:   Dress for the part. Although the meeting is definitely a special occasion, don't pick this moment to change your customary wardrobe. Wear your usual business attire, taking extra care to ensure that your outfit is freshly laundered and dry cleaned and that it is in top repair. Avoid flamboyance or sexual provocation. Err on the conservative side. It is also a big mistake deliberately to "dress down" for the occasion, as if to suggest that you cannot afford to look your best. This will not garner sympathy, nor will it make your boss feel guilty about your current salary. What it *will* suggest is that you cannot manage your personal resources and that you are not giving your best to your job. It is likely to get your boss thinking that if you can't get it together personally how can you manage your job or your department effectively?

STEP 10:   Make the appointment. In some organizations, it is possible to see the boss without making an appointment. In others, an appointment is necessary. It is also possible that the subject of compensation can be discussed appropriately only at an annual or semi-annual salary review. Even if you work in a firm in which a meeting with the boss is customarily spontaneous and casual, do make a specific appointment for this discussion. Moreover, be certain that your boss knows what the purpose of the meeting is. It is definitely not to your advantage to spring the salary negotiation on her. Don't let yourself believe that surprising your boss with a request for money will catch her off guard. Usually, a surprise proposition automatically elicits defensive resistance.

TIP

Your organization may or may not have a specific procedure for scheduling appointments with the supervisor. Whatever the details of the procedure, you should avoid "asking for" or "requesting" an appointment. Don't say, "Can I see you on . . ." but, "I need to meet with you to discuss a salary matter. Would Tuesday before 11 be good for you?" As in any sales situation (and you *are* selling your boss on the idea of compensating you at a higher level), your object is to move your "prospect" to act. The first act is agreeing to the appointment. Don't leave this up to your boss. Being specific and putting the request in the form of a statement rather than a question make it easy for her to act.

STEP 11:   Walk in and greet your boss as you normally would. Make strong eye contact and do your best to position yourself powerfully in the room. If she is behind her desk, pull a chair to the *side* of the desk, if possible, so that the desktop does not separate you. If this is not physically possible, sit as close to the desk as possible. Try to sit higher than or at the same level as your boss. In maintaining eye contact, be careful of your aim. From time to time, you may actually want to look slightly above your boss's eye level, a body-language signal that conveys subtle domination. Do not sustain this for too long a stretch, however, lest your healthy self-assertion be interpreted as arrogance.

STEP 12: Before getting to the point, begin with thanks for the meeting. This is not merely common courtesy (though it *is* that, too), it also reminds your boss that, in agreeing to the meeting, she has already invested something in you. Beginning with thanks enhances your value in her eyes.

STEP 13: Review the record. Then make your pitch.

Your script: negotiating a raise

Here's a raise-seeking scenario:

You: Thanks for seeing me, Jane [if you customarily call her by her first name]. I've been with Better & Better for five years now—two years in sales and the past three in marketing. I believe you know the quality of work I've been doing here. I mean, for example, since I took over the Lummox account, we've penetrated two major new markets and at least one new territory. And the year's not over yet! I am confident that we'll see similar results with the Flummox account, which I've just taken on. You've given me a lot of creative freedom, and I've really been able to run with that.

I've also been able to put together a terrific team: I'm supervising four people on the Lummox account, and I plan to put together a six-person team on the Flummox job, at least through start-up.

It's true that I've advanced pretty rapidly here, but, then, I've had to take on a lot of responsibilities. I believe that it's time for my salary to catch up to my level of achievement and responsibilities. Certainly, it's time for my salary to get into step with industry-standard compensation for the kind of work I'm doing.

Jane, what do you think?

In brief compass, you've presented your case and you have hinted at a salary range (industry-standard) without limiting yourself to a figure that may be too low. Having demonstrated that your performance merits a higher level of compensation, you've also given your boss the feeling that she is a fair person and a shrewd judge of talent and ability ("You've given me a lot of creative freedom . . ."). In effect, you are reflecting to your boss what she already thinks. You are reminding her that she has invested in you. Your "rapid advance" will not be perceived as a reason to slow down now, but as a precedent for advancing you some more. Just as your pitch is aimed at (subtly) telling your boss that she already thinks you are great, the conclusion of your pitch should leave her feeling that the proposed raise is *her* idea. You've set up the context that makes it possible for your boss to respond positively. As in any effective sales pitch, you've also made it possible for her to act. The decision, of course, is ultimately hers. The question at the end of the pitch, however, does not merely acknowledge this immutable fact, it empowers her to make the decision you want her to make. Not: Will you give *me* more money? But: What do *you* think?

- Successful persuasion shifts the focus from you to your prospect. It translates your self-interest into terms of the self-interest of the other person.

Overcoming resistance to your raise request

The most common form of resistance you are likely to encounter is a delaying tactic, your boss telling you that she can't consider the request now or that it will have to wait until later. If your firm has an annual or semi-annual salary-review procedure, it may well be appropriate to reserve salary discussions until then. However, if an off-putting response is merely a delaying tactic, attempt to set a specific appointment date for the review:

- "I understand. When will it be appropriate to have this discussion?"
  or
- "I'd like to reschedule, then, in two weeks. Can we set that up now?"
  or
- "The sales meeting is on the twelfth. Does the fifteenth look good for rescheduling this discussion?"

Don't leave matters hanging.

HERE ARE SOME OTHER COMMON NEGATIVE RESPONSES:

1. If it were up to me, there's no question you'd get a raise at this time. I can make a recommendation, but I'm pretty much powerless to make the final decision.

Reply with:

Should I have a conversation with [name of boss's supervisor]? Can I count on your recommendation to him?

2. To be perfectly frank with you, a lot of people here are doing great jobs, and they're not getting the kind of increase you're talking about.

Reply with:

I'm only talking about myself and what is appropriate in my case.

It is also likely that a genuine negotiation will develop. For example:

3. I can't offer you a 15 percent increase. Three, maybe 5 percent is more like it.

Reply with:

[Say nothing, but don't leave—and don't glare. You're not angry. You are introducing a strategic silence in order to make your boss uncomfortable enough to make a better offer or, at least, to prompt further negotiation.]

After a protracted silence, your boss says: "I'm sorry, but this is final. Five percent is as high as I can go."

Reply with:

Okay. I appreciate your consideration, and I'll work at that salary, provided that we have a firm understanding that in three months we will review what I've done and where I've taken the department. I'm committed to this job, and I'm prepared to wait three months before reopening this subject.

TIP

Be certain to follow up with a memo summarizing your understanding of the agreement, including the scheduled review.

What if the answer is simply no (usually something like, "I can't accommodate you at this time")? You might respond with:

- "Is there something I've done or failed to do?"

  or

- "What can I do to change your thinking on this?"

  or

- "Tell me what would make it possible for me to get more appropriate compensation."

As is the case with most negotiations, even one that fails to produce the desired result can be productive nevertheless. Use a negative response to gain knowledge about how you fit into the organization, about your boss's needs as well as your own.

- The only truly unsuccessful negotiation is the one from which you fail to learn.

In the worst case, you may learn that you should seek a different employer. *Worst* case? That may actually turn out to be the best thing that ever happened to you.

NEGOTIATING A PROMOTION

Seeking a promotion is similar to negotiating for a raise in that your task is to sell your boss on your value, negotiating a deal rather than making a demand or asking for something in return for nothing. Indeed, in many cases, it is more appropriate to seek a promotion than it is to ask for a raise. Many positions have formal or informal salary ceilings, and the next step up the compensation ladder is through a loftier position.

Is it harder to get a raise or to get a promotion? That's the same kind of question as the classic posed to optimists and pessimists: Is the glass half empty or half full? The pessimist will tell you that it's harder to get a promotion because you are asking for *two* things, more money *and* more responsibility. By the same token, the pessimist might also tell you that it's harder to get a raise because you're asking for more money without doing anything more for it. An optimist, on the other hand, may opine that a boss is more likely to yield on money than on power. Or the optimist may tell you that a boss is more likely to tie a raise to a promotion because she feels she is getting a better bargain—paying more, but also getting more.

The pessimist/optimist debate may be useful for anticipating possible responses, but it is not worth worrying about. Just take an optimist's position; after all, it's the only viewpoint that will do you any good in a negotiation.

If you have a choice between asking for a raise or asking for a promotion, begin by deciding what you want. Most people will choose the promotion, and if that's what you want, here is the best way to begin:

STEP 1: Adopt the attitude that you are offering to take on more responsibility in exchange for greater compensation. This not only has the potential for giving your boss positive feelings about parting with more money, even more important, it should allow you to feel less like a supplicant and more like a good businessperson: You are not simply asking for more, but you are offering value for value in a way that shows respect for yourself and a commitment to your company.

STEP 2: If you are turned down for the promotion, you are still in a position to negotiate a raise in your present position. This is a key advantage of asking for a promotion rather than a raise. Had you begun by asking for a raise, you would have had no such positive fallback position.

STEP 3: As with negotiating for a raise, it is far better to come into the discussion armed with a few solid accomplishments than with a collection of self-laudatory adjectives.

STEP 4: Building on a base of accomplishment, suggest that you could be even more useful in a position of greater responsibility.

TIP

For most of us, it is emotionally very difficult to *ask* for things. It is also true that most people would rather receive than give. Therefore, secure your promotion by offering rather than asking.

YOUR SCRIPT: NEGOTIATING A PROMOTION

Here's a typical negotiation:

You: I've been on the selling floor now for just about four years. Three out of those four years I've been among your top three salespeople. I have learned a lot here, and not only about selling shoes, but also about what *moves* and what does not. I've also learned that I have a lot to offer—and not just on a customer-by-customer basis. I know that Mr. Jones is moving up from assistant buyer; well, I'm ready to move up to working more closely with you. I've had a long and successful record of customer contact, but I've been concentrating as much on the product as on the customers. I have a very fresh perspective on what is selling here—what moves, what doesn't—and I'd like to put that knowledge to work for us as our new assistant buyer.

The most important point to note here is how the applicant turns a request into an offer. He states the facts and establishes his record of achievement, not with the object of proving that he "deserves" a promotion, but with the goal of selling additional services to the company.

> **TIP**
>
> You don't have to sell your boss on the fact that a promotion will benefit you. She knows that. Your task is to sell her on the idea that promoting you will greatly benefit the company—and, therefore, her.

NEGATIVE RESPONSES TO ANTICIPATE WHEN ASKING FOR A PROMOTION

1. I don't think you are ready yet.

Reply with:

What will it take for me to demonstrate that I *am* ready?

2. This is not the right time to talk about it.

Reply with:

When would be a better time? Can you pencil me in now?

3. You're doing such a good job where you are, that I'm afraid to move you out of the position.

Reply with:

Well, it sure is nice to be appreciated, but I'm confident that I can take the same skills and use them to greater advantage in an even more responsible position. I want to contribute as much as possible to our department.

5. I need to keep you where you are for at least another year.

Reply with:

I'd like to schedule a review before that time, to discuss my progress and my prospects. Can we plan on that now?

6. We're planning to fill that position with somebody from the outside.

Reply with:

Is that final? What would it take to change your mind? (Or: . . . to change company policy?) Can you tell me what it would take to get me in the running for this promotion?

PROMOTING AN IDEA OR PROJECT

It is difficult to prescribe any single strategy for promoting new ideas and projects, since the nurturing and reception of innovation are subject to the vagaries of a variety of corporate psychologies. Some bosses welcome and encourage new things, while others subtly or even actively discourage it.

- What is so intimidating about floating a new idea? The fear of meeting with hostility, discouragement, and derision.

The phrase that applies to this outcome is "shot down": *He shot me down. I was shot down.* Or even, *I went down in flames.* The vividness of the metaphor suggests the strength of the bad feelings associated with fear of rejection and humiliation.

If you happen to work in a corporate environment where innovation is indeed discouraged, nothing that can be suggested here will greatly affect your reality. If creativity and innovation are important to you, perhaps you should think about moving to an emotionally healthier company that welcomes these qualities. In the meantime, however, try to remember two things when you promote an idea or program:

1. If your boss habitually rejects innovation, *he's* the one with a problem, not you. Rejection of innovation is a sign of a very unhealthy manager. Unfortunately, your boss's illness also becomes your problem.

2. Painful as rejection can be, it is not really as painfully final as that "shot-down" figure of speech would suggest. I do not mean to minimize the bad feelings that rejection produces, but they are, after all, only feelings. They shouldn't be given the fiery gravity of death in aerial combat. You won't burst into flame.

> **TIP**
>
> What if you really *are* working for a company in which innovation can seriously threaten your job? If creativity is important to you, consider taking steps to move on to a different employer.

Bearing in mind that this situation presents a broad range of possible responses depending on varied corporate psychology, let's look at a best-case and worst-case scenario:

Best Case for Advancing Your Idea

The best case is promoting an idea or project to a boss who generally welcomes creativity.

STEP 1: Prepare thoroughly. The presentation may range from an elaborate proposal prepared in accordance with prescribed company policy to an apparently spur-of-the-moment remark at a meeting. At either extreme, preparation is not only possible, but essential.

STEP 2: If you present your boss with a ream of research material, give him some guiding remarks:

- "Here is the proposal for . . ."—then be as specific about the name of the project as possible.
- "As you look through the proposal, you might want to take special note of . . ."—then list a small number of *specific* highlights or key issues.
- "I'm especially concerned about . . ." Point out key issues you wish to discuss. Don't emphasize the negative.

- "It's been really exciting working on this, and I'd appreciate all the feedback I can get from you." (The object is not only to convey your own enthusiasm, but to let your boss know how much you value his response.)

STEP 3: If the introduction of the new idea is done informally, on the spur of the moment, be sure to brief yourself on the agenda of the meeting at which you wish to introduce the idea.

STEP 4: Arm yourself with notes. When you present an idea, you might preface it with a phrase such as, "This is something that just occurred to me," or "Here's something I think would be worth further thought," or "I just had a thought that might bear working up."

STEP 5: Secure involvement and commitment from the others: "Help me out with this one," or "What do you think about," "What's your quick take on," and so on.

Worst Case for Advancing Your Idea

In the worst-case scenario, working in an environment that does not routinely welcome innovation, you need to augment these steps with a strategy that seeks to give your boss a tangible stake in your idea or project.

STEP 1: You need to make your boss see himself as your partner in the project. For example: "As you look through the proposal, you might want to take special note of how I incorporated your thoughts in . . ." Or: "I'd like your take on what I did with the concepts you and I discussed last month."

STEP 2: Put even more emphasis on the importance of the boss's help: "I'd really be grateful for help with such and such," or "Such and such needs a lot more work. I need your take on it."

STEP 3: Make team-building statements: "It was great working with you on this."

YOUR SCRIPT: PRESENTING A NEW IDEA

Here's one way to introduce a new idea:

You: I'm very excited that I've completed the prospectus for the travel-book series I mentioned to you the week before last. Here it is. The potential here, I think you'll see, is in the combination of a fresh approach to a tested market and all the advantages of a series: a uniform design and format, a proven stable of authors, and a potentially unlimited number of titles. You'll see that I've run all the numbers here, and I'm confident you'll like what you see.

Now, I've given this a lot of thought, but I could really use your help with issues of format and size. This is one we can really run with.

- Communicate your enthusiasm and attempt to shape the desired degree of receptiveness. However, avoid bullying: "You're out of your mind if you don't go for this!"
- *Concisely* underscore the highlights of the proposal, giving specifics rather than adjectives; objective features rather than subjective attributes.
- Solicit your boss's input to get him on your team.

NEGATIVE RESPONSES TO ANTICIPATE WHEN PRESENTING AN IDEA

1. This one looks like a tough sell to me. I just don't know.

Reply with:

Well, they're all tough sells. What I ask is that you look over the proposal and look over the figures. *Then* let me know how tough it is. I'll trust your take on it.

2. I won't be able to get to this for a while.

Reply with:

I know you're busy here, but I'm confident you'll be excited by what you see in the proposal. It's worth making time for.

3. Look, we're putting all new projects on hold.

Reply with:

Even so, I'm so excited about this one that I'd really like to get your reaction to it and your advice on it—even if we can't act on it immediately.

4. We need to move cautiously. I don't want to rush into anything.

Reply with:

Neither do I. That's why I've taken time with the proposal, and that's why I don't want to rush it by you. I really need to get your response to it. Then I'll give it the time for all the revision and rethinking it may need.

RENEGOTIATING A DEADLINE

Bosses, even the most understanding of bosses, hate excuses, and nothing occasions more excuses than missing a deadline. Now, you might be able to get your boss to accept your excuse, but you will never be able to get her to like it. For that reason, it is best to give up on making excuses. Instead, recognize that extending a deadline is *buying* time, and like anything else you might "purchase," the buying of time is subject to negotiation.

STEP 1:   Persuade your boss to "sell" you more time in exchange for value received: "To do the most thorough job possible on this, I'm going to need a week more. I don't think it will do us any good to try to rush it and end up neglecting x, y, and z." Make it clear what the additional time will buy—a more thorough, more satisfactory job.

STEP 2:   Advise your boss as soon as possible of a time problem. No one likes to feel backed into a corner, and showing that you are on top of the schedule demonstrates that you are still in control, even if the deadline slips.

STEP 3:   Present the problem with the deadline as a simple alteration in schedule rather than as a crisis.

STEP 4:   Offer as many alternatives as possible. "I can get x done by Wednesday, y by Friday, and z early next week." Or: "If I postpone x, I can get you y and z by the original deadline." Avoid leaving your boss without choices.

YOUR SCRIPT: CHANGING A SCHEDULE.

Here's one approach:

You: I need to talk to you about altering the schedule for the XYZ project. All parts of the marketing report are scheduled for completion by March 15. I have enough information now to complete parts one through four by then, but a really thorough job on parts five and six is going to require an additional week of research. I don't see any point in throwing this together when, with a week's more time, I can do the job the way it should be done, and we'll have a document we can reasonably base decisions on.

TIP

Communicate control, the sense that altering a schedule is perfectly routine rather than something done in a hopeless emergency.

NEGATIVE RESPONSES TO ANTICIPATE WHEN RENEGOTIATING A DEADLINE

1. This is a serious deadline. I need you to move heaven and earth to meet it.

Reply with:

I take the deadline very seriously. That's why I'm talking to you about it now. I can give you a job I'm 75 percent happy with by the deadline. Give me another week, and I can promise 100 percent. Yes, the deadline's serious, but so is the project.

2. How are you guys spending your time down there?

Reply with:

One thing we're doing is thinking through the nature of the project and just how best to use our resources. If we cut corners now, it will cost us time later. That's why I'm asking for the modification of the schedule—to build a solid foundation now, so that we don't have trouble further on. That's my judgment on the matter, and that's what I'm asking for.

3. Can't you move any faster?

Reply with:

Yeah, sure. But I'm not going to be comfortable with the results, and how can I expect you to be confident if I'm not comfortable?

4. Can you guarantee that this will be the last delay?

Reply with:

I can guarantee that we'll do everything possible to ensure that the schedule won't have to be altered again.

ACCEPTING AN ASSIGNMENT

The manner in which you accept an assignment is a lot like how you shake hands. It is an initial act of communication that conveys far more than may be at first apparent. A handshake is a chance to transmit strength, warmth, eagerness, loyalty, a willingness to get the job done. Grip too firmly, and you convey the insecurity of one who feels it necessary to demonstrate dominance. Proffer your hand limply, and you telegraph weakness and hesitation. The way in which you accept an assignment presents similar opportunities and potential hazards.

If you happen to be thrilled with the assignment, your communication task is simple: just go ahead and express your feelings. It will give your boss pleasure to know that he has assigned you something you are excited about doing. It will also give him the feeling that he has chosen the right person for the job.

But what if you have reservations about the assignment? Before you react, you must make an important decision. Do you have a choice about whether you will accept the assignment? If you are in a position to decline, and that is what you wish to do, read the next section. If, however, you decide that you have no choice, it is not necessary to counterfeit joy. What you do need to convey is the message that you will work enthusiastically and professionally to get the job done. Generally, this is all you should convey, and you should do so without qualification.

But what if your reservations run deep? What if you believe the project is doomed to fail?

STEP 1: Neither feign enthusiastic confidence nor respond with panic-stricken negativity.

STEP 2: Respond positively, but mention that you'll be back with some questions: "I'll start looking it over right away and be back to you with some questions."

STEP 3: Give yourself time to review the pros and cons, the benefits and pitfalls of the project before you commit yourself to a definitive response. It is perfectly appropriate to buy time in this case, and it is certainly preferable to boxing yourself in with a thoughtlessly overconfident response on the one hand, or a rejection of the project on the other.

TIP

Even if you finally demonstrate the unfeasibility of an assignment, taking the time to consider it will still have conveyed your willingness to engage the task.

YOUR SCRIPT: ACCEPTING AN ASSIGNMENT

Here are several ways this discussion may go:

1. You: This is a very exciting opportunity. I've been preparing for just this kind of assignment, and I'll get on it immediately. I'm confident that you'll find my performance top-notch.

2. You: I'm prepared to get this under way now, and I know that you will be pleased with the results.

3. You: I'm very pleased that you've given this one to me. I've been wanting to work more closely with you on something, and now I have the opportunity. I look forward to it.

4. I'll look this over right away, and I should be back to you with some questions and issues over the next day or two.

- All of these responses are aimed at communicating enthusiasm and commitment that assure the boss that he has made the right choice.

Responses to Anticipate When Accepting an Assignment

1. Hey, hey. Don't let your enthusiasm run away with you!

Reply with:
I run *with* my enthusiasm. It's what drives me.

2. I'm counting on you.

Reply with:
I know you are, and I won't let you down.

3. Are you sure you're up to this?

Reply with:

You are making the right choice. I've prepared for this kind of assignment, I'm thrilled to get it, and I will make it work.

4. You seem to have some doubts.

Reply with:

What I have are some questions, and I need a day to review the assignment, formulate those questions, and come back to you with them.

5. I'd like to see more enthusiasm.

Reply with:

I'm being careful. I need to review the assignment, and I'll be back to you with any questions I have.

DECLINING AN ASSIGNMENT

You do *not* always have a practical choice about whether or not to accept an assignment. Just how much leeway you do have is something only you can judge at a given time and in a given situation. But observe this rule of thumb:

- If you are uncertain about an assignment, or even if you are certain you want to decline it, under most circumstances it is better to avoid an immediate negative response.

STEP 1: Faced with a distasteful or questionable assignment, respond that you will review it and that you will come back with any questions.

STEP 2: After you have reviewed the assignment, assuming that you are in a practical position to make the choice, decline.

Let's discuss the three ways to turn down an assignment:

1. You may attack the assignment itself, demonstrating that the project is unfeasible or unnecessary.

2. You may argue that, while the project is fine, you are not the best choice for it, either because of lack of qualifications, lack of experience, or because you are a resource better used elsewhere.

3. You may say that you prefer not to take on the project.

Each of these approaches has advantages and dangers. You'll need to exercise judgment.

Here are some guidelines to help you decide which strategy to employ:

- If you can demonstrate that a project is unworkable, you stand to save yourself as well as your company a lot of grief. But be strongly cautioned that the "if" here is a very big one. You should not protest the unworkability of an assignment just because you don't want to undertake it. This will benefit neither you nor your firm. If you are truly convinced that a project is doomed, present your well-reasoned doubts to your boss: "I mentioned that I'd be coming back to you on this project with some questions. I've reviewed the assignment, and, in fact, a number of very sticky points have come up. We'd better discuss and resolve these before we try to get this under way."

> **TIP**
>
> Note the transition from *I* to *we*. Don't deliver this message: "Wow! *You* have really stuck *me* with a turkey." Instead, express yourself this way: "*I* have reviewed the project and have discovered that *we* have problems."

- Don't toss the job back into your boss's lap or to make him feel as if you are shooting him down. It is one thing to criticize a project vigorously if you have been specifically asked to evaluate it. However, if your task was not evaluation but execution, you can safely assume that your boss thinks the assignment a good one and will be protective of it.

- Frame any criticism as positively as possible. Instead of rejecting the project out of hand, allude to "questions," "loose ends," "problems," "sticking points," and so on that need to be "resolved before proceeding." While this indicates that you are still engaged with the project, it also gives your boss an opportunity to acknowledge the difficulties for himself, which is better than your forcing the recognition on him.

What if there is nothing wrong with the project, but you are convinced that it is not right for you or, more accurately, you are not right for it?

STEP 1: The object here is to get your boss to see things your way in this *single case*, without prompting him to question your competence generally.

STEP 2: The safest course is to convince him that you are a resource better used on a different project. This, of course, is not always possible.

STEP 3: If the alternative project strategy is unavailable to you, do not blurt out your lack of qualifications, but begin the process of declining the assignment by securing time to review it, promising to return with questions.

STEP 4: Return armed with alternatives: "I've reviewed the project, and it seems to me that somebody in special sales would be better positioned to take this on. More than half the project, after all, depends on direct mail."

STEP 5: Don't dwell on your unsuitability. Focus on suggesting alternatives. Remember, your boss is primarily interested in getting the job done, not in specifically getting *you* to do the job. Nominate someone else for the assignment.

What if there is no alternative? Proceed with caution. The best thing you can do in this case is to make a demonstration of frankness and mature self-evaluation. If you were accepting an assignment, you would do well to bring up some recent past success to suggest that you can achieve the same results now. In declining an assignment, you may also want to bring up a past success:

- First, to suggest your general competence—the present assignment is a *rare* instance for which you are not the right choice
- Second, to contrast the kinds of strengths previously demonstrated with what the present assignment calls for

Even if your work situation permits you sufficient leeway to turn down an assignment at will, it is still best to offer alternatives and to have a good reason for declining an assignment.

> **TIP**
>
> Frame your rejection in terms of doing what's best for the company: "I'd like to take a pass on this one. Somebody like Fredericks can take this kind of thing and really run with it. I'm better at the conceptual end. The project will move faster with someone who's got this stuff down cold."

YOUR SCRIPT: TURNING DOWN AN ASSIGNMENT

Here are a few typical scenarios:

1. You: I've reviewed the project we discussed, and, as I thought, it raises a lot of questions. There are some formidable hurdles we'll have to consider before we get under way. I'd like to go over them with you one by one.

2. You: After thinking this assignment through, I've reached the conclusion that I'm not the most effective choice to get the job done as efficiently as possible. Half the work is technical analysis, and my specialty is *market* analysis. *That's* the part of the job I should be doing. Have you talked to Smith? He's the technical expert. We'd save a lot of time using him on this.

3. You: I've looked at this thoroughly, and I'd like to take a pass on it. It's not the kind of assignment I can really sink my teeth into. I've got some alternatives to suggest, however . . .

> **TIP**
>
> Successful responses *decline* an assignment without *rejecting* it. The key is to provide alternatives.

RESPONSES TO ANTICIPATE WHEN DECLINING AN ASSIGNMENT

1. I *really* want you to do this.

Reply with:

I would be glad to do it, if I didn't think there were people here who could do it more effectively. I strongly feel that my taking on this assignment would not be the best use of our resources.

2. How can you turn something like this down?

Reply with:

It isn't easy, and I'm grateful for the confidence you've shown in me. That's why I'd like us to sit down and review the project once more. Until we've addressed the issues I've mentioned, I can't in good conscience tell you that I can accomplish what we both want from this assignment.

3. I'm not accustomed to being turned down like this.

Reply with:

I'm not turning you down. I'm just suggesting that you reconsider your choice for this assignment.

TAKING A COMPLIMENT—WITH GRACE

This should be easy. Your boss says something nice to you. You thank her. And you're both happy. End of story

For many of us, not quite the end.

If you have a hard time taking a compliment gracefully and comfortably, you're not alone. From childhood, many of us have been admonished to be "modest," and we've been warned that people who get too full of themselves will, sooner or later, fall flat on their faces. Unfortunately, such injunctions against feeling good about our accomplishments don't produce true modesty, but instead make us seem graceless and ungrateful when we are complimented. Learning how to accept a compliment gracefully not only lets us claim our just desserts with poise, dignity, and pleasure, but also allows us to show the appropriate generosity to the person who gave the compliment. And when you're dealing with your boss, that's important.

STEP 1: Start with thank you. If you add the equivalent of "Coming from you, that really means something," you have a perfectly adequate response.

STEP 2: Consider using the occasion to build additional goodwill and good feeling between you and your boss. Begin by expressing your pleasure and gratitude. Express your regard for your boss.

STEP 3: Share the praise with others who deserve it. Name names. Recognize your colleagues and coworkers.

As important as it is to say the right things when you accept a compliment, avoid saying and doing the wrong things:

- Don't "confess" unworthiness. This does not make you look modest. It makes the person who paid you the compliment feel foolish.
- Don't respond with a long speech.

YOUR SCRIPT: ACCEPTING A COMPLIMENT

Here's a typical scenario:

Boss: Hey, Sarah, I want to tell you that I think you've handled Smith's problem very intelligently. That was good work.

You: Thanks. Coming from you, that's a real compliment. If there's one thing I've learned working in this department, it's to put the customer first. You've taught us to be good listeners, and that's the first step in customer relations.

TIP
Accept a compliment by giving a compliment—not just thanks.

RESPONSES TO ANTICIPATE WHEN ACCEPTING A COMPLIMENT

1. You deserve it.

Reply with:
I've had a good example set for me. You've given me a lot of support. It's meant a lot.

2. I don't give praise lightly.

Reply with:
I know you don't. That's why I'm thrilled with your remarks. They mean a great deal to me.

TAKING YOUR LUMPS—WITH DIGNITY

Let's face it: criticism from the boss is at best disturbing and, at worst, intimidating. Nevertheless, while you may never learn to welcome criticism, you can adopt strategies of responding to it in a constructive manner.

STEP 1: Accept criticism as an opportunity. All criticism, even unmerited criticism, is useful to you. Criticism, after all, may actually point out things you are doing ineffectively or poorly—things you could do better.

STEP 2: Fight the impulse to respond defensively. Listen and learn.

STEP 3: Realize that criticism is a perception, nothing more. Objective measurements—sales figures, for example—may indicate that you are doing a fine job, yet your boss may find something to criticize. Does this mean your boss is wrong or an ungrateful jerk? Quite possibly. But that conclusion should not prompt you to ignore the criticism. Explore, with yourself and with your boss, the reasons behind the criticism. Can you do something that will maintain the excellent sales performance you have achieved while also allowing your boss to *perceive* that you are doing a good job?

STEP 4: Do not meekly accept unjust or unfounded criticism, but don't reject it. Learn from it. Learn about creating more positive perceptions.

STEP 5: Seize the opportunity to respond to criticism, to communicate in a way that can strengthen and enhance your relationship with your boss.

STEP 6: While listening to criticism, demonstrate that you are hearing the criticism.

Send the right nonverbal signals to show that the criticism is registering with you:

- Make and maintain eye contact with your boss.
- Monitor your own signals of resistance, such as a hand placed over the mouth or on the forehead as if to shade—and partially conceal—the eyes, or arms folded across the chest. Such gestures are powerful signals of resistance that tell your boss you are determined *not* to hear her.

- If possible, both you and your boss should be seated during the discussion, since standing suggests and promotes face-to-face confrontation.

- If you must stand, it is best to keep your hands at your sides and to avoid the temptation to place your arms akimbo. This suggests defiance and sends a provocative message.

TIP

Your objective is *not* to appear passive, but open, willing to listen, to learn, to change, and to cooperate.

Your script: taking criticism

Some ways to profit from close encounters of the worst kind:

1. **Boss:** I don't want to run you down, but you should have been able to process those orders faster. Your trouble is that you need to delegate responsibility more effectively.

   You: I appreciate what you are saying. I'd be grateful for any advice you can give me on how to expedite these kinds of orders. I'm open to suggestion. I would certainly like to see the orders get out of here faster myself.

2. **Boss:** I have not been entirely pleased with the quality of the work coming out of your department. I want to talk to you about it.

   You: I wasn't aware of a problem, so it is very important that we talk and I get your input.

3. **Boss:** You've got some big, big problems here. A 2.5-percent reject rate is just too high. Let me tell you something, I just won't tolerate it.

   You: I'm aware of the problem, and I'd like to sit down and talk to you about it. I want to hear what you've got to say, and then I'll tell you how I plan to make improvements. It would be very helpful to get your opinion on the steps I plan to take.

TIP

Your boss may actually be spoiling for a confrontation. In all cases, your best verbal strategy is to avoid confrontation without, however, evading the underlying issues. Engage the issues rather than personalities. If you feel hurt, offended, or threatened, you'll just have to put those feelings on hold while you engage the issues.

Responses to anticipate when taking criticism

1. Look, you'd better shape up here.

Reply with:

I've heard your observations, and I need to review the problems you've pointed out. I'll come back to you with a plan that addresses these difficulties.

2. Generally, you do a fine job, but I hope that you can show improvement in the areas we discussed.

Reply with:

Well, your observations have been very helpful, and I'm confident that the problems you've noted can be resolved.

3. I hope you don't feel I'm picking on you.

Reply with:

If this is being picked on, I can use it. I need all the feedback I can get. To be frank, I don't agree with everything you've said, but you have given me a lot to think about. I'll review my methods and make some changes I think you will like.

4. I need to see significant improvement.

Reply with:

So do I. Let me review the situation. I have to say that my initial reaction is that you are overstating the degree of the problem, but I do agree that my department can perform at a higher level, and I will do everything possible to achieve that level. I appreciate your input, and we will do better. That I can promise you.

HANDLING SNAFU SITUATIONS

What was said about taking criticism applies as well to handling snafu situations. Yes, they're bad. No, nobody *wants* things to go wrong. But just about everything that happens in the workplace is an opportunity for communication, and communication can enhance relations between you and your boss.

- Most mistakes are not fatal or even beyond repair. Often, the more serious problem is the *feelings* mishaps produce. These can be truly destructive. Effective communication can minimize such damaging effect. In many cases, skillful communication can even produce positive feelings.

Accidents and errors contain at least one valuable element: the opportunity for forgiveness. If some of us derive satisfaction from affixing blame, it feels even better to forgive.

TIP

In apologizing for accidents and errors, never tell your boss (or anyone else, for that matter) how he or she should feel about it.

We'll deal with five major types of snafus, but all may be approached with the same basic strategy:

STEP 1: Acknowledge the error.

STEP 2: Let your boss know that he would be justified in getting angry, then thank him for his understanding and patience.

STEP 3: Make positive suggestions for working together to repair any damage.

When the Problem Is Your Fault

Report the error as soon as possible, since it's better coming from you than if your boss discovers it on his own or, even worse, some third party makes the revelation.

STEP 1: Do not run into the office in panic. The emotions you telegraph will strongly affect how your boss receives and interprets the news.

STEP 2: Try to take time first to assess the nature and degree of the error.

STEP 3: Try to prepare proposals for controlling and repairing the damage.

Armed with possible solutions, report the problem. However, it is not always the best idea to volunteer your assessment of the degree of damage. Use judgment before you deliver your assessment.

- An immediate assessment may be necessary for the good of the project or the company.
- If possible, however, report the particulars of error minimally. There is a strategic advantage in giving your boss the feeling that he is assessing the error for himself rather than having to take your "biased" version of it.

TIP

If you deliver a full report, try to go about it objectively. Avoid extremes— either bending over backwards to excusing yourself or beating your breast in a headlong rush to take all the blame.

Follow this overall plan:

1. Pause to assess the error.
2. Prepare potential remedies.
3. Report the error as concisely as circumstances allow.
4. Admit fault.
5. Acknowledge your boss's right to be angry.
6. Thank him for his patience and understanding.
7. Promise cooperation and swift action.

When It's Not Your Fault

When you encounter an accident or error for which you are not at fault, do not walk away from responsibility.

STEP 1: If possible, find the person who is responsible for the problem and discuss the matter with him as helpfully as you can, always focusing on constructive solutions rather than on blame.

STEP 2:   If it is impossible or impractical to identify the responsible person, and assuming it is a problem you cannot address and solve entirely by yourself or on your own authority, report it to your boss.

TIP

Beware of two harmful tendencies when we report problems caused by others: We tend to exaggerate the seriousness of the problem. We also tend to harbor a certain self-satisfaction.

- The key strategy here is neither to ignore nor to revel in problems caused by others but, rather, to try to discover the opportunity within the problem.

It is to your advantage if your boss perceives you as a problem solver. You *need* a problem. Find one, report it, and suggest solutions.

It's Not Your Fault, But It Is Your Problem

Subordinates and others may cause problems for which you are not directly responsible, but which are, nevertheless, your problems.

STEP 1:   If you can handle such problems immediately, efficiently, and effectively without resorting to higher authority, by all means do so. Reporting such errors and accidents can be a delicate and tricky matter.

STEP 2:   When you must make a report, communicate your adherence to Harry Truman's universally respected motto: *The buck stops here.* You may assess fault—your subordinate failed to do something, a supplier failed to deliver, and so on—but you *must* demonstrate your willingness to take ultimate responsibility.

STEP 3:   Turn the event into something positive with a strong response that tells your boss that you are a problem solver.

When You're Baffled

It's bad enough when problems or errors occur. Bad as this is, it can get worse. Sometimes things go wrong for—as far as you can tell—no particular reason at all. You're baffled. You're in an uncomfortable spot. If you cannot get an immediate handle on the problem, you cannot instantly demonstrate mastery of the situation. This may scare you, and it certainly won't make your boss happy.

What you need is an ally.

And who would that be?

Your boss.

STEP 1:   Admit the difficulty calmly: "I need your help." This simple phrase is practically a magic formula, which even the hardest-hearted boss will find difficult to resist. "I need your help. We are missing three customer files. I don't know why, and I don't know where they could be. Rather than waste more time hunting for them, I'd like to call the clients. How do I do it without embarrassing us?"

> **TIP**
>
> Don't *dump* the problem in your boss's lap, but do enlist his aid. Suggest as much of a course of action as you can, but don't try to go it alone. Transform the situation from *I* to *we*. Work out a solution together.

What To Do When a Project Fails

Mistakes, errors, glitches. They happen. So does failure. A product line you've developed doesn't sell, a client you've courted doesn't buy, a contract you've angled for goes to someone else. In cases like this, depending on your employer and your track record, your job may or may not be on the line. Your ego, however, *certainly* is. And it is very hard to communicate strongly and positively when you are feeling bad about yourself. Yet it is essential that you do just that, salvaging whatever you can from the wreckage.

Much that you salvage is valuable. At the least, you may gather information that will help you learn from your mistakes. What you are salvaging—saving—is the future. And it is the future that constitutes the core of your strategy when you confront your boss in the wake of failure.

STEP 1:   Avoid such phrases as "should have," "wish I had," "if I had only," and so on.

STEP 2: Use phrases like "next time," "in the future," "we"—not "I"— "learned a lesson for the future," "we won't do it this way next time," and so on.

STEP 3: Accept responsibility for the present, but hold on to the future: potential and opportunity.

Your script: dealing with failure.

Here are some viable approaches:

1. **You**: I made a mistake in the report I submitted to our client. The figures for items two and seven are wrong. I tried to catch the documents before they went out of here, but I was too late. I've prepared a corrected report with a cover letter that I'd like you to read. Assuming you approve, I'll send this to our client by messenger. I'll call them to tell them it's coming. In the future, I see, we're just going to have to build in a full day's proofreading and fact-checking time.

- This is the forthright approach. Error is admitted, and no excuses are offered. Nor is there any wallowing in guilt. The emphasis is on what to do in the future.

2. **You**: The figures are in on the client's promotional program. I'd be lying if I said I wasn't disappointed in the performance of what I thought would be a big sale. We worked hard on this, and it's rough on us all when things don't turn out as we had hoped and expected. I'd like to schedule a meeting with you to review the project and see what we can learn from it. I don't want to be disappointed the next time we promote our client's product.

- In this approach, there is a willingness to learn. No excuses are offered, but perspective is maintained.

Responses to anticipate when admitting failure.

1. Don't be too hard on yourself.

Reply with:

Thanks. I appreciate that. Don't worry. I know that tearing myself up is not going to keep this kind of thing from happening again. What I want to do is take a good, hard look at the problem, analyze it, learn from it, and then discuss it with you.

2. Frankly, you're not being hard enough on yourself. You're letting yourself off too easy, I'm afraid.

Reply with:

I take full responsibility for what happened. If I thought an elaborate demonstration of remorse would do anything for our bottom line, I'd be in here with a cat-o'-nine-tails. I promise you that I will be very hard on whatever caused this error. That's what I'll devote my energy to. We won't let it happen again.

COMMUNICATING YOUR DECISION TO QUIT

Termination of employment—whether voluntary or not—shouldn't bring communication to an end. Depending on what you do for a living, the business world can be quite small, and it is possible that you and your boss will cross paths again. You may even return to the firm. Termination can be a positive event; don't let your words make it negative. But even when termination comes under bad circumstances, don't turn a bad thing into something even worse. Use words to keep your termination as open-ended as possible.

Quitting—either you make a decision to go into business for yourself or you've found another job.

- Before you announce your resignation, *think*. Do you absolutely want to quit?
- Or do you want to use the job offer you've just gotten as a bargaining chip with your present company?

Unless you are firmly bent on leaving, you should approach the "terminal" conversation *as if* you are willing to entertain (or are even seeking) a counteroffer from your boss.

STEP 1: Avoid beginning with something like, "I have accepted an offer from . . ." Instead, start with "I have *received* an offer from. . . . "

STEP 2: Give the particulars, including money and other conditions that make the offer attractive.

STEP 3: Even if you are certain that you don't want to use the offer as leverage in your present position—that what you want is *out*, period—don't rush to slam the verbal doors behind you.

STEP 4: Regardless of your reasons for leaving and your feelings about the job and the boss you are leaving, your "terminal" conversation should be framed as positively as possible. Don't lie, but do avoid concentrating on the negative reasons that have motivated your decision. Emphasize the positive: "I've decided to accept a position that offers me the kind of opportunities for advancement that, at least for now, we can't match here."

> **TIP**
>
> Use phrases such as "at least for now" or "at this time" to keep the door ever so slightly ajar. The object is not to soften the blow of your departure, but to demonstrate that you are a valuable person, a business asset, and that you are fully aware of your value.

STEP 5: Plan your departure carefully, so that you can offer your boss something more than good words. Make it clear that you will do everything possible to ease the transition for your replacement. Engineering a smooth transition will go a long way toward defusing any smoldering resentment.

Your script: quitting your job

Some parting scenarios:

1. **You:** This is the hardest thing I've ever had to say to you, so I better just come out and say it. I've been offered a position as senior analyst with XYZ at a salary of $XX,000. As you know, that's more than we're in a position to ante up here. Add to that the way management is structured over there—well, I've got a faster track to account executive than what might be offered here. This place has been like family to me, but for the sake of my career I don't see how I can turn down the offer.

   • This is a good example of an opening that reflects a sincere intention to leave the company, coupled with equally sincere regrets about doing so, yet leaves the door ajar for a possible counteroffer.

2. **You:** I've been approached by XYZ Products with an offer of a position as assistant sales manager. I haven't said yes yet, but I've got to tell you that it is a very attractive offer—despite the loyalty I feel to our company and to you personally. The salary is XX percent higher, and the opportunities for advancement seem considerably greater. They want me to start in four weeks.

- This leaves the door open wider, more deliberately inviting a counteroffer.

3. **You:** I've worked here six years, and during that time I've gotten very close to a lot of people, including you. That's why it's not easy for me to tell you that I am accepting an offer from XYZ Printing Company as a press manager. The money, the hours, and the job security are just too inviting to pass up. Even with all that, it's a hard decision. I've learned a lot here, but it is time to move on to a position of broader responsibility.

- This approach closes the door firmly, though not rudely. Unless your boss is very devoted to you, this type of announcement will garner no counteroffer.

RESPONSES TO ANTICIPATE WHEN YOU QUIT

1. What would it take to make you change your mind?

Reply with:

I'll admit it. I would love it if you could make it impossible for me to take the offer. [Then list what you want: salary, hours, vacation, working conditions, position, etc.] That's what I would need to turn down the offer in good conscience.

2. You *can't* leave at a time like this.

Reply with:

I know this isn't the best time for the company. But it is when the offer came. For me, it is a case of act now or miss the opportunity, and this is an opportunity I cannot afford to miss. I've got three weeks. You have my assurance that I'll do whatever is necessary to ease the transition for you.

3. I feel betrayed. Stabbed in the back.

Reply with:

I'm sorry you feel that way. You must know that my leaving has nothing to do with you or with the company. It's a matter of opportunity for me. I don't see this as leaving ABC Company, but as doing what is necessary to build my career. If I could do it as effectively by staying, I would. It is very hard for me to leave.

4. I've enjoyed working with you, and I wish you the best of luck.

Reply with:

Thanks. Coming from you, that means a great deal to me. I know that we'll be staying in touch, and I am grateful to you for having made this a rewarding experience.

HOW TO RESPOND WHEN YOU'RE FIRED

People tell you that getting fired is not the end of the world. But when it comes, it might as well be. Your emotions may overwhelm you—feelings of failure, embarrassment, anger, and fear.

- The fact is that people are fired every day. It is a normal—not inevitable, but normal—phase of the employment cycle. Almost certainly, you will survive the experience, and you might even get a better job.

For the moment, your objective is to achieve effective verbal management—no small task when you are assailed by powerful emotions. Your strategy should be to make it possible for your boss to leave the door open—even just a crack—after she hands you your walking papers. How feasible that objective is depends on why you've been dismissed. If it's "for cause"—failure to do your assigned job, misconduct, excessive absenteeism, poor performance, and so on—the going will be rough. More often, however, dismissal comes as a result of economic conditions, corporate reorganization, or phase-out of a program. In these cases, do what you can to make reentry possible.

TIP

Dismissal for cause does not usually come out of the blue. It generally follows warnings and employee conferences. If you feel that you are being treated unjustly, plan to seek counsel from the appropriate union or professional or governmental agency. You may want to secure legal advice as well. At the time of dismissal, it is generally best to threaten nothing. Do, however, make clear your position that you are being treated unfairly, that you have endeavored to perform well for the company, and that you feel you deserve better treatment. You might ask, quite straightforwardly, if there is an alternative course available: temporary separation during a review process, for example.

STEP 1: In cases where the dismissal is made without prejudice, perhaps even with regret, because of economic or other circumstances, respond by letting your boss know that while she has fired you, you have not dismissed her. You are greatly dismayed by the news, of course, since you have found working here such a rewarding experience.

STEP 2: Determine, in conversation with your boss, whether the dismissal is permanent or temporary. Might you expect to be hired in this or another capacity at another time?

TIP

Beware of prompting false hope from the boss. She may tell you what you want to hear because she finds the experience of letting you go painful.

STEP 3: Ask what circumstances would make continuation of this position—or hiring in another position—possible.

YOUR SCRIPT: HANDLING TERMINATION.

Some ideas for making the final scene less final:

1. **Boss:** I'm afraid that, due to corporate restructuring, we're going to have to let you go, effective two weeks from today. I wish there were something I could do about it.

You: I don't have to tell you, this is a shock. Let me digest this news for a day or two, and then I'd like to discuss the situation with you.

- If you have some advance warning, it is best to delay your response rather than stammer something while you are under the most pressure. When you return later for a conversation, raise the possibility of alternatives to dismissal or layoff, discuss the permanence of the layoff, and go over with your boss ways in which she is willing to help you find another job.

2. **Boss**: As you know, we have not been satisfied with your performance. I'm afraid at this point I have no choice but to let you go. The severance is effective immediately. I've prepared a severance check for you.

   You: I would be lying if I told you this is entirely unexpected. I had hoped, however, that we could work out some alternative to dismissal. I've enjoyed working here, and I believe I've given this company a lot. Since your decision does seem final, I'll leave without further discussion—except to tell you that you are losing an able, skilled, and loyal employee.

- When there is obviously no room to maneuver, leave with dignity, including a statement meant to set the record straight.

3. **Boss**: It's clear we're not getting along together, so I've decided to terminate our working relationship, effective two weeks from today.

   You: I am sorry you feel this way and, of course, even sorrier that you feel you must take such an extreme action. Since your decision seems to be based on feeling, it would help me very much if we could talk again before I leave. It would also be very helpful—and, I think, appropriate—if you could put your reasons for my dismissal more concretely and specifically, perhaps in the form of a letter. I have enjoyed working here, and I sincerely believe that I am good for this company. I don't want to leave without knowing exactly what went wrong.

- This response accomplishes three things: It leaves the door slightly ajar. It does not let your boss off the hook so easily, but compels her to review her decision. And it underscores your commitment to the firm.

RESPONSES TO ANTICIPATE WHEN YOU'VE BEEN FIRED

1. We have nothing further to discuss.

Reply with:

I don't agree. Other than knowing that you are somehow dissatisfied with my performance, I have very little idea of why I'm being fired. That is what we have to discuss, and I would like to discuss it.

2. I can't hold out much hope for another job here soon.

Reply with:

I'm not asking for much hope. I want to leave here with good feelings on all sides, and I want you to know that, no matter where I go from here, I'm always eager to hear of opportunities at XYZ.

3. The matter is closed.

Reply with:

For you it may be, but I have a lot of questions without answers. I would like to ask them, and I would like to hear the answers. I don't intend to argue. I just want to find out what went wrong.

CHAPTER 5

Putting Yourself Across . . . to Colleagues

SELF-TEST YOUR SAVVY IN COMMUNICATING WITH COLLEAGUES

The following is a simple diagnostic test. A smaller and more selective version of the self-test in Chapter 1, its purpose is not to test your knowledge of communication theory or techniques, but to help you gauge how effectively you communicate with your colleagues in a day-to-day business context. For the most part, you will find it easy to guess the "right" answer. But getting the "right" answer is not the point of the test. Respond honestly, even if you feel that your response is not the best one possible. This is *not* a contest. The object is solely self-inventory.

1. There's a lot of backstabbing that goes on where I work. T/F ____

2. I am open with my colleagues. T/F ____

3. I am pretty effective at getting my colleagues to cooperate with me. T/F ____

4. I am afraid my colleagues will steal my ideas. T/F ____

5. I ask my colleagues about what interests and concerns *them*. T/F ____

6. My colleagues respect me. T/F ____

7. My colleagues are jealous of me. T/F ____

8. I criticize issues and actions rather than people. T/F ____

9. I criticize only what I believe can be remedied, improved, or eliminated. T/F ____

147

10. I criticize constructively.   T/F ____

11. A dispute has a winner and a loser.   T/F ____

12. I don't make waves.   T/F ____

13. I dread making apologies.   T/F ____

14. I drink *lots* of coffee.   T/F ____

15. I enjoy the people I work with.   T/F ____

16. I enjoy conversation with my colleagues.   T/F ____

17. I feel like part of a team.   T/F ____

18. I get plenty of sleep.   T/F ____

19. I'm good at "brainstorming."   T/F ____

20. I handle stress well.   T/F ____

21. I have "championed" projects and ideas.   T/F ____

22. I have a happy home life.   T/F ____

23. I know my colleagues and their jobs, duties, and areas
    of expertise.   T/F ____

24. Our office is *very* political.   T/F ____

25. The people I work with waste my time with too much talk.   T/F ____

26. I share ideas with my colleagues.   T/F ____

27. If someone gets angry, I tell them to calm down.   T/F ____

28. I think business meetings are a waste of time.   T/F ____

29. I try to respond fully and informatively to my colleagues'
    ideas and projects.   T/F ____

30. I usually get my way.   T/F ____

31. Sometimes you just have to holler and argue the
    other person down.   T/F ____

TOTAL T/F   ____

Score 1 point for each "True" response and 0 for each "False" response, EXCEPT for questions 1, 4, 7, 11, 12, 13, 14, 24, 25, 27, 28, and 31. For *these questions only*, SUBTRACT 1 point for each "True" response. Record your total. A score below +17 indicates that you would benefit from practicing the communication techniques discussed in this chapter. (Note: It is possible to have a negative score.)

WORDS TO USE WITH COLLEAGUES

adapt	merge
admire	modify
advice	objective
advise	open
agree	opinion
collaborate	our
combine	respect
confer	results
consult	rethink
contribute	reveal
contribution	revise
cooperate	straightforward
data	study
differ	suggestion
disagree	synergy
efficiency	talk
efficient	team
facts	tell me
feasible	thought
goal	thoughts
handshake	together
honest	us
input	we
may I	

PHRASES TO USE WITH COLLEAGUES

constructive criticism

get your opinion

get your take on

great idea

How would you like me to proceed?

let's talk about it

let's work it out together

pick your brain

seek your advice

team effort

value your opinion

value your thoughts

What do you need?

What would you like me to do?

work together

work this out

WORDS TO AVOID WITH COLLEAGUES

absurd	insane
bad	refuse
can't	ridiculous
crazy	stupid
doomed	unworkable
failure	wrong
impossible	wrong-headed
incompetent	

PHRASES TO AVOID WITH COLLEAGUES

Are you out of your mind?

bad idea

don't know what you're doing

don't know what you're talking about

don't know your job

no good

won't work

you wouldn't understand

you're crazy

BODY-LANGUAGE STRATEGY FOR COLLEAGUES

The key element of body-language strategy in successfully working with colleagues is to establish openness. Look and act approachable. Generally, the more communication you invite, the better.

- Walk with arms at your sides.
- Smile.
- Make eye contact.
- Use open hand gestures—palms slightly upturned.

BODY LANGUAGE TO AVOID WITH COLLEAGUES

If the key strategic element is openness, obviously any postures and gestures that communicate standoffishness should be avoided.

Avoid:

- Walking with hands in pockets
- Walking with arms crossed
- Walking with head down; this suggests that you are "lost in thought" and do not want to be disturbed

- Averting eye contact
- Frowning
- Lip biting
- Gesturing with hands near mouth or face
- Shaking head "no"
- Pushing gestures—using the hands as if to push people or things away
- Sitting with hands to head

HOW EVERYONE CAN WIN WHEN COMMUNICATING WITH COLLEAGUES

Putting yourself across to your colleagues is more than just getting along with people—although that element is essential, and the body-language strategies just discussed will go a long way toward conveying, nonverbally, that "get-along" message. Beyond this, successful, persuasive communication with colleagues also requires creating an atmosphere in which everyone feels that something has been gained. Everyone needs to be a winner. If you look at communicating with colleagues as a zero-sum game, in which someone must lose if someone else wins, you make effective colleague communication almost impossible. If talking to you means losing, few will venture down that road.

Setting up a win-win communication environment depends on four principles:

1. *Demonstrate respect for your colleagues.* You can think of this as the Golden Rule: Do unto your colleague as you would have him or her do unto you. Listen to coworkers. Hear what they have to say. Then demonstrate that you have heard them and that you value what they say.

> **TIP**
>
> Respect for colleagues may be shown in many ways, big and small. But it is the small gestures that are often the most cumulatively effective. Make clear how you value what your colleagues say by punctuating conversations with such phrases as "That's interesting," "It's worth thinking about," "I never thought of that before," "I see," and so on.

2. Establish ground rules, define responsibilities, and refine and modify these definitions as necessary.   Human beings are territorial animals. Much workplace hostility and many barriers to communication are "turf" disputes. Indeed, it is amazing how many companies misuse—and also frustrate—their human resources by failing adequately to define responsibilities and areas of authority. This can happen even when so-called official job descriptions exist.

Create a relatively threat-free atmosphere by openly discussing your responsibilities and "turf" areas. Understand them and agree on them. Be sufficiently flexible to alter them as the demands of your business may require.

> **TIP**
> Consensus on responsibility is a key not only to efficient operation, but to successful ongoing communication.

3. Don't suffer in silence. When necessary, "sound your horn."   Avoid unpleasant, even hurtful, encounters with coworkers by alerting them to any problems they may be causing you. If something bothers you, discuss it in a calm but firm and unmistakable way—a way that educates and informs rather than scolds or threatens.

4. Make creative small talk.   Contrary to what all too many managers believe, small talk in the workplace need not be a waste of time. Indeed, it can be an important medium through which coworkers bond into an effective team by learning to appreciate and respect one another as human beings, not just as job titles. Demonstrate an interest in your fellow workers by asking about families, hobbies, interests, and outside activities. Small talk builds morale and improves cohesiveness.

> **TIP**
> Don't let small talk get out of hand. When enough is enough, and it's time to get down to the task at hand, terminate the small talk by politely and specifically pointing out what you have to do. Avoid saying, "Bill, I've got work to do." Instead, try: "Tom, you'll have to excuse me, but the XYZ report has got to get done by the ten o'clock meeting." If you don't have a pressing task, cite one that is as specific as possible: "Bill, I'm just settling down to catching up on my mail. Let's talk later."

SECRETS OF GETTING BIG RESULTS FROM SMALL TALK

"So now I have to *learn* to shoot the breeze?"

Of course not. But you may find useful some advice on shooting the breeze *effectively*. By "effectively" I mean using casual, day-to-day small talk to

- Help build a team.
- Establish and strengthen your position among your colleagues.
- Give you leverage to enable you to secure support and compliance.
- Generally make the workplace more harmonious.

All this from "shooting the breeze"?

Not quite. If you enjoy making conversation, ask yourself why. If the answer—the *honest* answer—is that you like to hear other people talk so that you can learn about them, congratulations. You are already well on your way to making *effective* small talk. But if most people answered this question honestly, they would say that their pleasure in small talk derives from hearing *themselves* talk. Now, there is nothing terribly wrong with this. Why shouldn't you get pleasure from holding court? But if you want to harness the power of small talk to enhance your position and influence among your colleagues and to improve the work environment, you're going to have give up some of that listening to yourself and start devoting more of your small-talk time to hearing others.

The easiest way to begin is to reduce the number of declarative sentences you utter and to increase the number of questions you ask.

Let's say you run into Joe Schmidt from accounting in the hall. You like Joe. Ordinarily, you might say something like this: "Hey, Joe! Listen, I just saw a movie over the weekend that you've got to get yourself to . . ." Friendly, warm—nothing wrong with that. But here's a more effective approach to small talk in the workplace: "Hey, Joe! Do you like movies?"

Now, let Joe talk. Let him tell you something about himself.

Is this just being polite? Well, it *is* considerate, and if being polite is making other people feel good, it certainly is true that showing interest in another person usually creates good feelings.

But asking questions is more than being polite. You already know what *you* like and don't like. You already know about yourself. You already know what you want and don't want. You already understand which are your hot buttons. Why waste valuable small-talk time going over what you already know? Instead, use it to learn something new.

Knowledge, the well-worn cliché goes, *is power*. The more you know about Joe Schmidt, the stronger your basis for communication with him.

- Small talk can be the key that unlocks the needs, wants, wishes, thoughts, and inclinations of those with whom you work. The more you know about your colleagues, the more effectively you can communicate with them.

Remember, effective communication—which, at its most effective, we call *persuasion*—depends on a perception of gain. It is difficult to persuade someone to act in a certain way or to do something if that person feels either that he will not gain from compliance or, even worse, will lose as a result of compliance. It is, therefore, to your advantage to appeal to the self-interest of others. Small talk can help you learn about that self-interest.

TIP

Use small talk to learn about your colleagues—what drives them, what upsets them, what pleases them, what interests them. Don't squander small talk on yourself—your own interests and needs.

GETTING INFORMATION OR HELP FROM COLLEAGUES

On a day-to-day basis, what you need most frequently from your colleagues is information and help. But before you ask for information or help, you need to identify the best sources. This may be obvious to you, but if it is not, ask yourself the following questions:

1. Who does what job?
2. Who seems to command influence and enjoy respect?
3. Who seems to be "in the loop"—communicating with upper levels of management most frequently and effectively?
4. Who has been climbing the corporate ladder?
5. Who answers questions frequently?
6. Who is frequently quoted?

7. Who makes the key decisions?

8. Who writes the significant memos?

9. Who runs the meetings?

Identify these people, get to know them, and cultivate them as your primary sources of information and aid.

Asking for information or help is, of course, *taking* rather than *giving*. So you need to find something to give in return for information and help. What you can always give is your interest.

STEP 1: Cultivate the people you identify as key by taking an interest in what they do and say.

STEP 2: Engage them in conversation about what interests them.

STEP 3: If you run across an article or memo concerning a subject of interest to them, copy it or clip it and send it along to them.

STEP 4: Building on the key person's interests is a great way to build an information-sharing and helping relationship.

Accelerate the development of the information-sharing relationship by *asking* for a conversation rather than demanding help or information. Use such phrases as:

- "I'd like a chance to speak with you."
- "What's a good time to talk about something?"
- "I need to find out ____, and I'd really like to talk to you about it. What's a convenient time for you?"
- "Mind if I pick your brain?"

SECRETS OF SUCCESSFUL MEETINGS

In business, it's difficult to make any statement that doesn't invite disagreement. Make this one, however, and you're likely to get closer to universal agreement than you ever thought possible:

Most meetings are a waste of time.

In fact, the chorus of assent is likely to be interrupted by only one thing: a call to the second, third, or fourth meeting of the day. The masochistic irony of it all is that, even while most of us decry and deride meetings, we call for them, set them up, attend them, and endure them, all the while complaining that, really, the best ideas come from informal discussions held in the corridor.

Well, sometimes that's true. And sometimes—maybe even most times—formal meetings are boring and unproductive.

But there is a big problem with corridor spontaneity. It's just so—well—*spontaneous*. You can't control it. You can't summon it up at will. Potentially, the greatest advantage a formal meeting offers is a forum and format for "forcing" spontaneity. Used this way, meetings can be transformed from hollow time wasters to exciting generators of ideas. You can work with your colleagues to effect this transformation. Here are some techniques:

1. *Problem polling.*   Gather an impromptu meeting in a room with a blackboard or the equivalent. Ask the participants to call out the problems and issues of greatest concern to them. Have someone write them on the board. Do not discuss the problems or issues. Do not analyze. Do not interrupt the flow until the flow stops. Then restate each concern in positive terms. For instance: "I'm worried about quality control" becomes "Our objective is to improve quality control in order to reduce returns by 15 percent."

2. *Brainstorming.*   This is a tried-and-tested method for generating ideas. It works in small peer groups—usually of eight participants or fewer. Define an issue, then ask for ideas. You objective is quantity rather than quality. Allow no discussion of the ideas. Allow no judgment or criticism or, for that matter, praise. Have someone write each of the ideas on a blackboard. After the flow of ideas peters out, begin to analyze the ideas, focusing on how to establish criteria for judging the value of each idea. In this way, you should be able to winnow the welter of ideas down to a few viable ones.

3. *Small-group discussion.*   Break larger groups into small groups (four participants is a good number), each of which is assigned a particular problem or issue to discuss. Appoint a leader of each group, whose job it is to keep the talk focused. Another participant should record the results of the discussion. After a period of time, reconvene the smaller groups into a larger group and ask the recorders to share the results of the individual discussions.

PROMOTING AN IDEA OR PROJECT TO YOUR COLLEAGUES

Whether within the context of a single meeting or a series of meetings, the key to promoting a project or an idea is to get your colleagues—not just your supervisors—to invest in it, to claim a stake in it. The successful development of ideas and projects requires a champion, someone willing to fight for the idea or project, pushing it through, over, and around the many organizational and human obstacles that threaten to mire it in the muck of inertia. From among the ranks of colleagues and coworkers, the champion recruits "investors" in the idea or project.

What Is a Champion?

In the early 1950s, the U.S. Navy solicited proposals for the development of the Sidewinder missile. The Navy generated a long and stringent list of specifications. What William B. McLean, the physicist in charge of a missile-development team at the Naval Weapons Center, China Lake, California, understood, however, is that specifications suffer from a serious drawback: They force both customer and would-be contractor to presume they know the answers before they have any experience with the product. McLean, a scientist, wanted to get the answers first. Accordingly, he sheltered the Sidewinder program from internal critics and even from the "customer"—the U.S. Navy. He ignored the specs as issued and concentrated instead on developing concepts that his own actual experiments indicated would work.

McLean carried out these experiments on his own time, in his garage, in effect designing about 85 percent of the missile himself. Working within—as well as around—"The System," he scrounged money from other projects, and he scavenged spare parts from wherever he could, including junkyards in and around Pasadena. Once he developed a prototype, it failed. Actually, it failed 13 times—more than enough to kill the project. In fact, the Sidewinder officially ceased to exist. But McLean persisted, taking what he had learned from the 13 "failures" to make modifications and launch one more test, on September 11, 1953, which landed right on target. As quickly as it had been officially killed, the Sidewinder was officially reborn, and the Navy took an interest.

But now the Air Force balked. Not to be daunted, the Sidewinder's champion proposed a "shoot out" against the Air Force's favored Falcon missile. The challenge was accepted, the contest took place, and the Sidewinder won. First tested in 1953, it remains a key part of the U.S. arsenal, a weapon of incredible longevity. And it owes its existence to the man who championed it.

Your script: championing an idea

Here is an exchange in which a "champion" recruits a colleague "investor":

Champion: Sue, before we go into this meeting, I'd like to give you some advance information on the new widget idea. This is information you should have before it goes to a general discussion.

Note the approach. "Advance information" is made available exclusively to Sue. This makes her feel that her opinion is truly valued, that she is perceived as a special and powerful person within the company. This is a much more effective approach than simply saying "I need your support." "I need your support" is *asking* for something, whereas providing "advance information" is *giving* something.

Note also the phrase "the new widget idea." The champion avoids the possessive pronoun *my* and is careful to substitute the neutral article *the*. The object is to avoid laying claim to the idea or project. You want the "investor" to feel that she has a personal stake in the proposal.

Sue: Well, thanks. I'll look it over.

Champion: Great. This really needs not just your support, but your tender loving care. It needs your expertise. I want you in at a stage where you can contribute to shaping the project. Also, I know that, with you behind it, this thing will sail through the meeting to the next stage.

The champion continues to stress the value of Sue's involvement. She will make a genuine contribution. This is team building.

TIP

The champion must choose his allies wisely. Keep the group small enough to promote "ownership" of the project. A small group of "investors" is most effective in building reception of the project to critical mass, at which point consensus kicks in, and the project is in the best position to gain the support of management.

HANDLING DISSENT FROM YOUR COLLEAGUES

Working well with your colleagues is hardly about avoiding disputes, and when you champion an idea or project, you can count on at least some opposition. The key strategy here is not to suppress opposition, to ignore it, or to beat it down. Instead:

STEP 1:   Identify issues on which you differ and then separate these issues from the personalities behind them.

STEP 2:   Pit issue against issue, not personality against personality or ego against ego.

TIP

Focusing on opposing points of view on a particular issue or problem will not, of course, magically resolve the dispute, but it is essential to molding a cooperative team out of disparate personalities. Team members may have differing views, but they must be committed to common goals. Assuming your project goes into development, you do not want it subject at some later stage to sabotage, whether deliberate or unconscious, by disgruntled colleagues.

STEP 3:   In the course of a dispute, work toward shifting the focus from the disagreement to some alternative or set of alternatives on which agreement can be reached. Bring about a shift from a negative to a positive.

YOUR SCRIPT: HANDLING DISSENT

Colleague: Look, you're just out of your mind if you think the consumer will pay $25 for this widget.

The bait has been offered: "Out of your mind" is a provocative, offensive, and personal attack. You can take the bait and pitch the argument at an unproductive, even destructive, personal level, or you can shift the dispute productively to *issues*.

You: So you think the price point is wrong for the market?

No emotional, personal words here. Just business: "price point," "market." Note that the possessive pronoun *my* is also absent: not "my price point," but "*the* price point."

> **Colleague**: That's right. Your idea will never sell.

The other fellow persists in keeping it personal: "*your* idea." Refocus.

> **You**: Let's forget about the price point for just a minute. What about the product? What's your take on that?

Still refusing to take the bait, you look for some point of agreement.

> **Colleague**: The product is fine—great—but what good is it if we can't sell it at $25?

With this point of agreement, you've got something to build on.

> **You**: Maybe we *can* lower it. What if we increase initial rollout . . .

And so on. The keys to handling dissent are:

1. Keep the focus on the issues and away from egos.
2. Look for areas of agreement. Build on these.

But isn't point number two just evading the tough issues? What good is finding agreement if the obstacles remain?

The answer to the first objection is no, looking for areas of agreement is not simple evasion. However, there is no guarantee that, first, you'll find areas of agreement and, second, that finding them will bring about ultimate harmony and cooperation. But by finding areas of agreement and building on them, you prompt your colleague to make an investment in the project, which, in turn, motivates her to find a way to make the idea work.

TIP

Moving from 100 percent disagreement to 50 percent (or 20 percent, or 10 percent . . .) agreement is a positive step. It's now up to you to decide whether the glass is half empty or half full. Proceed accordingly.

RESPONDING TO THE IDEAS AND PROJECTS OF OTHERS

Just as it is important to secure the support and cooperation of colleagues for the ideas and projects that you champion, you owe it to those you work with—and to your company as well as to yourself—to respond fully and informatively to ideas and projects your colleagues may propose and champion. Effective responses fall into two categories: positive reinforcement and constructive criticism.

Providing Positive Reinforcement to Colleagues

In general, *all* of your responses to the ideas and projects proposed by others in your organization should be positive. This does not mean giving mindless, unqualified approval; however, the most effective response identifies positive elements of an idea or project and comments on them before identifying and criticizing problems.

> **TIP**
>
> Once you reject an idea or project as 100 percent worthless, you and your colleague have very little reason to communicate and virtually no reason to communicate constructively.

Obviously, the task of communication is easiest and most pleasant when you *can* give unqualified approval to a project or idea. But, even in these cases, it is important to be specific.

- Responding to an idea or project with something like "That's great!" is not helpful or effective.
- Respond instead: "That's great! I'm especially excited about A, C, and E, which should greatly improve F, H, and I." Identify specific strengths in your response.

The more specific you are in your positive reinforcement, the more clearly you establish and demonstrate

1. The degree to which you value the project

2. The degree to which you are willing to cooperate to develop the project

Being specific also provides the basis for

1. Modifying parts of the project—emphasizing some aspects, reducing others
2. Providing criticism

The second point is especially important. The fact is that "unqualified" approval is rare in business. You may find an idea or project 99 percent wonderful, but it is to everyone's advantage for you to carve out a credible position that allows you to criticize that remaining 1 percent. Being specific about positive reinforcement earns you the right to be specific about criticism as well.

> **TIP**
>
> In contrast to most other business situations, providing positive reinforcement *should* take in personality and character. Praise the virtues of the project or idea, but also compliment the person or persons responsible: "This shows real creativity. You guys worked hard on this. It's great to be working with people like you."

The key to an effective positive reinforcement strategy is to think in terms of process rather than of product:

- Provide reinforcement at steps along the way of idea, project, or product development. The objective of reinforcing remarks is to further the process, increasing the prospects for the success of the next stage, and the stage, after that, and so on.
- Even if you are praising a finished product, look to the future—how the product fits into the ongoing process that is your business. Don't praise it as a done deed, a dead end.

> **TIP**
>
> Positive reinforcement should energize, encourage, and build. It should help to enable further achievement.

Here's an example of responding positively and effectively to an idea during the development of a product:

> **You:** I just want to congratulate you, Mary, and your team for coming up with the solution to problems A, B, and D. The scheme you've proposed for fast-tracking production is really innovative, but what's great about it is that, innovative as it is, it uses proven methods. I'm eager to work with you on this, and I'm confident that your team will now be able to come up with a satisfactory solution to C, which, I think, we're all agreed, still needs work in three areas . . .

Offering Constructive Criticism to Your Colleagues

Let's not kid ourselves. Responding *critically* to a colleague's idea or project is more difficult, more demanding, and more risky than providing positive reinforcement. But, like praise, criticism can also be positive. It can build relationships, foster a team spirit, and improve performance and productivity.

Constructive criticism is appropriate when:

1. Your colleagues are not functioning well.
2. A situation is threatening your working relationship with a colleague.
3. You have a sincere desire to upgrade a colleague's performance for the good of the organization.
4. A project or idea requires improvement or modification.

Even though criticism in these cases is justified and necessary and, therefore, positive, you may meet with negative responses:

1. You may be confronted with hostility.
2. You may be confronted with defensiveness.
3. You may be told that you have misunderstood the situation.

It is also possible that the criticism may be welcomed. If so, you'll hear responses like these:

- "I didn't realize I was doing that."

- "I didn't think there was a better way."
- "I was totally unaware of that."
- "You're right. I could be doing a better job if I approached the problem your way."

The objective of your criticism should be

- To correct or improve a problematic situation, faulty colleague performance, problems with ideas or projects
- To secure a positive response from the person or persons to whom the criticism is directed

You can maximize the chances for a positive reaction—and a positive outcome—by observing the following guidelines:

1. *Make certain the situation really does call for criticism.* You *should* be hesitant to offer criticism. Make certain that your criticism is motivated by a genuine problem or issue, not by your personal dislikes or frustrations. Make certain, too, that the problem or issue is serious enough to warrant criticism. After all, you are risking the creation of bad feelings. Make certain that the "cure" is not apt to be worse than the "disease."

2. *Don't go blundering into the criticism.* Practice finesse. Instead of opening up with your big guns, ask your colleague if she would *like to hear how* you feel about what she's doing. That is, ask her permission to offer criticism. This will help translate "criticism" into "feedback"—which is far more neutral and apt to trigger less defensiveness than criticism.

3. *Choose the right place and time.* Never criticize a colleague in front of others. Instead, find—or create—an appropriate time: "George, there's something I need to discuss with you. When would be a good time for us to have a few uninterrupted moments together?"

TIP

Avoid delivering criticism first thing in the morning—especially Monday morning. Avoid delivering it right before quitting time, especially before a weekend. You don't want to send a colleague home to stew about something you've said.

TIP

Don't deliver criticism in the heat of anger—for example, right after some incident has occurred. Try to cool down and reflect before offering criticism.

4. *Back up your criticism with substance.* The most frustrating and enraging kind of criticism is delivered in vague generalities. Be concrete. Use specific incidents, instances, and events. Also, concentrating on specifics will help to keep the criticism from degenerating into a personal attack.

5. *Offer alternatives.* It's easy to criticize, but much harder to come up with positive alternatives. Generally, you should not offer criticism to a colleague unless you are prepared to offer alternatives that will be helpful to him and to the organization.

6. *Be friendly.* This does not mean that you should approach your colleague in a phony, sickeningly sweet, or patronizing manner. However, be considerate and sensitive. Don't tease or taunt. Don't raise your voice. Watch your vocabulary. Avoid such phrases as "you must," "you should," "you have to," "you never," "you always," and the like.

7. *Where possible, combine praise with criticism.* This is not just to soften the blow, but to let your colleague know that you appreciate her value, her qualifications, and her abilities.

8. *Criticize only what can be improved or corrected.* Make certain that you don't lay the blame for some essentially uncorrectable problem at the feet of your fellow worker.

9. *One at a time, please.* Don't lay multiple criticism on anyone. Tackle one issue at a time.

10. *Follow up with positive feedback.* If the situation improves or the issue is corrected, offer praise, congratulations, and thanks. Express your admiration.

Your script: giving construction criticism.

Here is an example of establishing a positive basis and maintaining the focus on issues rather than personalities or abilities:

You: What's working very well in this proposal is A, B, D, and F. These are cost-effective and, I think, very attractive in the present market. However, C and E pose serious problems. Here's what I mean: [explains the problems in detail].

With most of the proposal looking so sound and affording such advantages, we have to come up with solutions for C and E. Mary, you and your team have done wonderful things with A, B, D, and F. I would like to offer my support in resolving the problems with C and E.

APOLOGIZING FOR ERRORS AND MISUNDERSTANDINGS

If you find it difficult to apologize, you're hardly alone. Few people look forward to apologizing. Yet I would suggest that a revision in attitude is in order. While it is true that there is never anything to cherish about the reason for making an apology—that is, a mistake or misjudgment or misunderstanding—there is a good reason to value the apology itself as an opportunity for building and strengthening relationships with your colleagues.

It's relatively easy to get along with your colleagues when things are going well. The relationship is tested, however, when a crisis occurs. How you and your colleagues work together, help one another in the wake of an error or other crisis, is the test and the builder of effective coworker and colleague relationships.

When an apology is called for, observe the following:

- *Make it timely*. Don't wait to be asked for an explanation or apology. Be proactive. Take the initiative.
- *Be helpful*. Don't just apologize. Offer whatever help you can to make things right again. Such a response may not only repair damage, it can actually improve relations.

Common sense tells you that the most important component of an apology is the offer of a remedy. This is largely true, but of nearly equal importance is *how* you arrive at the remedy:

STEP 1: Apologize; say that you are sorry.

STEP 2: Sympathize; express understanding of the other's feelings.

STEP 3: As you work toward a remedy for the situation, structure the conversation so that the words "you" and "I" become "we": "We'll repair this situation."

TIP

Your colleague will appreciate your apology. But make sure you give him what he probably needs most: help. Render aid, and you will become a hero, even if the problem was your fault to begin with.

TIP

Recognize the difference between an explanation and an excuse. You owe the wronged party an explanation—an outline of the facts and circumstances surrounding the error—but she will not want to hear an excuse: why the problem wasn't your fault. If the explanation—an outline of the facts—serves to exonerate you, great; if not, offer no additional excuse.

YOUR SCRIPT: APOLOGIZING TO A COLLEAGUE

Here's an apology for being late with information a colleague needs:

You: I'm very sorry that I was late with the report you needed. I know that put you in a tight spot.

Colleague: Well, yes, it sure did. The boss was angry.

You: I'm willing to explain to him that the problem was on my end. We didn't get the results back from the first three tests on time. There was nothing I could do about that, but I should have warned you that the problem was coming. I'd like to explain that to the boss.

Colleague: Well, I'd appreciate that.

You: Yeah. I know he can be pretty short-tempered about things like this. I'm sorry to have put you on the receiving end of *that* blast.

DEALING WITH AN IRATE COLLEAGUE

What if we could keep our emotions out of our work? Wouldn't that be wonderful? Sometimes. Expressions of outright anger in the workplace range from disturbing to downright frightening. Of course, if our work consistently failed to engage our emotions, if we just didn't care, the quality of what we do would suffer. Loud and visible anger in reaction to errors may result from passion about one's work, but other factors may also figure in the picture:

- A fight with one's spouse
- A fight with one's children
- A lingering disagreement with someone else at work
- A miserable morning commute in bumper-to-bumper traffic

Who knows what else? You cannot, of course, control all the stressful and enraging factors in your colleague's lives, but you can recognize that an enraged response from you in return will only fuel the anger. In contrast, a calm, businesslike response will make it that much more difficult for your colleague to maintain rage.

Successfully coping with the rage of others requires that you take steps to deal with the causes of stress in your own life. These nonverbal steps will help you deal more effectively with strong emotion in the workplace:

1. Get more sleep. Fatigue reduces your patience and tolerance, making you susceptible to angry outbursts.
2. Try to handle difficult colleague situations, such as apologies, after breakfast or after lunch—not when you or your colleague is hungry.
3. Moderate your intake of coffee. Caffeine heightens anxiety and rage levels.
4. Turn up the air conditioning. Too much heat makes most people more irritable.

5. Do what you can to make yourself more comfortable. Ditch the buzzing fluorescent tube. Get rid of the clock that ticks too loudly.

So much for what you can control. An error occurs. You are responsible. You apologize. Your colleague flies off the handle. Here's what you do:

STEP 1: Start by doing little or nothing. Let the person vent.

TIP

It is difficult to sit and take it from an irate colleague, but doing so will allow him to bleed off some of that pent-up energy.

TIP

Avoid *telling* an irate colleague to "calm down." This will only stoke the fire. Avoid telling your colleague to do anything or to feel or behave in a certain way.

STEP 2: After the first wave of rage has washed over, "play back" the gist of angry message—minus the rage: "If I understand you correctly . . ."

STEP 3: If you believe that you have a satisfactory remedy for the colleague's issue, propose it—quickly.

STEP 4: If no immediate remedy is available, lay the burden on your colleague: "How would you like to resolve this?"

TIP

Rage is directly proportional to a person's feeling of powerlessness. If you ask your colleague to tell you what he wants, you give him power and, therefore, reduce his feeling of powerlessness.

STEP 5: If your colleague makes a proposal and you can agree to it, tell him that you will take the necessary action.

STEP 6:   If you are unsure that you can comply with the proposed remedy, ask for some time to consider and investigate. Arrange a specific time and place for a follow-up discussion.

STEP 7:   If your colleague's solution is unfeasible, negotiate an alternative: "I can't do that, but here's what I can do."

STEP 8:   Do what you can to transform "I" versus "you" into "we" versus "the problem."

TIP

If your colleague becomes abusive or threatening, remove yourself from the situation—immediately: "John, this is getting out of hand. I'm going to leave. I'll return in a half hour. Let's try to cool down and discuss this productively then."

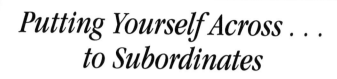

CHAPTER 6

Putting Yourself Across . . . to Subordinates

SELF-TEST YOUR SAVVY IN COMMUNICATING WITH SUBORDINATES

The following is a simple diagnostic test. A smaller and more selective version of the self-test in Chapter 1, its purpose is not to test your knowledge of communication theory or techniques, but to help you gauge how effectively you communicate with your subordinates in a day-to-day business context. For the most part, you will find it easy to guess the "right" answer. But getting the "right" answer is not the point of the test. Respond honestly, even if you feel that your response is not the best one possible. This is not a contest. The object is solely self-inventory.

1. It's a bad idea to be friendly toward your subordinates. T/F ____

2. I'm a leader because my boss says I'm a leader. T/F ____

3. *Never* admit that you are wrong. T/F ____

4. Employees *always* complain. You can't take it seriously. You just have to go on. T/F ____

5. I am frank in assessing employees who are not performing up to par. T/F ____

6. Questions are usually a waste of time. T/F ____

7. Threats are not effective motivators. T/F ____

8. I ask for feedback. T/F ____

9. I ask permission to criticize. T/F ____

10. You can't depend on your subordinates.   T/F _____

11. I care about my subordinates' personal goals, but they must mesh with the firm's.   T/F _____

12. Sometimes criticism is brutal. That's just the way it is.   T/F _____

13. My department is a democracy.   T/F _____

14. My department is a team.   T/F _____

15. I do issue verbal reprimands, but I summarize them afterwards in a written memo.   T/F _____

16. I don't *say* anything. I put it *all* in writing.   T/F _____

17. Insubordinate employees should be fired—quickly.   T/F _____

18. I expect my people to get it right—the *first* time.   T/F _____

19. I give *very* clear directions.   T/F _____

20. Subordinates have to be watched at all times.   T/F _____

21. We have an employee handbook with clear statements of workplace policy.   T/F _____

22. When I criticize a subordinate I hope to help him or her develop and improve.   T/F _____

23. I invite questions.   T/F _____

24. Criticism is part of mentoring.   T/F _____

25. Reprimand is a normal part of employee development.   T/F _____

26. Termination is a process, not an event.   T/F _____

27. It is quite possible to say no to an employee without alienating him or her.   T/F _____

28. Work is not fun.   T/F _____

29. Loyalty is important to me.   T/F _____

30. Call it what you want, criticism *is* finding fault.   T/F _____

31. Sometimes it is necessary to "terminate" an employee.   T/F _____

32. All management owes the employee is a paycheck.   T/F _____

33. I may be upset by the complaints of my subordinates, but I listen and try to learn. T/F ____

34. I never get involved in disputes between subordinates. That's dangerous. T/F ____

35. My people can do what I tell them to, or they can find other employment. T/F ____

36. The people who report to me have to *perform*. Period. T/F ____

37. I always resist requests for salary increases. T/F ____

38. I see myself as a coach. T/F ____

39. Some things just aren't worth criticizing. T/F ____

40. When things go wrong, I try to offer not only an apology, but a remedy. T/F ____

41. I try to combine criticism with praise. T/F ____

42. Mature workers do not require profuse positive reinforcement. T/F ____

TOTAL T/F ____

Score 1 point for each "True" response and 0 for each "False" response, EXCEPT for questions 1, 2, 3, 4, 6, 10, 12, 13, 16, 17, 18, 20, 28, 30, 32, 34, 35, 36, 37, and 42. For these questions only, SUBTRACT 1 point for each "True" response. Record your total. A score below +20 indicates that you would benefit from practicing the communication techniques discussed in this chapter. (Note: It is possible to have a negative score.)

WORDS TO USE WITH SUBORDINATES

advice	future
advise	glitch
analyze	help
assist	invest
consider	lead

WORDS TO USE WITH SUBORDINATES, *cont'd*

control	learn
cope	lesson
counsel	manage
determine	navigate
discuss	plan
evaluate	reconsider
expedite	rethink
formulate	revise

PHRASES TO USE WITH SUBORDINATES

ask your advice

build on this

consult with you

create progress

create satisfaction

Do you understand?

full cooperation

get your input

give guidance

hear your take on this

How do you want to proceed?

How may I help you?

improve even more

join the team

make progress

realize our goals

team effort

What part is unclear?

What would you suggest?

WORDS TO AVOID WITH SUBORDINATES

blame

catastrophe

crisis

demand

destroyed

disaster

exploded

fault

force

foul-up

hopeless

idiotic

impossible

mess

misguided

must

snafu

PHRASES TO AVOID WITH SUBORDINATES

better shape up

can't do it

don't ask

don't come to me about it

don't want to hear it

don't worry about it

figure it out yourself

know what's good for you

no choice

not allowed

you wouldn't understand

you'd better

BODY-LANGUAGE STRATEGY FOR COMMUNICATING WITH SUBORDINATES

The basics of effective body language apply in conferences with subordinates:

- Make and maintain eye contact.
- Smile.
- Keep hands away from the face and mouth, but use many open-handed gestures.
- If you feel the need to achieve subtle domination, direct your glance to the subordinate's forehead rather than meeting his or her eyes directly.

Your approach is simple. It pays to come across as open and receptive. Of at least equal importance to the nonverbal cues you transmit is learning how to read those you receive. When you speak with a subordinate, how do you know that you are getting through? Do you know because the person *tells* you she understands? Or because he *promises* to do better "next time"?

In part, it's just this simple and obvious. *Ask* for feedback: "Am I making myself clear?" Or: "Is this helping you?" But you need to go beyond this.

- Particularly in situations in which you must deliver criticism and correction, you should expect instances of *verbal* compliance combined with the *nonverbal* signals of resistance.

Look out for:

1. Avoidance of eye contact, which suggests that you are not getting through
2. Hands to face or mouth, which suggests that the employee is not being fully honest with you
3. Arms folded across the chest or hands on hips, which suggests resistance, even defiance
4. Rubbing the back of the neck or, if the employee is seated, nervous leg movement, which suggests a desire to leave—*now*

If you pick up any of these nonverbal cues, try to bring the issue of communication out into the open:

STEP 1:   Verbalize: "I get the feeling that I'm not communicating as effectively as I would like. Do you agree with such-and-such?" Or: "Does what I say disturb you? Does what I say seem inaccurate to you?"

STEP 2:   Do not accuse the subordinate of *failing* to listen or *failing* to understand. In reacting to nonverbal cues, put the burden on yourself rather than the subordinate: "Am *I* making *myself* clear?"

BODY LANGUAGE TO AVOID WITH SUBORDINATES

Supervisors are notorious for telegraphing their emotions through frowns, narrowing of the eyes, pouting expressions, and so on. Endeavor to smile as much as possible, but when that is inappropriate, cultivate a neutral expression or "poker face." In addition, avoid:

- Gestures of hands over or near the mouth
- Running the hands through the hair or rubbing the back of the neck. These gestures transmit frustration
- Folding the arms across the chest—a gesture that indicates a closed mind or resistance
- Avoidance of eye contact
- Leg movement—which indicates a desire to be elsewhere, to get away
- Violent gesturing, including jabbing, pointing, and pounding fist

COMMUNICATING YOUR MANAGEMENT STYLE

You can choose to manage your department or your business like a dictator. In the short term, providing limited choices and unlimited threats may actually be effective. This style tends to produce immediate results; however, among those immediate results are employee dissatisfaction and, ultimately, a high turnover rate. Dictatorial managers do not create successful teams—certainly not for the long haul.

What about going to the other extreme? Giving little direction and communicating scant feedback can be effective if you have the right team assembled. But that is a big *if*. And to meet adversity with anything like passive resistance usually leads only to frustration—for you and your employees.

Generally speaking, the most effective managers resemble the legendary Notre Dame football coach Knute Rockne more than either Adolf Hitler or Mahatma Gandhi. They lead, but by inspiration rather than fear. They let team members discover the best within themselves, but they do so with positive criticism and encouragement rather than inscrutable silence.

The most effective managers are able to foster personal dedication not by persuading the staff that they work for a great and beneficent manager or company, but by convincing them that their personal goals mesh with those of the company; that is, personal success depends on the success of the corporate endeavor.

For the long term, showing the connection between personal goals and company objectives works well, but on a day-to-day basis an even more direct way to manage employees for optimum performance is to create in them a sense of personal loyalty to you. This is mostly a matter of communication, of conveying the following:

1. That you are accessible
2. That you are willing to hear—and respond to—grievances and complaints
3. Absolute clarity about your expectations
4. Generous positive feedback
5. Helpful and constructive criticism
6. A sense of fun and enjoyment in your directives

Listening to Complaints from Subordinates

Let's take a closer look at what it means to be willing to listen to complaints. It is a willingness that requires strength on your part. Most managers can get candor from their staff—at least once. It is how you respond to candor that determines whether the productive honesty will continue.

The most effective opening strategy is a what's-bothering-you-let's-talk-about-it approach.

STEP 1:   "Sam, you look really upset about something. I want to hear about it. Go ahead. Don't pull any punches."

Just be certain that *you* can roll with those punches. The object is to learn from complaints, not to become enraged or offended by them. The most destructive thing you can do is ask for honesty, only to react to it with anger.

STEP 2:   After the employee gets the gripe off his chest, try to translate the negative into a positive solution. If Issue A upsets Sam, ask him what can be done to resolve Issue A and improve the situation.

STEP 3:   If no immediate solution is possible, indicate your willingness to work toward a solution.

Strive for Clarity in Your Communications

Effective management is not magic. Much of it is effective communication, and, in turn, effective communication consists largely of clear and precise directions.

1. Clarity is often best achieved by writing out your instructions in the form of a memo.
2. Use plain English. Quantify instructions wherever possible: how many, when, where, how much time, and so on.
3. Always invite questions.

Getting the Best from Your Subordinates

To cultivate the best in your team requires the development and nurturing of enthusiasm. Now, enthusiasm is not a robust commodity. Fragile, it is easily stifled by insensitive supervision and can be dissipated utterly by cynicism. The inspired manager circulates among her team, infusing it with enthusiasm. Upbeat, she

- Talks with team members
- Works closely with the group
- Suggests new approaches to stubborn problems

- Expresses empathy in difficult situations
- Tirelessly consults and coaches

Enthusiasm is a creation. Through frequent meetings and conferences, the manager

- Shares her observations
- Reinforces positive achievements and attitudes
- Continually corrects the team's direction and focus as required

You may hear "hard-nosed" managers protest that mature workers do not require profuse positive reinforcement. Look around: The world is full of rewards and awards and ceremonies of public recognition. Positive reinforcement is hardly a new idea, nor is it peculiar to the workplace. It is, quite literally, ancient history, and its utility is just common sense. Indeed, the effective manager should consider holding regular reinforcement meetings.

- Such meetings should be positive and upbeat; their objective is to reward, refresh, and, if necessary, refocus.
- Invite staffers to bring up their concerns, but defer full discussion of these to separate meetings if they threaten the upbeat tenor of the reinforcement meeting.
- Introduce an element of pleasure into each meeting. Serve refreshments, perhaps, or share a funny story.
- Greet your staff with kind and pleasant words: "You guys, as usual, look great!"
- Keep the tone of the meeting light, warm, and friendly.
- Be specific in your positive reinforcement. Invite the staffers you single out for praise to talk about their success.
- Spend less than an hour in the meeting—enough time to cite, in detail, several positive examples. Allow ample time for questions, discussion, and clarification.

TIP

Reinforcement meetings should not be lectures. Make them interactive.

In between reinforcement meetings, motivate your staff with continual feedback designed to reassure subordinates that you have confidence in their skills and abilities.

TIP

Be specific in your feedback. To the degree that it is possible to do so, stress the positive. Practice delivering feedback in a sincere tone. When you criticize, always suggest alternatives. Never simply demean an employee or reject his work.

TIP

The best managers enjoy what they do. Put some *fun* in your directives. Don't turn them into jokes, but feel free to use imagination when you give directions, discuss ideas, or deliver feedback.

Giving Constructive Criticism to Your Subordinates

Offering constructive criticism to subordinates is similar to criticizing your colleagues, except that you are in a more authoritative position with subordinates. This has its advantages as well as its liabilities. For while your subordinates are more likely to accept criticism—and to expect it—there is a greater potential for anxiety and, with anxiety, resentment of you. This can undermine your effectiveness as a manager and lead to resistance among your staff.

STEP 1: Avoid creating resentment by communicating criticism in the manner of a mentor or a coach.

STEP 2: Make it clear that you are committed not just to your department's or company's bottom line, but to the development of the employee as a long-term member of the team.

STEP 3: Before you criticize, *be certain of your need to criticize.* Avoid using criticism merely to vent frustration, anger, or irritation.

TIP

If your remarks are not likely to improve the situation, don't make them.

STEP 4:   Ask permission to criticize. Asking permission to criticize will actually enhance the effectiveness of your remarks. Instead of starting out with something like, "You're not doing an effective job with so-and-so," begin with "We have a problem with so-and-so, which I would like to discuss with you."

STEP 5:   Be certain that the cure will not be worse than the disease. Even sensitively expressed, criticism can damage a fragile ego. Use judgment to decide whether the problem or issue is worth the risk that critical words entail.

STEP 6:   Do not criticize subordinates in front of others. Take the person aside—subtly. "Alice, I need to speak to you about an important matter. When is a good time for us to get together for a few minutes of uninterrupted time?"

STEP 7:   Avoid criticism first thing in the morning or at quitting time. Criticism is not a good way to start or end the day.

STEP 8:   Be specific and avoid issuing blanket criticism or generalized criticism. Cite specific issues and incidents.

STEP 9:   As far as possible, quantify your criticism objectively: "Turnaround time in your area is a good 15 percent more than we need it to be."

STEP 10: Maintain your perspective. You are both on the same team; therefore, approach the subordinate not just as an employee, but as a member of *your* team. Be friendly.

STEP 11: Always address issues, never personalities. Resist the temptation to tell an errant employee what you think of him. Focus on the issue.

TIP

If necessary, it is appropriate to focus on a particular negative or harmful behavior—just be sure it is a behavior in a certain circumstance or set of circumstances. Be specific.

STEP 12: Combine as much praise as possible with the criticism. You might observe that, in general, you are pleased with the subordinate's work, but that, as regards issue A, an improvement needs to be made.

STEP 13: Limit your criticism to what can be changed. It does no good—and may do great harm—to criticize a subordinate for something over which she has little or no control.

STEP 14: Address one issue at a time. Avoid bombarding the subordinate with a cluster of faults and problems.

YOUR SCRIPT: GIVING CRITICISM TO SUBORDINATES

Here is an example of constructive criticism:

You: Mary, I liked the way you handled that customer's complaint. It was done quickly and politely.

Mary: Thanks.

You: May I just share with you a few observations, some points that might help you to deal with such complaints even more effectively?

Mary: Well . . . sure.

You: You came up with a course of action very quickly. There's a lot to be said for such decisive action; however, in cases where more than a few options are available, it would be more effective to ask the customer what he wants. Empowering the customer in this way increases your opportunity to create satisfaction. Am I expressing myself clearly?

Mary: I'm not sure. Are you saying I did something wrong . . . ?

You: No. Not at all. I want you to know that you handled that customer well, but there is an even more effective approach, I think. When you have choices to offer, give more power, more authority to the customer. Don't be too quick to propose a single solution. If the customer needs help deciding what to do, by all means, jump in.

Mary: But doesn't this take too much time?

You: That's a very good point, Mary. It *does* take time. But time spent with the customer in a case like this is valuable for us. It builds satisfaction. It turns a problem into an opportunity.

Note that the criticism, though expressed clearly and in detail, is softened by the generally positive context surrounding it. This boss offers positive reinforcement, then asks permission to offer criticism, then approaches the criticism as a mentor—not as a monitor.

WHAT TO SAY TO SUBORDINATES WHEN YOU ARE WRONG

Tyranny. Now *there's* a motivating force. It has sparked rebellion after rebellion, including our own American Revolution. Tyranny may be manifested in many ways, running the gamut of economic and physical oppression. But, at bottom, all tyranny is founded on injustice, a refusal either to recognize the differences between right and wrong or to admit wrong.

Supervisors and managers make mistakes. Sometimes those mistakes are hurtful, financially to the company or personally to an employee. Forgiveness may or may not be possible, depending on the problem, the magnitude of loss or harm, and the prevailing attitude of the company and the employees.

- But you can be certain of *not* being forgiven for one thing: a refusal to own up to the mistake, to admit error, and to work toward amends. That failure is tyranny.

STEP 1:   Assess the error, problem, and damage.

STEP 2:   Do not rush into a confession of guilt and do not wallow in remorse. Assess the degree of your culpability.

STEP 3:   Apologize and explain the problem or mistake.

STEP 4:   Listen to the affected employees. What do they need you to do?

STEP 5:   Empathize.

STEP 6:   Propose remedies.

STEP 7:   Explain and justify limitations to the remedies proposed.

Your script: telling a subordinate you're wrong

An employee submitted to you a request, with documentation, for travel-expense reimbursement. Three weeks after submitting this, he asks you about the status of his reimbursement. You tell him you'll look into it—and then discover that your accounting people never received the request from you. After further investigation, you realize that you've misplaced—*lost*—the employee's request and documentation. What do you say? What do you do?

You: Tom, I've traced the source of the delay in getting you your reimbursement.

Tom: Great!

You: Well, not so great. It's me. I don't know how it happened, but I have lost your request and documentation. Do you have any copies?

Tom: Well . . . I have a copy of the expense form, but I didn't make copies of the documentation.

You: Okay. Well, I really screwed up, and I'm sorry. This is what I propose to do. Give me the copy of the form. I will reimburse you out of petty cash immediately, and I'll submit the copy to accounting with an explanation that I have misplaced the documentation and have initiated a search. I'm really sorry to hang you up like this.

Tom: I'll get that copy to you right away.

You: And I'll draw the money for you. Again, sorry!

The employee does want to hear an apology, but what he wants even more is a fix for whatever went wrong. Offer the apology, but don't belabor it. Move as quickly as possible to the fix.

REFUSING REQUESTS—WITHOUT ALIENATING EMPLOYEES

In a perfect world, you would be able to grant the wishes of everyone who reports to you. Of course, in a perfect world, no one would ask you for anything. In our far-from-perfect world, they do ask, and sometimes you have to say no. The best you can do?

- Say no clearly and unmistakably.
- Say no gently.

- Provide a reason for your being unable—or unwilling—to meet the request.
- If possible and appropriate, offer alternatives.

TIP

Try not to emphasize what you can't do, but shift the focus to what you can do—even if this is substantially less than what you were asked for.

In general, take these steps to refuse a request without alienating the employee:

STEP 1: Listen without interruption—unless you need a point clarified.

STEP 2: Show that you have understood the request by rephrasing and summarizing it.

STEP 3: If there is any part of the request that you *can* satisfy in some degree, begin with that.

STEP 4: Express regret that you cannot satisfy the request or that you cannot satisfy it completely.

STEP 5: Explain why you cannot. This step is the most important of all.

STEP 6: Put the request in perspective; develop your negative response in the context of department or company needs and goals, which will ultimately benefit the employee.

STEP 7: Express your wish that your refusal will cause no great hardship or disappointment.

STEP 8: If possible and appropriate, suggest an alternative.

TIP

Be careful! In suggesting an alternative, beware of "volunteering" others to satisfy the request.

STEP 9: Offer *rational* hope. Are there conditions under which the request might be satisfied at some future time? Be as specific about this as circumstances allow.

STEP 10: Thank the employee for understanding.

TIP

Don't let the *no* cut off communication. Make it clear that you are responding negatively to the proposal, the request, or the idea—*not* to the *person* bringing you the proposal, request, or idea.

When a Subordinate Requests a Raise

Saying no to a request for a raise is one of the really hard things a manager has to do.

- Make the situation easier for you and the employee by establishing clear guidelines and policies, including annual or semi-annual performance reviews.

If you have to say no, your approach should be straightforward and unemotional. Avoid being either judgmental ("You don't deserve a raise!") or apologetic ("Aw, gee, shucks, darn it all . . .") Give a straightforward reason for your response and, if at all possible, offer rational, realistic, and clearly defined hope for the future.

YOUR SCRIPT: HANDLING A RAISE REQUEST

After four months on the job, Sally Smith wants a raise. She's doing a *very* good job, and the last thing you want to do is discourage her. But you can't give her a raise at four months. Offer praise and whatever promises you can honestly make:

You: Sally, I am thrilled with the job you've been doing for us in the four months you've been here. In that short time, you've already made a difference. But, look, it *has* been a *short* time. Policy is very clear: I can't even consider a raise before one year of employment. Now, that's the bad news. The *good* news is that you are not an "ordinary" employee. So here's what I would be willing to do: hold a salary review with you in May. You will have been here six months then. Assuming you maintain or even improve your level of performance, I will do whatever I can to secure an increase before the one-year mark.

Saying no to a request for a raise from an employee whose performance does not merit one can be a particularly difficult and unpleasant experience. However, try to look at it as an opportunity to help an employee improve performance and to develop professionally.

> **TIP**
>
> Keep this meeting as positive as possible. Avoid self-righteous outrage. Avoid threats.

Ostensibly, the object of the meeting is to deliver the bad news to the employee. It is more important, though, to use the occasion to outline the performance conditions that will make a raise possible in the future. Make this an educational experience.

You: Sid, before we can consider a compensation increase, we have to review your job performance. I have to tell you that your present level of performance does not merit a salary increase. I need to see improvement in three areas before I will consider a raise.

- Note the phrase "at present," which implies the possibility of improvement and the possibility of a raise later. Be certain to enumerate the three (or two or four or whatever) areas requiring improvement. Explain yourself. Make your requirements clear.

On this occasion or in a subsequent meeting, which you set up on this occasion, establish clear objectives and goals for each of the improvement areas you outline.

Conclude positively. The most positive—honest—conclusion you can reach is to reaffirm your bond with the employee.

You: Sid, I know that, together, we can bring your performance to a level that will merit an increase—and that will improve performance for all of us here and also increase your job satisfaction.

Perhaps even more painful for you are those occasions when a fine employee, whose work merits an increase, requests a raise, but your finances won't allow you to give her one. Even this cupboard-is-bare scenario can be turned to advantage. Emphasize to the employee that she has a real and immediate stake in the company's performance.

You: Esther, you deserve a raise. There is no question about that. The problem is that we, as a company, have not reached a revenue level this quarter that would make that raise possible. It's a tough one. I hope you realize how much I value your contribution to this team. While I'm sorry I can't increase your salary now, I do feel confident that, with your continued maximum effort, we will reach the level of revenue necessary to give you an increase. I promise that we'll review this situation at the end of the next quarter.

- Unless the employee in question is working under certain contract and union guarantees, regular periodic raises are not an unalienable right.

In the case of an employee who is doing a better-than-satisfactory job, you may not want (or be able) to grant a request for a raise if his compensation is already appropriate to his position. Saying no to a raise in this situation is an opportunity for mentoring, for developing the employee.

You: Ed, you do a wonderful job as production coordinator. That fact should be recognized and rewarded. And it *has* been. You are now at the top level of compensation for your position. If you want to grow financially, you're also going to have to grow in terms of the scope of responsibility you're willing to take on. Let's talk about how you can get to the next level.

TIP

Don't make the mistake of seeing salary issues in terms of an absolute yes or no. If you can't swing a raise in salary level, perhaps you can offer

- A compromise amount
- Enhanced benefits or perks
- Additional paid vacation
- Flexible hours

Be certain to respond positively. Don't stress what you *can't* do, but what you *can*.

You: "Helen, I am thrilled with your work. I agree that an increase is called for. But you have been with the company only a little over a year now, and the figure you propose is inappropriately high. I'm prepared to offer a 3 percent increase now, and at your two-year review we can revisit the matter.

When a Subordinate Requests a Promotion

Turning down a request for promotion may be even more difficult and trying than rejecting a bid for a raise. The dangers of offending pride, of injuring self-confidence, of implying that you do not appreciate the employee's accomplishments, or that you simply do not believe him capable of handling greater responsibility—all of these dangers are real and can be terrible for morale and motivation.

> **TIP**
> Avoid making the employee feel that he has reached a dead end and should seek opportunity elsewhere.

STEP 1:   Say no, but give a full an explanation for the no.

STEP 2:   If possible and appropriate, provide hope for the future. Be as specific as honestly possible. Lay out the conditions and performance expectations under which a promotion might be made in the future.

STEP 3:   Agree on mutual steps that may be taken to make the promotion possible at some future time.

STEP 4:   Without promising any action, do try to set a precise date for a new performance review.

Employees often want to move up faster than appropriate. Mary wants to move from associate to head widget inspector, even though she's been on the job for no more than six months. Your task is to respond prudently, but without curbing her ambition, enthusiasm, and commitment to the company or department.

> **You:** I appreciate your ambition and enthusiasm, and it is clear to me that you are fully committed to this firm. I certainly see a move up to head widget inspector, and I don't think you need to stop there, either.

However, the earliest I could consider a promotion is in August. I promise we'll meet then.

Often, a promotion is simply not yours to give freely. Many companies operate in conformity to a seniority policy, which can be a source of great frustration both to staff and managers. If you must refuse a promotion due to seniority requirements, do your best to minimize the frustration.

STEP 1: Do not use the phrase "company policy" to justify the refusal. This will be taken for exactly what it is: arbitrary and inflexible.

STEP 2: Soften the blow with an encouraging, positive assessment: "Penny, I want to see that you grow here, and I want to accelerate that process. However, as you know, promotion here is guided by seniority status. You've done a great job in the time you've been here. However, right now, it would not be fair for me to put you ahead of others whose commitment and performance are comparable to yours. They've put in their time, and that counts for a lot. We reward commitment, and one of the chief measurements of commitment is, for better or worse, time."

In some cases, you may want to promote, but, for one reason or another, the firm is not filling the appropriate position at this time. Your challenging task becomes saying no without turning off a valuable member of your team. The most effective strategy is to *join forces* with the employee in mutual limitation.

You: I wish I could move you up to the position, but, at this time, management has made the decision not to fill it. Now, I don't believe this is a permanent situation. It will be reviewed, and I promise you that I'll let you know when the review takes place. At that time, you'll be very high on the list for that position, when it does open up.

When Subordinates Request Assorted Perks and Privileges

Outside of salary and promotion, employee requests range from the perfectly reasonable to the outlandish. Most requests fall somewhere in between. For example, one of the people you manage asks for a change in working hours. He's thinking—quite naturally—of himself, rather than of the needs of the team, the department, and the company. You are in no position to shuffle the staff around.

Of course, you can simply say no. You're the manager. But a more effective way to handle the matter is to position your no somewhere along the road to a solution.

> **You:** Gil, just now, we need you to be available as you are presently scheduled. I'm not in a position to shake up the entire department. But maybe *you* can do something about it. Why don't you discuss the matter with your colleagues? Perhaps one of them would be willing to swap hours with you. I would be open to that.

TIP

Demonstrate your willingness to take all requests seriously and in good faith. Employees may be disappointed if they don't get what they ask for, but they are downright enraged if they feel that their requests are dismissed out of hand by a boss who doesn't listen to them.

Your scripts: responding to employee requests

1. **Employee:** The folks in the shop really want you to consider giving us an additional coffee break in the early afternoon. It's something we all need.

   You: Harry, a third coffee break would cut too deeply into our productive time. It's just not right for us. It won't work. Look, I understand that some of you may feel the need to get up and stretch and get a cup of coffee. Do it on your own, once in a while, and that's fine. But I can't afford the downtime of a third formal coffee break. That would just take too much time from everyone's schedule. It would impact the entire team.

2. **Employee:** Boss, I'd really like to get a new computer. Everyone else has one.

   You: I understand. But, actually, only two people in the department have computers purchased within the past six months or so. But, more important, Bill, your day-to-day needs don't call for a new computer. Look, you do very little word processing and no accounting. If you need faster Internet access from time to time, you can use the machine in the shipping department. That's open to everyone. I just can't justify the expenditure—based on what your job calls for.

Employee: Well, it doesn't seem fair . . .

You: Bill, if you can show me something in your job that I am overlooking, I'd be happy to reconsider. Why don't you give that some thought.

3. **Employee**: . . . So it seems to me about time that I got my own office. I could be much more productive.

You: Claire, it wouldn't be appropriate for me to assign you a private office at this time. Here's why: First, your job doesn't require client conferences or other private meetings. Second, other staffers with positions equivalent to yours have not been assigned private offices. Third—and this is a big one—our building facilities are strictly limited, and we don't have the remodeling budget to fund additional private office space.

   Now, look, I'm sure you're not thrilled to hear all this, but I believe that you can appreciate my reasons for saying no.

4. **Employee**: Parking is a real pain. I really, *really* want to put in for a reserved space in the lot.

You: I agree that parking is becoming a problem here, and we're working on it. The lot will be expanded within the next year and a half. For the present, however, reserved spaces are assigned on a seniority basis, period. I don't have the authority to override that. You're right, certainly, that, at present, we have far fewer reserved spaces than people who want them.

   All I can tell you is that I appreciate your willingness to tough it out until more spaces become available in about 18 months. The consolation I can give you is that you're not alone.

RESPONDING TO COMPLAINTS AND CRITICISM FROM EMPLOYEES

Being unreceptive to complaints and criticism will not make the sources of criticism and complaint go away. It merely puts you in the position of the proverbial ostrich: head uncomfortably in the sand, rear end dangerously exposed. Yes, complaints and criticism can be emotionally difficult to hear, but they give you valuable insight into what's working well and what isn't. In addition:

- Listening to criticism and complaints tells you about the morale of your company or department.
- It gives you the opportunity to affect—directly—morale.
- It gives you the opportunity to build or build up your team.

Listening to complaints and criticism does all this *provided* that

- You really do listen.
- You don't respond judgmentally.
- You don't respond defensively.

> **TIP**
>
> The worst thing you can do is to invite criticism—only to snap at a subordinate for accepting your invitation. If you ask for frank feedback, prepare to hear it and hear it out.

- Do not invite criticism and complaint if you have no intention of making any changes. Of course you do not have to act on each and every criticism and complaint—some will be groundless, and others will be impossible to remedy—but you do have to be willing to change what can and should be changed.

Unbearable Workload

Complaints about workload should be taken very seriously. They are rarely made idly, and they require action.

- Consider the possibility that your expectations of the employee in question are excessive or unrealistic.

• Consider the possibility that the workload would be burdensome to anyone. You may need to hire additional personnel.

Your overall strategy should be to present yourself to the employee as receptive and nonthreatening. Be certain to begin by expressing your appreciation of the employee's comments and his willingness to come to you with them. Here's how a typical conversation might go:

Employee: Boss, we've got to do something about handling the volume of work here. We're going to burn out sooner or later.

You: I agree that your work load is indeed heavy, and I have always greatly admired and appreciated your willingness to take it on. The problem we face is limited funding, which prevents our hiring additional personnel anytime soon.

Now, this doesn't mean that I intend to ignore the situation. Let's get together with the supervisors of the other departments to work out some strategies for making life more bearable around here.

Unpleasant Working Conditions

Managers are often all too quick to respond to complaints about working conditions by taking the attitude that the workforce is spoiled. But a physically comfortable and attractive working environment promotes productivity, communicates a high regard for quality, and generally increases employee satisfaction, which translates into better relations with customers and clients, resulting in greater customer satisfaction and a reduction in expensive employee turnover. It pays, then, to take complaints about working conditions seriously.

Again, as with other complaints, it may or may not be possible to remedy the problem. Serious problems that do impact on productivity and general employee satisfaction and well-being should be addressed, of course, but it is almost less important to remedy these problems than it is to listen and respond to the complaints. Communicating to your subordinates a feeling of teamwork, making them feel that they have a voice in the department or the company, is extraordinarily valuable in creating an effective workforce.

Here is a typical working-conditions complaint scenario:

You: Hank, I'm very pleased that you and the others have taken the time and effort to report to me on the problems with employee facilities here at XYZ Company. I wish I could respond by telling you that I can address all of the issues you raise and totally refurbish the facilities. But I cannot. Our funding for the physical plant is far too limited to make all the improvements we would like. That said, I want to make it clear that I agree with you: Improve-ments are needed. This is what I suggest we do. The department staff should choose a delegation of three or four representatives to meet with me in order to determine which items on your "want list" are most pressing. Based on that evaluation and the available funds, we can determine just what changes can be made now, which ones can be put off until a later date, and which can be shelved at least for the time being. How does that sound to you?

Employee: It sounds like a good idea. I'm grateful.

You: Well, you folks decide on your representative group, and let's get started.

Differences with Coworkers

Managers are often reluctant to involve themselves in disputes between employees. Such managers argue that these matters should be resolved between the employees involved, that intervention from higher up will bring bad feelings on all sides. Certainly, there are risks associated with intervening in employee disputes.

- One party to the dispute may believe that you have shown favoritism to the other.
- *Both* parties to the dispute may believe that you have shown favoritism to the other.
- Employees may feel intruded upon.
- Employees may feel that their differences haven't been resolved—just ended by arbitrary authority.
- Resentment may be turned against you.

All of these risks are real. However, the consequences of failure to intervene can be far more devastating. They can, in fact, include all of the above, except that, instead of feeling intruded upon, employees may feel that you are indifferent to their problems. In addition, other negative feelings may result, including:

- Employee impression of weak or nonexistent authority
- Employee feeling that the workplace is unjust
- Poor performance
- Compromised productivity
- Increased frequency and volume of errors
- A poor, unprofessional image projected to customers and clients
- The creation of a hostile work environment

TIP

The phrase "hostile work environment" is all too familiar to anyone who has been involved in labor-related litigation. It is the language of harassment suits. If you allow a hostile work environment to develop, you expose your company to significant liability.

As with most management decisions, the decision whether or not to intervene in an employee dispute should involve a judgment of degree. Minor disputes probably are best left to the resolution of the employees themselves. But if you judge a dispute to be acute or critical, on the one hand, or chronic and long term, on the other, you should act.

STEP 1: Avoid snap judgments.

STEP 2: Meet with the employees involved and acknowledge the existence of a problem.

STEP 3: Listen to all or both sides *without comment*. Interrupt only to seek clarification, but withhold judgment.

STEP 4: After hearing all or both sides, ask those involved what *they* would like to see happen.

STEP 5: Do not render a judgment now. Say that you need time to evaluate the problem. Set another meeting time.

STEP 6: Assert the necessity of working cooperatively together—for the good of everyone. Don't *ask* for cooperation. Say that you *expect* it.

STEP 7: Study the problem.

STEP 8: Call another meeting and announce your decision. This may be in the form of suggestions or directives, as appropriate.

YOUR SCRIPT: HANDLING EMPLOYEE DISPUTES

Here is an example of a response to an employee who brought a problem to the attention of the boss.

> **You:** Let me begin by telling you how pleased I am that you came to me to discuss the problems you and Fred are experiencing. I'm not saying I'm happy that you're having problems, but that you approached these problems rationally and productively by bringing them to my attention. Now, let's set up a meeting for Thursday. I want to speak with both of you.

Before the second meeting, review the records of both employees.

> **You:** I have reviewed your personnel files, and I have to say that you are both really top-notch performers. Everyone agrees on that. There is no record of any complaints or negative comments concerning either of you. This being the case, I am confident that the two of you can work your problem out together in the same rational spirit in which you approached me.
>
> Now, I do have a few suggestions for how you may resolve your differences.

You give your suggestions.

> **You:** Do you have any thoughts on these suggestions?

After listening to the employees' remarks, continue:

> **You:** What outcome would you both like to see? Tell me, Fred, you first.

After listening to the employees' comments, conclude:

You: Look, you are both extremely valuable to this company, and I certainly enjoy working with you. I am eager for you to work well together. I am eager for this because we can't function as a team with any personal agendas in operation. It's bad for productivity, it makes a very bad impression on our clients, and it just makes the workplace—well—ultimately intolerable. That's why I am intervening. Here, at this company, a dispute is not just a personal, private matter. It *can't* be. Too many people depend on us.

Unsafe Conditions

Any report of an unsafe condition must be addressed immediately and taken seriously.

STEP 1:   Gather the facts.

STEP 2:   Ask employee(s) reporting the condition to do so in writing.

STEP 3:   Document your response in writing.

STEP 4:   Ensure that you follow company and governmental regulations concerning the condition.

STEP 5:   Act promptly.

TIP

Always express appreciation for prompt, accurate reporting of an unsafe condition. Encourage such reporting. Never let employees feel that making such reports constitutes grumbling or idle complaining.

REPRIMANDING YOUR SUBORDINATES

Reprimands should serve three important purposes.

1. They should furnish creative, constructive criticism to correct or improve a particular situation.
2. They should aid generally in the development of an employee.

3. The verbal reprimand, memorialized in writing, serves as a documentary record of employee performance.

Let's address this third point first.

- Verbal reprimands are more immediately effective than written reprimands.

- Verbal reprimands should always be followed up by a memo recording and summarizing the reprimand. The memo should note any action that is to be taken, including corrective action promised by the employee. The memo should also record any consequences of failure to remedy the situation.

- The written record of the verbal reprimand is valuable as a rationale for declining a request for a salary increase or promotion, for disciplinary action, or, in extreme cases, as backup for termination.

TIP

Ours is a most litigious age. Disciplining an employee is sometimes necessary—ideally, to improve performance, but also to build a case for termination. Failure to document this case—the progressive steps that led to termination—exposes you and your company to potentially expensive legal liability.

Assuming you wish to retain the employee, the tone of your reprimand should be as positive and constructive as the situation permits.

TIP

Never attack the employee personally. Never make threats—though you should, as appropriate, advise the employee of possible consequences if the problem is repeated or remains unremedied.

STEP 1: If possible and appropriate, begin by acknowledging the generally positive nature of the employee's performance.

STEP 2: Clearly state the nature of the problem, infraction, or issue.

STEP 3: Explain the effect of the employee's error, bad behavior, or poor performance on the welfare of the company (on which, after all, his own welfare also depends).

STEP 4: Suggest remedies and appropriate steps to resolve the situation.

STEP 5: Ask the employee for comments and suggestions.

STEP 6: Clearly advise the employee of consequences to himself if the infraction is repeated or the situation goes unresolved.

> **TIP**
>
> If termination is a realistic possibility, advise the employee of this; however, do not make idle threats.

STEP 7: Assure the employee of your willingness to work with him to correct the problem.

Habitual Lateness or Early Departure

Failure to adhere to prescribed business hours is typically an insidious problem that comes on gradually. Coming in five minutes late or leaving ten minutes early becomes a habit. On occasion, the five or ten minutes grows to a half hour. The manager's task is to establish and enforce arrival and departure times without seeming (or being) petty and unreasonable.

STEP 1: Ensure that arrival and departure times are clearly stated and understood.

STEP 2: Establish definitions of what constitutes legitimate reasons for arriving late or leaving early.

STEP 3: Establish a policy of clearing late arrival or early departure with a designated supervisor.

> **TIP**
>
> Of course you don't have to provide a reason for your on-time policies; however, you can expect greater compliance if you make clear the rationale behind enforcement of starting and quitting times: It is essential to productive operation that people be where they are expected to be.

Here is a statement of on-time policy, to be used in speaking with an employee who is habitually late or habitually leaves the workplace early:

You: Pat, I don't want to make you feel as if you've got to punch a clock. That's not the kind of work environment any of us here would be happy with. However, we *are* a team, and, as a team, we depend on all our people being where they are supposed to be when they are supposed to be there. I expect that, and so do the others. Starting time is nine, and quitting time is five. Do you anticipate any further problems with adhering to those times, Pat?

Absenteeism

If habitual tardiness or early departure are problems, even worse is absenteeism. As with late-arrival and early-departure problems, the most effective cure is prevention.

STEP 1: Establish firm policies on sick days and personal days.

STEP 2: Make it clear that everyone is essential to the team. Attendance is, therefore, critical.

Your script: handling attendance problems

Here is a typical corrective scenario:

You: Mary, you've been out X number of days during the past three months. We've missed you—I mean *really* missed you. It's critically important that you be here. We *need* you.

Mary: Well, I was sick a lot.

You: Well, Mary, I've never felt comfortable establishing a limit on the number of "sick days" an employee may take. After all, how can you predict how many days you might be sick? But I do rely on employees to use sick days only when absolutely necessary. Mary, if you're having a problem with chronic illness, we need to discuss it.

Look, you are a valuable part of this operation. I need to be able to depend on you—and that includes being able to depend on your being here.

Rude to Customers and Clients

The danger in reprimanding an employee for rude behavior is becoming rude oneself. Because you are addressing an issue of character and personality, it is difficult to keep from criticizing or attacking the employee personally. Difficult though it is, you must resist this temptation. Keep the conversation focused on a particular incident or incidents. Let the facts—deeds and words—speak for themselves.

Your script: handling rudeness to customers

Here is one way to handle an issue of rudeness to customers:

You: Ben, I received a phone call yesterday, which disturbed me very much. One of your customers—who was (understandably) angry enough to take her business elsewhere—described some very rude treatment from you, including what I would consider abusive language. Now, that's her story. What's your take on this incident?

After listening to the employee, continue:

You: We are a service organization. We pride ourselves on treating each customer as someone who is special to us. *That* is the message we need to convey, one customer at a time. It's service, customer service, that gives us our edge. It's as important as any other product benefit we sell. Now, can you deliver courtesy?

Ben: Yes, I promise, I can.

You: I would like to suggest that you apologize to the customer. How do you feel about that?

Ben: Yes, I could do that.

You: Great. I'll leave it to you. Do you intend to call or write? I'd suggest a call. I know it's difficult, but I believe it would be more effective.

Insubordinate or Uncooperative Attitude

Insubordination and general lack of cooperation and compliance can be the result of many causes:

- Emotional instability
- Job dissatisfaction
- Personal crisis
- Failure to understand the nature of a job or assignment

Whatever the cause, the important thing is to recognize the insubordination or lack of cooperation, to call the employee on it, and to discuss with her the consequences of the behavior and acceptable alternatives to the behavior.

YOUR SCRIPT: DEALING WITH INSUBORDINATION

Here is a dispassionate, controlled response to an instance of insubordination:

You: When you started working here, Meg, you agreed to take direction from your supervisors. Now, yesterday, I asked you to do some filing. You refused because, you said, you didn't think the job was part of your job description.

Well, Meg, filing *is* part of your job description. But that's not nearly as important as the fact that here at XYZ Company we need to be able to rely on one another without a lot of discussion or second guessing. You need to do your job.

Meg: Well, it seems to me that you don't want the boat rocked. I mean, filing just isn't very creative. I thought a more junior person could do it.

You: Meg, the last thing we want here is an army of unthinking robots. If you're unhappy with your present position, let's talk about ways that you might move into something else. I'm also open to legitimate objections to certain things you might be asked to do, and I welcome alternatives. But a simple refusal to perform assigned work, well, that's insubordination, period. It's not acceptable.

Meg, I'm going to prepare a memo of this meeting. This is a reprimand, and it is a warning. If you are not willing to live up to the obligations, you must also be willing to recognize that we cannot and will not long retain your services.

The next move is yours. Where do you want to go from here, Meg?

Repeated Errors

Occasional mistakes are all too human, but a *pattern* of error is a quality-control problem, which you cannot afford to ignore.

STEP 1: Gather the facts.

STEP 2: Don't look for a person to blame, but do look for sources of the error.

STEP 3: Review procedures as necessary.

STEP 4: Do not criticize the employee(s) involved without also furnishing direction and alternatives.

STEP 5: Take a team approach. Work with the employee(s) involved in order to break the pattern of error.

Your script: handling repeated errors

A meeting devoted to repeated errors must not be allowed to degenerate into a blame fest. Here's a productive exchange:

You: Ron, have you had an opportunity to look at the summary of error reports generated by customer service concerning your accounts?

Ron: Yes, I have.

Start out with facts—evidence. Avoid subjective assessments, which are subject to emotion-charged dispute. Focus on events and results, not on issues of skill, ability, talent, or character.

You: Taken in and of themselves, none of the errors is very serious. But it's the pattern of errors that bothers me. We shouldn't be making so many mistakes. Somewhere in our system and procedures, we're being sloppy. Now, since the errors fall into your area, you are the person who is going to have to be most responsible for creating improvement.

Let me give you my instructions, then I'll ask for your comments and suggestions.

First, I want you to review your customary processing procedures to ensure that your routine meets the requirements of company policy.

After you complete this self-review, I want to see a report to me no later than the fifteenth. Here's what I want in that report: First, describe what—exactly—has been going wrong. Second, why has it been going wrong? And third, what do you think you—and the rest of us—need to do to reduce the rate of error?

Ron, you are typically highly productive, which gives me confidence that once you enumerate and confront these errors head-on you will be able to improve overall performance.

Do you have any questions and comments?

Ron: I'm not so sure the situation is as bad as you think it is.

You: That's why I asked for the report. Let's assess it together.

Inadequate Record Keeping

As the pressure mounts to produce results *fast* and to turn out product *fast*, certain routine and superficially "nonproductive" functions may begin to suffer. Keeping files and records up to date takes time, and by putting on the pressure to produce, you may also be contributing to deficiencies in areas that are perceived to be secondary. Be aware of this when you speak to an employee about record keeping.

YOUR SCRIPT: CORRECTING RECORD-KEEPING PROBLEMS

You: Sarah, no one is more aware than I am that we move fast. No one is more aware of it, because I'm in large part responsible for setting the work pace. It is not tempting to cut corners, and I'm afraid I've even encouraged that. Well, the fact is that whatever else we must do to get the job done, there is one corner we cannot afford to cut.

Note that the boss includes himself in the "reprimand." If you are part of the problem, shoulder your fair share of the responsibility.

You: We must always take the time to keep accurate and full records in strict accordance with company policy. I have to tell you frankly that I was quite disturbed last week when I asked you for the file on the Jones account and found that a number of records were either missing or incomplete, including . . .

Be specific about what is missing or inadequate. Avoid mere subjective appraisal.

You: Sarah, you will need to set some time aside to begin reviewing your files, one by one, and bring each of them up to company standards in terms of completeness of records.

Look, don't drop everything to do this, but I do want to see a proposed schedule for completion. I'd like that schedule by Wednesday.

Disclosing Privileged or Proprietary Information

Information leaks can be highly destructive. The practical as well as legal strength of trade secrets depends on your company's ability to keep them secret. Other sensitive information may create critical problems if it falls into the wrong hands.

Communicating the seriousness of breaches in security or discretion is easier if you and your firm establish a clear policy on protecting privileged information, trade secrets, and other proprietary data. That is the first step to take. Beyond this, if a breach does occur, act swiftly.

TIP

It is critically important that you document verbal reprimands concerning disclosure of privileged information. The written record may figure in subsequent disciplinary or legal action.

Your script: handling security breaches. Act swiftly and decisively

You: I am not happy to find myself obliged to remind you, Max, that you hold a position of significant sensitivity and confidence. I enjoyed seeing you at the annual trade convention reception last night, but I was alarmed to overhear you talking—even in the broadest terms—about our upcoming line of products.

You must know that, under no circumstances is such information to be considered a topic of casual conversation. To take such information outside the company is at the least squandering a portion of our investment in present research and future markets. At worst, Max, it is theft. It's grounds for dismissal.

Max: Oh, come on, boss! This was casual party conversation—not industrial espionage.

You: Max, it really is as serious as I say, and it will be taken that way.

Do not concede that the security breach was harmless. Indeed, make no judgment, other than pointing out the *fact* that sensitive information was inappropriately discussed.

You: Your careless conversation was improper, unwise, and dangerous. Max, I do not want this happening again. I am writing a memorandum of this conversation and placing it in the file. You will regard that as an official reprimand and as a warning. Future indiscretions will not be tolerated, and I will have no other choice than to act in strict accordance with company policy and the terms of your employment. Discussing privileged information with unauthorized persons is grounds for dismissal. Max, it really is that serious. Please, *please* be more discreet in the future. Is there anything I've said that is unclear to you?

Sloppy Appearance

Some managers find this a difficult subject to discuss. They feel that they are intruding into matters of personal taste and, perhaps, even matters of one's pocketbook.

STEP 1:   Remove subjectivity from criticism of appearance by establishing (or working with your supervisors to establish) clear and specific guidelines for dress and grooming on the job.

STEP 2:   When you discuss personal appearance with an employee, make it clear that your concern is essentially about communication: the message the employee's dress and grooming is transmitting to customers and clients.

YOUR SCRIPT: DEALING WITH SLOPPY APPEARANCE.

Approach this matter as specifically as possible.

You: Bob, I want to talk to you about something—about *confidence.* You know that whatever else we sell here, there is one "product" we must sell before we can promote anything else. That is *confidence.* Our customers have to feel comfortable dealing with us, and they can feel that way only if they believe in us.

We begin to sell confidence before we speak a word. We sell it by the way we present ourselves. It is important that we look professional and successful.

Now, Bob, we have never had a formal dress code at XYZ, but we have always depended on our employees to dress with taste and, above all, to dress neatly. It is all part of the package we are selling.

Taste is pretty subjective, Bob, but there are aspects of your appearance that aren't subjective at all. Lately, your clothes have been wrinkled, shirts occasionally unlaundered, tie loose. Look, I'm not saying that you go out and buy a new wardrobe, but I do ask that you make an extra effort to see to it that the clothing you wear is clean and neatly pressed. And, please, it is also important to the image we must create that you wear a necktie and that you keep it neatly tied.

Bob, you understand, I hope, that I'm not criticizing you personally. But I am concerned that we consistently send the right messages to our customers. Do you have any questions?

ACCEPTING RESIGNATIONS FROM SUBORDINATES

It's over, right? What more is there to say?

- Are you sure you want to go?
- Is there anything I can do that would change your mind?
- Congratulations!
- Let's stay in touch.

Moreover, accepting a resignation should never be casual. Document the event in writing. The employee should be asked to submit a written resignation, but if she does not, you should acknowledge the verbal resignation in a letter written to him and copied into your files.

TIP

It is extremely important to distinguish between a voluntary resignation and dismissal. Documentation of the voluntary resignation may be your only defense against severance claims and other legal actions.

In accepting the resignation, take the following steps:

STEP 1:   Acknowledge the resignation.

STEP 2:   Accept it with congratulations, regret, or whatever emotion is appropriate to the circumstances.

TIP

Keep the response as positive as possible. If you accept with regret, do not tinge that with personal bitterness. If you are happy for the employee, show it. If you are relieved to see her go, be as courteous as possible.

STEP 3:   If appropriate, share a memory, comment on years of service, and so on.

TIP

Why bother to personalize the moment? To begin with, there is nothing wrong with human decency and warmth in business. But, of more pragmatic import, the world of business can be remarkably small. You may well have dealings with this employee again. Let her leave with good memories of you and the company.

STEP 4:   If appropriate, invite reconsideration or later return.

STEP 5:   Wish the employee success in her new position or endeavor.

STEP 6:   Review the facts: date the employee wants to leave, status of projects, and so on. You may wish to set up a separate meeting for some of these matters.

Congratulating the Departing Employee

Accepting the resignation of an employee who is growing, going on to a well-deserved position that you are not in a position to provide, is the easiest of all resignation scenarios:

You: Well, Pete, I'm sorry to see you go. You know that. But this sounds like a great, great opportunity. I congratulate you on it.

Go on to Step 6, in the preceding section.

Asking the Employee to Reconsider

Inviting a resigning employee to pause a moment to reconsider can be a delicate matter, especially if you don't have a competitive incentive to offer.

STEP 1: Acknowledge the news.

STEP 2: Ask the employee what it would take for her to reconsider.

STEP 3: Negotiate, if you have the authority.

STEP 4: If necessary, ask for time to formulate a counteroffer.

STEP 5: If the employee does not want to entertain a counteroffer, offer your congratulations and proceed to clarify such items as last day, status of projects, and so on.

YOUR SCRIPT: ASKING THE EMPLOYEE TO RECONSIDER

An invitation to reconsider should never be a plea. It should be an *invitation*.

TIP
_____
Do not appeal to feelings of guilt, even in jest.

You: Jane, I am not surprised that someone of your abilities should have attracted the attention of ABC Company. Would you entertain a counteroffer? I sure don't want to see you go.

Jane: Well, I . . . sure. I'd be willing to consider it. I'm flattered . . .

You: Okay. I need two days to formulate our counteroffer. Can I have that?

Jane: Yes.

Employee Resigning Under Unfavorable Circumstances

When an employee resigns under unfavorable circumstances—essentially to avoid dismissal—your task is as follows:

STEP 1:   Acknowledge the resignation.

STEP 2:   Maintain a neutral stance. Do not betray emotion.

STEP 3:   Do not comment on the employee's precarious position. To do so could render your firm liable for a severance settlement.

STEP 4:   State the procedure for the employee's departure, including the exact date, what to do with company property, company car, and so on. All of this should be furnished in writing.

STEP 5:   Ask for a written report on the status of the employee's projects.

YOUR SCRIPT: ACCEPTING THE RESIGNATION

You: Dan, I accept your resignation. Can we agree on March 3 as your last day?

Dan: Yes.

You: Please remove your personal belongings from your office by that time. I'll have Gail available to assist you, if you like. Now, Dan, your separation from us is subject to the policy set out in the Employee Manual. I will have a copy placed on your desk. On the day before you leave, I would like to get from you a report on the status of your projects. Do you have any questions?

Dan: No.

You: Very well. I wish you luck in your new endeavors.

Get no more emotional than a simple, polite "good luck" wish. Anything more intense than this may create an unwanted scene.

TERMINATING AN EMPLOYEE

Employee termination is usually a process rather than an event. It is often the culmination of "progressive discipline," a procedure that begins with supervisory counseling and progresses through warnings and, perhaps, a probationary period, ending at last in dismissal, if problems and deficiencies aren't cured.

> **TIP**
>
> The prospect of termination can be a powerful motivator. It should never be used as an idle threat, but a problem employee should be put on notice, in the course of progressive discipline, that termination is the ultimate consequence of failure to improve.

Of course, termination may be due to circumstances outside the employee's control, such as plant closings, layoffs, and so on. In such cases, sympathetic understanding is called for, but you should not put yourself in the position of apologizing for the company's actions.

Why expend much thought and energy on how you terminate an employee? After all, she is about to be history . . .

- Terminated employees do not vanish from the face of the earth. They move to other companies, and they talk about your company. For the sake of your firm's reputation and image, it pays to terminate with a sense of fairness and dignity.
- Losing a job puts a major dent in anybody's day. You can make feelings better or worse with words. Make them worse, and you may be more likely to find yourself with litigation on your hands.
- The world of business can be mighty small. You may want to rehire the terminated employee someday, or you may, in some capacity or other, end up working with him again. Don't create bad blood.
- Most of us want to behave as decent human beings. The process of termination affords ample opportunity to be decent and humane.

Communicating Probationary Status to an Employee

Management is frequently inclined to procrastinate when faced with a poorly performing employee. While it is true that termination need not be brutal and sudden, it is often well worth the effort to try more training, more coaching, and more counseling. But don't use these activities merely to prolong the agony for all involved. Make it clear to the employee that she is on probation and that how she performs and the degree of improvement she shows will determine whether she retains her job.

STEP 1: Probation is partly about avoiding surprises. Even while you coach and train the employee, be clear with your criticism and be clear about the consequences of failure to improve:

- **You:** Pat, you are still performing below the minimum expected standards. We're going to continue with the training, but if we don't get a turnaround by August, I will need to release you from the company.

STEP 2: State and define all of your expectations in specific, quantifiable, and measurable terms whenever possible:

- **You:** Pat, you turn around an average of five units per week. The departmental average is ten. I think you'll agree that five units is not an acceptable level of productivity. Is this the right job for you? How do you propose to increase your productivity?

STEP 3: Document, document, document. Document performance in writing, using as many objective measurements as possible.

STEP 4: Be specific about performance goals and about time lines.

STEP 5: Make it clear to the employee that failure to achieve the goals will result in termination.

TIP

It's easy to call for immediate improvement, but not so easy to be explicit about the consequences of failure to improve. Tell the employee that he is in danger of losing his job.

Your script: putting an employee on probation.

Here is a sample probationary statement:

You: Max, your performance is not improving. I don't think you are going to survive here. But this is what I propose to do. I will allow another 60 days for additional training. By the end of that period, I expect you to achieve the following: (lists goals). If you haven't achieved these goals by November 15, I will let you go.

Max, I suggest you do two things between now and then. First, work on achieving the goals we have just discussed. Second, use some of your time to explore other employment opportunities for which you may be better suited.

Now, just so that all of this is very clear, I will prepare a written summary of this conversation. You'll have a copy tomorrow.

- Notice that the tone is frank—humane but unapologetic. You owe it to your company and the employee not to disguise the gravity of the situation.

Dismissal "for Cause"

In contrast to dismissal for poor or inadequate performance, termination for cause is characteristically sudden. It is motivated by such problems as

- Simple failure to perform
- Failure to perform assigned tasks
- Gross insubordination
- Wrongdoing, such as theft, sexual harassment, drug use, and so on

In instances of dismissal for cause, your objectives are:

- To amass adequate documentation
- To separate the employee quickly and quietly

TIP

If reasons for termination include possible criminal activity—drug use on the job, pilfering, embezzlement, theft, violence in the workplace, sexual misconduct, and so on, management must seek legal counsel. If you believe that you are dealing with a potentially dangerous person, the police and/or your company's private security officers should be present during the dismissal.

YOUR SCRIPT: DISMISSING FOR CAUSE.

Most terminations for cause do not result from dramatic instances of misconduct. Here is a typical scenario:

You: Gail, three days ago I brought to your attention discrepancies in your petty-cash records and asked that you prepare an explanation of them by this morning. I indicated to you that if the explanation was not satisfactory in all regards, you would face termination for cause. Have your prepared something for me?

Gail: No.

You: Then I have no choice but to tell you that you are released from the payroll effective immediately. I am asking security to meet you at your office while you remove your personal belongings. Within the hour, I will have a final check issued to you, which will include pay for unused vacation days and three days' additional pay in lieu of notice. You are to leave the building by five this afternoon.

Gail: I . . . I . . . Look, I'm sorry . . .

You: I understand that you are, but this decision is final. You are released from the payroll.

Gail: But can't I explain . . . ?

You: You had that opportunity. Now this is what must happen.

Gail: Are you going to call the police?

You: What legal action the company takes, if any, will be decided in consultation with our attorneys.

Gail: But I need to know.

You: Gail, I'm telling you all I know at this time. I am preparing a letter summarizing the terms of this dismissal. Please go to your office and collect your personal belongings now.

Keep the termination for cause as emotionally neutral as possible. Do not scold, do not lecture, do not express regrets. Above all, do not apologize. You have nothing to apologize for. Make no statements concerning future civil or criminal litigation.

Termination Due to External Circumstances

This is the most difficult termination scenario, both for the manager and the employee. Typically, you are in the position of having to lay off a good employee. It hardly seems fair, and it hurts.

Your strategy is to separate yourself and the employee from the action. "It" is happening. "It" is a fact. There is nothing either of you can do about it.

STEP 1: Make a background statement: why layoffs are happening.

STEP 2: Tell the employee he is being terminated.

STEP 3: Give him the effective date of termination.

STEP 4: Tell him any positive measures that can or will be taken on his behalf, including (for example) severance pay, salary for unused vacation, placement assistance, your willingness to write letters of recommendation, and so on.

STEP 5: Provide instructions regarding collecting his final check, performance during the notice period, return of company property, and so on.

STEP 6: Express sympathy, but do not apologize beyond remarking "I'm sorry this had to happen." Always stress the inevitable, unalterable nature of the layoff.

STEP 7: An official notice must be submitted in writing.

Your script: terminating due to external cause.

Here is a typical conversation:

You: Cutbacks at the corporate level have made it necessary for XYZ Corporation to reduce personnel. Jack, you are among the employees being released from the payroll.

Your employment here will end on November 18. Your final check will be issued at that time. It will include any vacation pay you may have coming. There is also two weeks' severance pay.

The company offers a placement-assistance program, which you may find helpful in securing new employment. Personally, Jack, you know that you can come to me at any time for letters of recommendation or for a phone call to a prospective employer. I'll be happy to give you the fine recommendation you deserve.

Jack, I'm handing you a letter putting this termination in writing and spelling out the terms in detail. The letter also explains how you can continue health-insurance coverage and other benefits.

I'm sorry this had to happen, and I wish you all the luck in finding a great job.

CHAPTER 7

Putting Yourself Across . . . to Prospective Clients and Customers

SELF-TEST YOUR SAVVY IN COMMUNICATING WITH PROSPECTS

The following is a simple diagnostic test. A smaller and more selective version of the self-test in Chapter 1, its purpose is not to test your knowledge of communication theory or techniques, but to help you gauge how effectively you communicate with prospective clients and customers in a day-to-day business context. For the most part, you will find it easy to guess the "right" answer. But getting the "right" answer is not the point of the test. Respond honestly, even if you feel that your response is not the best one possible. This is *not* a contest. The object is solely self-inventory.

1. I always use a soft-sell approach. T/F ____

2. I always use a hard-sell approach. T/F ____

3. I always try to smile when I talk to a prospect on the phone. T/F ____

4. I approach the sales call systematically and step by step. T/F ____

5. I care less about making a sale than I do about creating a customer. T/F ____

6. Resistance is the customer asking for more information. T/F ____

7. Don't let the customer ask questions. You'll lose the sale. T/F ____

8. My main focus is to *make the sale*. T/F ____

9. To make the sale, speak quickly. T/F ____

10. I never "wing" a cold call. I prepare notes to work from. T/F ____

11. I seek to *educate* my customer.   T/F ____

12. I sell value.   T/F ____

13. I sell price—the cheaper the better.   T/F ____

14. Never take *no* for an answer.   T/F ____

15. I try to get my prospects to ask questions—*lots* of questions.   T/F ____

16. I want my customer to understand his or her choices.   T/F ____

TOTAL T/F   ____

Score 1 point for each "True" response and 0 for each "False" response, EXCEPT for questions 1, 2, 7, 8, 9, 13, and 14. For *these questions only*, SUBTRACT 1 point for each "True" response. Record your total. A score below +7 indicates that you would benefit from practicing the communication techniques discussed in this chapter. (Note: It is possible to have a negative score.)

WORDS TO USE WITH PROSPECTS

absolute	authorize	confirm
accessories	authorized	consider
accommodate	availability	convenient
act	available	convinced
acute	benefits	create
advise	choice	deadline
agree	choose	debate
alternative	client	decide
answer	close	decision
appreciate	comfort	demand
appropriate	commitment	demonstrate
approval	competitors	desire
assist	complacency	direct
assure	completion	directly
authorization	confident	disbelief

WORDS TO USE WITH PROSPECTS, *cont'd*

discerning	need	savvy
discuss	offer	schedule
do	okay	serve
enjoy	opportunities	service
enjoyable	option	smart
enjoyed	order	solution
ensure	our	solve
especially	partners	sophisticated
establish	percentage	special
expedite	personal	style
experience	pleased	substantial
extra	pleasure	successful
features	possible	supply
final	pressure	sure
fresh	price	talking
furnish	problem	target
generous	productive	terms
give	promise	testimonial
guarantee	quality	time
help	questions	trust
immediate	real	truth
immediately	relationship	try
information	reliability	understanding
inventory	require	unique
liabilities	requirement	value
listen	resolve	vendor
low	sale	welcome
minimum	satisfaction	winner
more	satisfied	yes
move	save	

PHRASES TO USE WITH PROSPECTS

always available
answer your objections
ask our advice
available for immediate shipment
best price
best effort
beyond my control
challenge the status quo
committed to you
confirm the availability
confirm that
confirm our understanding
count on the order
create a new market
deal direct
demand has been unusually high
do something good for yourself
do yourself a favor
don't cut any corners
enjoyed talking
exactly what you want
expect extra effort
expect more
expect your order
extend special terms
follow-up
generous terms
give us a try
go that extra mile
good news

PHRASES TO USE WITH PROSPECTS, *cont'd*

great product

greatest value for your dollar

have no choice

height of the season

here to serve you

hold the quantities promised

hold the prices promised

I think you'll agree

I understand completely

in the long run

industry leaders

lead time

let us help

let us help you

listen to you

little room for doubt

lock in your order

look forward to hearing from you

look forward to working with you

low prices

make certain

meet or exceed the specifications

no later than

no compromise on quality

our busy season

our situation

over the long haul

personal service

PHRASES TO USE WITH PROSPECTS, *cont'd*

price that's right for you

production times

prompt attention

proven winner

pure pleasure

put us on trial

put us to the test

ready to ship

reaping the benefits

right combination

self-indulgent

serve your needs better

special offer

special value

start-to-finish

target date

tell us what you need

to my attention

unique opportunity

very special price

we don't want you to get shut out

we won't leave you

we can

we can help

we care

we're here to help

we listen

what do you need?

you can talk to us

WORDS TO AVOID WITH PROSPECTS

bargain	costly
buy	cut rate
cannot	expensive
cheap	impossible
cheapest	sacrifice

PHRASES TO AVOID WITH PROSPECTS

be a fool to pass up

can't do it

cut to the bone

don't ask

I don't know

never again

no choice

once in a lifetime

think it over

BODY-LANGUAGE STRATEGY FOR COMMUNICATING WITH PROSPECTS

Let's begin by observing that, these days, much sales prospecting is done by telephone. Obviously, body language plays no role in that, right?

Well . . . wrong.

Consider adding two nonverbal elements to your prospecting calls:

1. Make the call standing up instead of sitting down. Talking while standing imparts more power and authority to your voice. (Few operatic arias are sung from a seated position!)

2. Smile as you talk. Even though the callee can't see your smile, she can *hear* it in your voice.

In addition, remember that, in general, the lower the pitch of your voice, the more conviction and authority it conveys. This is true whether you are a man or a woman.

- Pitch your voice lower than normal.
- Speak slowly and distinctly.

> **TIP**
>
> Some authorities advise salespeople to speak a little faster than at a normal conversational rate. Actually, it is advisable to speak a little more slowly than normal, especially during telephone calls. This not only makes your message clearer, it helps to defeat the negative image of the "fast-talking salesperson."

- Open your mouth when you speak into the telephone. Don't mumble.

In face-to-face sales situations, your object is to convey openness, trustworthiness, and honesty. Practice and apply the following:

- Establish and maintain eye contact.

> **TIP**
>
> In person-to-person sales situations, eye contact is the single most important nonverbal element of presentation. Eye contact conveys sincerity and character.

- Use open gestures, hands slightly spread, palms turned upward, as if offering something.
- When you stand, do so with feet slightly apart and firmly planted.
- Smile.
- Provide frequent nonverbal feedback. Gently nod to show that you are hearing and taking in what the prospect tells you.

BODY LANGUAGE TO AVOID WITH PROSPECTS

In general, avoid gestures that

- Suggest closedness, resistance, or that you are hiding something or "holding back"

- Convey nervousness
- Suggest evasiveness, shiftiness
- "Push" the prospect

  Negative nonverbal gestures include

- Avoidance of eye contact
- Folding arms across the chest (suggests closedness or concealment)
- Hands on hips (suggests defiance)
- Shifting weight from side to side while standing (generally distracting and suggests that you don't want to be where you are)
- Leg movement when seated (distracting and suggests that you want to make a getaway)
- Hands near face or mouth (suggests evasiveness and concealment)
- Pointing, gesturing with a fist (coercive; likely to elicit resistance from the prospect)

FOUR-STEP FORMULA FOR BUILDING A CUSTOMER BASE

Working with a sales prospect can be broken down into four essential steps, which may be expressed in an operatic acronym: AIDA:

*A*ttention
*I*nterest
*D*esire
*A*ction

Getting Attention from the Prospect

Get your prospect's attention. These days, we all swim in an ocean of information. Data stream by and around us. Is the result universal enlightenment?

Hardly.

The continual flux of information is often less enlightening than it is mind and emotion numbing. Your first task, then, is to get your prospect's attention. Here's an example of a telephone sales call:

You: Hello, Mr. Smith. This is Clara Barton at XYZ Company. I'm calling because we had a conversation a short time ago concerning high-performance widgets. I wanted to let you know that we are now stocking the brands we spoke about . . .

The caller gets the prospect's attention by recalling the past.

1. This is not a *total* stranger calling.
2. You and I had a conversation once.
3. You wanted something at that time.

Remind the prospect that he wants something, and you will get his attention. Identifying a need your callee has will also command attention.

Developing the Prospect's Interest

But attention is too brief to last through the close of a sale. You need to develop that attention into interest. Do this by showing your prospect how you can fill the need you've identified.

You: . . . and I think what we've got will suit your needs just perfectly. Even better, we're able to offer the widgets at a special introductory price. Are you interested?

TIP

Ask questions. Sales is not just about presenting information and speaking persuasively. It's about continued customer involvement, interactive feedback, opportunities for the customer to express himself and tell you what he wants.

Prospect: Yes, sure. I'm interested.

You: Great! I'll tell you about what we have.

Creating Desire in the Prospect

Interest certainly broadens attention, but it is still usually not enough to move the conversation along the road toward a close. This is the point at which you must make the merchandise attractive and irresistibly appealing.

TIP

The more you know about your prospect's taste, wants, and needs, the better chance you have of closing the sale.

You: Mr. Smith, in our earlier conversation you had mentioned (enumerate key points the prospect previously raised). The exciting news is that these widgets can do all of that—and more. For example: (enumerate key features).

Pause a beat to let this sink in. Then ratchet up the desire another notch:

You: But there's even more. Installation is *much* easier than it used to be for products of this type. Let me explain (explain improvements in installation).

One of your strongest selling points is value. You've built up desire. Now show that the desire *can* be satisfied:

You: Now, Mr. Smith, let me ask you something. How much have you been paying for widgets?

Prospect: (Answers with a figure.)

You: Here's a very pleasant surprise. The base price for these new widgets is $XX, with options extra. I think that you'll agree that this represents a spectacular value.

Prospect: Sounds pretty good to me.

You: Well, you won't pay that amount. We're offering a special introductory price, with the options package: $X! How does that sound to you?

This question is critical. Obtain a response to the price. This not only will further involve the prospect, bringing him closer to commitment, but will also allow you to gauge how close you are to closing the sale.

Prospect: I'm not sure . . .

You: Well, let me just add one other feature—our warranty. To begin with, warranties are quite good in this industry. Your typical widget warranty runs X years. *Ours* goes to XX years.

You know that our price is excellent, but you also know that price is meaningless without value. In terms of features, benefits, warranty, *and* price, well, you can't beat it, can you?

Prospect: It *does* sound good.

Moving the Prospect to Action

Once you receive a "buy signal"—an indication that the prospect is on the brink of commitment—move to close the sale. This critical point is not as difficult to reach as you may think. If the prospect is now ready to buy, all you have to do is make concluding the transaction easy.

> **TIP**
>
> Close the sale by making quick, easy, direct action possible.

You: Mr. Smith, the introductory pricing period will end on June 5. If you place your order now, I can guarantee units available at the price of $X. I can take a credit-card number right now.

MAKING THE SALE VERSUS CREATING A CUSTOMER

Sales professionals are typically told to concentrate on The Sale, and to make "one sale at a time." They are drilled in the ABC formula: *Always Be Closing*. The truth is that, for all the mystique and mystery in which selling is so often immersed, making "one sale at a time" is neither all that difficult—nor all that worthwhile. With practice and a halfway decent product to sell, you can probably close with a significant percentage of those you approach.

But why settle for that?

- Far better than the one-sale-at-a-time strategy is the one-customer-at-a-time approach.

A sales opportunity comes, you make the sale, and the event is over, finished. If, instead of making the sale, you create a feeling of trust and confidence in the customer, the sales *event* becomes a sales *process*. It doesn't just come and go. It develops. Approach selling as an opportunity to create satisfaction, to create, that is, customers.

- A sale is a one-shot event.
- A customer is a person who may generate sale after sale.
- Your best customers are your current customers.
- Your best advertising is the word of mouth of current customers.

Customers are a key asset. Develop the asset. Develop relationships. Develop trust. The payoff is plural sales, rather than *a* singular sale.

> **TIP**
>
> Not only are satisfied current customers great sources of word of mouth, they are often ideal consumers, consumers custom made for you. Cultivate them. Learn about what they want and don't want. Use this information to appeal to them, to make each sale that much easier.

ESTABLISHING AN EFFECTIVE COLD-CALL STRATEGY

A cold call is an unsolicited sales call: an attempt to sell someone something she hasn't asked for. At least, that's the simple and traditional view of the cold call. The cold call can be made more effective by preparation:

STEP 1: Don't make random calls to a random list of people you don't know.

STEP 2: Warm up cold calling by selecting names from special-interest lists you purchase or lease.

STEP 3: Call customers from your own data files.

STEP 4: Consider research efforts to identify potential customers; then call them.

Just as you should base your cold calling on some form of consumer research, prepare your presentation in advance.

TIP

It is usually an exhausting mistake to attempt absolute spontaneity. Prepare.

Preparation for cold calling may include:

- Composing fully scripted pitches, which are read over the phone. Many direct marketers use this method. It is most practical for carrying out large-scale campaigns.
- For smaller campaigns that you handle personally, consider finding a middle ground between spontaneity on the one hand and a fully scripted pitch on the other.
- Prepare the "spontaneous" cold call by creating clear notes to yourself, including selling points, ways to meet and overcome objections, and so on.

Your phone notes should consist of fact sheets or "cue cards" listing the most important sales points of the merchandise or services you offer.

- The material on your cue cards should be just comprehensive enough to "hook" your customer. Avoid overselling, boring the prospect with details he doesn't want to hear.

TIP

Avoid falling into the detail trap by asking the customer for feedback: "Do you want to hear more?" Or offer: "I can recite the whole spec sheet, if you like."

Should You Sell Soft or Hard?

Selling styles may be divided into two broad categories: soft sell and hard sell.

Soft sell is more conversational in tone than hard sell. It is a style that *pulls* the customer, gently, toward a close. Hard sell, in contrast, *pushes* the prospect, headlong, to a close.

Which approach is better?

This depends on the nature of the four major variables of any sales situation:

1. The perceived character of the seller
2. The skill of the seller
3. The needs and desires of the buyer
4. The intrinsic desirability—quality and value—of the product or service

In general, the more sophisticated these four variables are, the more appropriate is the soft-sell approach. The simpler these variables, the more likely it is that a hard sell will produce results.

YOUR SCRIPTS: MAKING COLD CALLS

Here's an example of soft-sell cold call:

You: Ms. Davidson, I'm taking the liberty of calling you at your office rather than your home to add yet one more call to your busy morning. Ms. Davidson, how many times has the phone rung this morning? How many problems have you handled? How many fires have you put out? How many meetings have you sat through? How many battles have you fought?

Prospect: Plenty . . .

You: If you're like most people in high-responsibility positions, you find it difficult to get through the day without taking some evidence of the pressure home with you: a knot in the stomach, an ache in the head, a pain in the neck.

Well, I won't use any more of your time to tell you how you feel. Let me get right to my offer: a place to go and work off all that tension. A place to do something kind and good and healthy for yourself.

XYZ Spa is a health club for professionals. We offer a complete gym, indoor track, two pools, sauna, and steam room. We're geared to offer you a vigorous breakfast-time workout before work, or fast and efficient lunchtime workout at midday, or something more when you have the time at the end of the day.

Ms. Davidson, what time is best for you?

Prospect: I really don't know.

You: Does the prospect of membership in a highly flexible and convenient health club interest you?

Prospect: I'm not sure.

You: Well, then, what you need is information. May I send you a brochure that describes our various programs? I think once you see the brochure, you'll be ready to pick a program that's right for you. You'll also find telephone numbers for fitness counselors, who can help you decide what would be best for you.

Here is a similar pitch, but done as a hard sell:

You: Mr. Tompkins, I'm calling to tell you to "Just do it."

Prospect: What?

You: Just do it. It's more than the slogan of a popular brand of running shoe. It's good advice. Especially now.
    Mr. Tompkins, have you ever thought about getting into better shape, or maintaining the shape you have, or just finding a time and place to unwind and have some fun?

Prospect: Are you trying to sell me a health-club membership?

You: Now is an excellent time to stop thinking and start doing.
    Yes, sir, I am offering an opportunity to join XYZ Club at special discount rates. Would you like me to explain?

Prospect: Yes, sure. Why not?

You: (Briefly outline the available plans, with promotional bargain prices.) Mr. Davidson, XYZ offers state-of-the-art facilities, including a Nautilus-equipped gym, indoor track, two pools, sauna, and steam room. We are located near your office, at First and Third Streets.
    You may be asking yourself, *Is there a catch?*
    Well, yes, there is. You must act now. This is a one-time telephone offer. To get the prices and services I just mentioned, you'll have to sign up today.

Now, we don't expect you to spend your money on blind faith. Here's the second part of the offer. Sign up and pay today, and you will be given a free 14-day trial membership. Here's how it works: If you join now, two weeks will be added—free—to your membership. If you join today and feel that you are not getting all that you had hoped for, just drop into our downtown office before November 12 and ask for a full refund. You risk nothing.

We've made it extra easy for you to "just do it." Just use your major credit card. Once you come into the club, you can put together your own health program, or you can talk with one of our fitness counselors. And remember: there is no risk. Try us for 14 days. If you don't like us, your money will be refunded—on the spot.

FOCUSING THE PROSPECT'S NEEDS

The great Chicago master of nineteenth-century retailing, Marshall Field, put his selling philosophy into a single phrase: "Give the lady what she wants." That is a fine philosophy—provided the lady, or the man, *knows* what she or he wants. In many selling situations, however, neither fulfillment of a clearly stated want nor persuasion of a need is called for. In many situations, selling is a process of education and discovery. It is up to the salesperson to help—yes, *help*—the customer focus his or her needs.

- In selling sophisticated or complex goods (personal computer equipment, for example), the educational component of the sales process may be especially significant.
- In selling high-ticket items, requiring a substantial investment from the customer, education plays a key role.
- In selling bulk items, it is often important to help the customer determine just what and how much of the product he or she needs.
- In selling merchandise intended to solve specific problems ("What flea shampoo is best for my dog?"), education is critical.
- In selling items that involve more than one purchase or financing option, education plays a key role.
- Selling merchandise incorporating new technologies requires educating the customer.

Salespeople of the old school—and salespeople who do not respect their product—discourage customer questions. They believe the salesperson should remain "in control," that questions bring on thought, thought brings on doubt, and doubt halts the momentum that makes a sale.

All of this is true—if you see the sales process as essentially cheating the customer out of his or her money.

If, however, you see sales as trading value for value, and, furthermore, if your objective is not merely to make a single sale, but to create a customer—a source of repeat business and word-of-mouth advertising—then you will make an effort to elicit questions from the customer.

> **TIP**
>
> A question is an investment. It takes initiative, positive action, and effort to ask a question. The customer who asks questions has, in effect, made a down payment on the merchandise you offer.

The process of focusing needs typically begins when you pick up the phone and the caller tells you that she's looking for some "information" on the style and prices of widgets you carry. "I just want to get information," she warns, in an almost scolding tone, as if to put you on notice that she has no intention to make a purchase at this time.

Now, you may take this implied warning at face value. Or you may give it a little thought. While there are people who "window shop" on the phone, filling empty few moments with idle requests for information, it is more probable that the caller asking for "information" is really doing two things:

1. Shopping
2. Calling for help

The best way to handle the call is to offer:

1. Selling
2. Helping

If the caller's question is sufficiently specific, reply: "I can help you with that." If it is vague, ask questions to bring the caller's questions into clearer focus.

Better yet, let's establish a STEP 1 for focusing needs:

STEP 1: When you pick up the phone, greet the caller, state your name, the company's name, and then ask: *How may I help you?*

Let's talk about this step. The phrase is important. It's not *May I help you?* or *What can I do for you?* but *How may I help you?* That single word *how* is a powerful tool for focusing the caller. The word prompts her to tell you what she wants. If all goes well, it will evoke a response such as, "I'm looking for a good, solid widget—not the cheapest, but I don't want to go overboard, either."

The *How may I help you?* approach is also very effective in face-to-face sales situations. In a retail setting, for example, you see a customer browsing certain items. The usual approach is to walk up to the customer and ask "May I help you?" There are two problems with this phrase:

1. It does nothing to focus the customer's needs.
2. It may be answered *yes* or *no* and is, therefore, quite possibly a dead end.

TIP
A good salesperson asks questions and invites questions, but avoids asking questions that can be answered yes or no. The object of a sales-oriented question is to define needs and to get the customer to invest time and effort in the sale, thereby increasing the customer's stake in the sale and the likelihood of the sale's coming to a close.

Once you have a response to *How may I help you?* begin to develop the response into a sale. Here, then, is STEP 2:

STEP 2: Make the caller or browser feel that he has come to the right place. Now is the time for the *I can help you with that* response.

STEP 3: Work with the caller or browser to develop the initial statement into whatever you need to make an informed and helpful response that will likely result in a sale.

TIP

Sales fail to close for many reasons. One of the most common is misunderstanding or inadequate understanding. This is a result of insufficient information, and that—let's face it—is *your* fault. It is up to you to ensure that the information you receive and supply is adequate and clear.

STEP 4:   Be prepared to make an adequate commitment of time. It takes time to make a sale because it takes time to determine what information the customer requires, to provide that information, and to ensure that the customer understands the information. The time required to "persuade" the prospect is actually slight. Invest your time in information.

STEP 5:   Do not avoid asking questions. This is how you gather the information you need to help the caller and to convert an "information-only" call into a sale.

YOUR SCRIPT: FOCUSING THE PROSPECT'S NEEDS

Here is a call-answering scenario. The phone rings, and you pick it up:

You: XYZ Company. This is Bill Smith. How may I help you?

Caller: I am interested in widgets.

You: I can help you with that. May I have your name?

Caller: Mary Clark.

You: Ms. Clark, we offer a wide variety of widgets. Let me just ask you a few questions so that we'll find just what you're looking for.

Be sure that you have at the ready a list of questions relating to the product you sell. Make it your business to know what buyers of your product are most interested in. In general, avoid talking about price until questions about product features and benefits have been answered.

You ask the questions, and the caller responds. After this, you continue:

You: Great. Now I have a clear picture of what you're looking for. Based on what you've just told me, I suggest that you consider either widget A or widget B. Both will do everything you've just told me you need; however, widget A also does (list additional functions). Would you like me to tell you more about those additional functions?

Caller: Well, what will they cost me?

The caller tries to introduce his own agenda. You don't want to give the impression that you are evading the question, but it is important for the caller to know more about the additional features *before* additional costs are discussed. If price is mentioned before interest in the additional features is developed, it will be difficult to develop that interest.

You: Let me quickly review these features in order to give you that information. (*After* explaining the additional features, the widget A price is given.) Now, widget B is priced at $XX, and widget A, with the additional features I mentioned, is $XXX.

I think you'll agree that both prices represent excellent value. Both widgets are of the same quality. The difference is in available features. If you want the additional features, the additional cost is certainly justified. But if you're looking for something more basic, which still fits the requirements you mentioned, you might want to spend less on widget B.

Is there anything more that I can tell you about the additional features—or the basic features, for that matter?

If there are more questions, handle them. Do not *push* the caller toward the more expensive product, but do make the additional features and value seem attractive. Once you have responded fully to the caller's requests for information, you have also set up a sale. Why not attempt to close? Ask:

You: May I take your order for widget A or widget B?

Maybe you'll get an order. However, if the customer hesitates or simply says that he is not yet ready to order, ask another question:

You: Is there any more information I could supply to help you make your choice?

TIP

Choice is a word you should always use in preference to *decide* or *decision*. *Decision* suggests compulsion, but *choice* connotes empowerment and freedom. It helps to put the sale in a positive context and gives the customer the feeling that he is in control.

You may have to be patient and review the information again. Be careful, though, not to bombard the caller with too many choices. This may lead to discouragement, the customer's feeling that he isn't sufficiently competent to make the decision. You may lose the sale. In complex sales situations, consider drawing up a "decision tree" or a "flow chart," with the yes and no responses branching from one decision to another, in order to help your sales staff "walk" customers through the options and help them clarify their needs.

GENERATING URGENCY IN THE PROSPECT

Generating a sense of urgency does not mean creating an aura of panic, hysteria, or ballyhoo. Rather, it requires demonstrating that *now* is the time to buy. Options for creating the sense of urgency include:

- There are price incentives.
- We can promise current availability of a high-demand item.
- You owe it to yourself to make the choice *now*.
- Why wait to begin enjoying the product benefits?

Your script: generating urgency.

Here are some examples of creating an appropriate sense of urgency:

1. **You:** There's a good reason to act now. I can deliver the widget to you for only $XX. That's a savings of $X. But this is a limited-time promotional price.

2. **You:** We sell an awful lot of these. Right now, I can guarantee immediate shipment. I can't promise *anything* about future orders. Demand is high, and production doesn't always keep up with it.

3. **You:** Why not do something good for yourself and buy now? You could own this widget today.

4. **You:** We're agreed that the widget will make your operations more efficient and cost-effective. My suggestion is that you put these product benefits to work for you right away.

OVERCOMING RESISTANCE BY THE PROSPECT

Resistance may be in the form of an outright "No, I'm not interested," but, more often, is expressed as "I don't know . . ." or some more specific phrase, such as:

- "Isn't that terribly expensive?"
- "I've heard those things don't work."
- "I've heard a new model is going to make that obsolete."
- "I've always used Brand X."
- "I don't have the staff to operate it."

Perhaps the most frequent expression of resistance is postponement:

- "Can you call me about it later?"
- "I've been too busy to think about it."
- "I'm not ready to buy yet."

The most effective strategy for overcoming resistance depends on the type of resistance you encounter. Answer the "I don't know" or more specific types of response by educating the prospect:

Prospect: It's too expensive.

You: You are right The widget does require an investment. But our experience has shown that it *is* precisely that: an *investment*—a cost-effective investment of resources. On average, in installations we've done for firms the size of yours, the initial outlay is amortized within less than a year. Of course, we also offer you a wide range of financing choices for you.

TIP

Resistance is not just something a customer puts up to thwart you. It is an obstacle that both you *and* the customer confront. Overcome resistance by showing your customer how to get around the obstacle. Never argue. That's negative. Instead, show the alternatives. These are positive.

The other type of resistance—postponement—may be overcome by exploring and removing some of the uncertainty that is typically at the heart of the resistance:

- "What can I do to help you make your choice?"
- "What additional information will help you move on to the next step?"
- "How can I help you define your options?"

WHEN TO WALK AWAY FROM THE PROSPECT

Old-time hard-sell sales forces were taught never to take no for an answer. This was thought to be a highly admirable approach. There are problems with it.

- Pursuing a nay-saying customer is exhausting and demoralizing for the sales staff.
- Pursuing this customer takes time away from more productive sales opportunities.
- Pursuing this customer will alienate him or her. *No* need not be a permanent state. Failure to make this particular sale is not a good reason to see to it that you lose this customer, who represents the possibility of *future* sales.

The key is to recognize the difference between resistance, hesitation, and uncertainty on the one hand and no on the other. It's really simple. If the prospect declares that she is "not interested" or that she is "not in the market for" your product, you may ask "Is there anything I can do that will change your mind?" If the answer is still no, *thank* the prospect for her time and stake a claim for the future: "Ms. Johnson, needs change over time, so I hope that you will think of us if you ever find that you do need to purchase a widget."

CHAPTER 8

Putting Yourself Across . . . to Current Clients and Customers

SELF-TEST YOUR SAVVY IN COMMUNICATING WITH CUSTOMERS

The following is a simple diagnostic test. A smaller and more selective version of the self-test in Chapter 1, its purpose is not to test your knowledge of communication theory or techniques, but to help you gauge how effectively you communicate with current clients and customers in a day-to-day business context. For the most part, you will find it easy to guess the "right" answer. But getting the "right" answer is not the point of the test. Respond honestly, even if you feel that your response is not the best one possible. This is not a contest. The object is solely self-inventory.

1. When a customer calls for information, I try to sell him something.   T/F _____

2. I am unable to resist a request for a favor.   T/F _____

3. I am willing to negotiate many things.   T/F _____

4. I ask the caller's permission before I put him or her on hold.   T/F _____

5. I call the customer if I know I will have a problem meeting a deadline.   T/F _____

6. Informing customers about new products and accessories is *helpful to them*.   T/F _____

7. A customer's call for information is a nuisance that should be quickly disposed of.   T/F _____

8. I don't panic when I'm going to miss a deadline.   T/F ____

9. I don't repeat back other ordering information a caller gives me. Too tedious.   T/F ____

10. I encourage the customer to order.   T/F ____

11. I *explain* costs and prices.   T/F ____

12. I feel good about asking for a favor.   T/F ____

13. I *hate* asking for favors.   T/F ____

14. *Everything* is negotiable.   T/F ____

15. I know how to upsell.   T/F ____

16. I know the products/services I sell.   T/F ____

17. I know how to turn informational calls into sales.   T/F ____

18. I let the customer know that I am eager and able to help him.   T/F ____

19. I never *demand* information from a customer. I ask.   T/F ____

20. I offer my customers guidance *and* choice.   T/F ____

21. Company policy is of supreme importance in dealing with customer requests.   T/F ____

22. I smile while I'm on the phone.   T/F ____

23. I sometimes try to avoid calls from customers.   T/F ____

24. I take the extra time to "error proof" orders.   T/F ____

25. I take customers' orders accurately and efficiently.   T/F ____

26. I try always to tell a customer what I *can* do, not what I *cannot*.   T/F ____

27. I understand rapport and how to establish it in the first few seconds of a phone call.   T/F ____

28. I won't take no for an answer.   T/F ____

TOTAL T/F   ____

Score 1 point for each "True" response and 0 for each "False" response, EXCEPT for questions 1, 2, 7, 9, 13, 14, 21, 23, and 28. For *these questions only,* SUBTRACT 1 point for each "True" response. Record your total. A score below +17 indicates that you would benefit from practicing the communication techniques discussed in this chapter. (Note: It is possible to have a negative score.)

WORDS TO USE WITH CUSTOMERS

able	exceptional	key
advance	excited	latest
answer	expect	money
answers	expected	new
anticipate	expedite	nominal
approach	experience	opportunity
assume	expertise	options
attention	extensive	outstanding
attitude	extra	personal
biggest	facts	please
client	features	pleasure
colleagues	figures	pledge
competitive	fine	prefer
complete	folks	pride
confidence	free	project
conversation	great	promised
customer	hope	prompt
deliver	impressive	provocative
delivery	improvements	purpose
detailed	include	quality
direct	inclusive	questions
discount	innovative	reaction
eager	inquired	ready
easier	interest	realize
enterprise	invite	requirements

WORDS TO USE WITH CUSTOMERS, *cont'd*

response	small	time
responsive	special	upgrade
review	specifications	warranty
save	standard	willing
send	style	winner
service	support	
shrewd	thanks	

PHRASES TO USE WITH CUSTOMERS

across the board

as you requested

bear in mind

brand-new

competitive edge

complete satisfaction

complete confidence

complete—with absolutely everything you need

comprehensive selection

compelling investment opportunity

cost savings

crystal-clear specifications

customer-support program

deeper level of service

detailed prospectus

discussed with you

drop by our showroom

even more useful

exceptional warranty

experience tells me

extended warranty

PHRASES TO USE WITH CUSTOMERS, *cont'd*

free customer support

full range of

give you

great numbers

just came in

just received

just gotten

key to success

let the document speak for itself

locked in and guaranteed

look forward to

many options

may I direct your attention

most popular

my direct line

no unwelcome surprises

not to be missed

nothing in this world is risk free

our relationship

our single most important product: ourselves

pass those savings on to you

personal attention

pleased to send

points of special interest to you

pride ourselves

prove it to yourself

ready, willing, and able

right away

risk free

save you plenty of time

see for yourself

PHRASES TO USE WITH CUSTOMERS, *cont'd*

significantly upgraded

special effort

special highlights

special offers

special price

special pride

talking with you

total commitment

trailblazing

uncompromising quality

very personal

virtually unlimited number of options

walk that extra mile

want very much to work with you

wide range

willingness to help

without risk

your bottom line

your thoughts on

WORDS TO AVOID WITH CUSTOMERS

bargain	expensive
buy	impossible
cannot	lost
cheap	sacrifice
cheapest	sidetrack
costly	unload
cut rate	wait
delay	

PHRASES TO AVOID WITH CUSTOMERS

back burner

be a fool to pass up

can't do it

check on you

cut to the bone

don't ask

haven't bought anything in a while

I don't know

inactive account

inactive customer

minimum purchase

never again

no choice

once in a lifetime

think it over

waiting list

BODY-LANGUAGE STRATEGY FOR COMMUNICATING WITH CUSTOMERS

The body-language strategy for dealing with current customers is the same as that for dealing with new customers and prospects, except that you might try to approach these current customers as you would acquaintances and friends. The approach may be informal, friendly. Make the customer feel that he or she has established a relationship with you.

BODY LANGUAGE TO AVOID WITH CUSTOMERS

See the discussion on this subject in Chapter 7.

BUILDING CUSTOMER RELATIONSHIPS BY PROVIDING INFORMATION

Most customer contact involves nothing more—or less—than conveying information. That's just fine. No matter what products or services your company sells, it deals in information. You need to know what your customers want, and they need to know what you have to offer, how much it costs, and how they can obtain it.

STEP 1: Save timed by focusing informational calls with the question "How may I help you?" As discussed in the previous chapter, be sure that you include the *how* in this question. It will help the caller to focus her request, to be specific.

STEP 2: When the caller answers that question, be prepared to focus it further. This may be done by echoing back to the caller what she has asked for, but modifying the statement to define it more precisely: "You want the *complete* price list, or the price list for the standard models only?"

STEP 3: Once you have a clear understanding of what is being asked, provide the information.

TIP

If you must obtain information in order to handle a caller's request, *ask* permission to put the caller on hold: "May I put you on hold so that I can look up the answer? It will take about 30 seconds." Note that you should give the caller an accurate estimate of the amount of time she will be on hold.

TIP

If you are using a computer to obtain information, remember that your telephone customer cannot see what you are doing. Let her in on the action: "I'm going to search for that record right now. I'm typing it into the system . . . and it's searching . . . should be another few seconds. Yes. There. What's come up on my screen is a pair of orders from you, one dated June 5 and the other July 1."

STEP 4: If appropriate, conclude the call by asking for an order. "Will you be ordering those widgets today?"

STEP 5: If the customer does not want to order, ask "Have I answered all of your questions?"

STEP 6: Ask: "May I help you with anything else today?

STEP 7: Conclude the call by inviting future calls—directly to you: "Ms. Carlson, please feel free to call any time. Just ask for me. I'm Jake Barnes."

TIP

Don't give *too much* information. Be sure to give the caller all the information she has asked for *plus* any information you judge necessary or useful, but do not overload the caller with marginally useful or confusing data.

Taking an Order from a Customer

Taking an order: it's the most basic exchange of information there is, right?

Absolutely. But taking an order should not stop with exchanging information. The process should also establish or build on a positive, business-growing relationship between your firm and the customer.

- Take the order quickly and efficiently while communicating an attitude of helpfulness, service, pride, and accountability.
- Do not use the caller's time to advertise your company.
- Review each order with the customer to ensure accuracy.
- Confirm verbal orders in writing.
- Create an order-taking process that has you doing the work, not the customer. That is, don't force the customer to look up item numbers or to memorize his account number or to perform any task. You should never be in the position of having to demand information from the customer.

YOUR SCRIPT: TAKING A CUSTOMER'S ORDER.

Here is the scenario for a straightforward order:

Caller: I want to order a dozen widgets.

You: I can help you with that.

In a single sentence you have told the caller that he has come to the right place and that you are ready to *help*. You are willing to serve. You continue:

You: We will need some information. May I have your name?

Here is that vital transformation that is at the heart of most successful business communication. Move the conversation from *I* and *you* to *we* as quickly as possible. This pronoun shift is the basis for rapport. Why do you need rapport? After all, *you* are filling an order at the *customer's* request. True. But, to fill this order, you must ask for information. See to it that this comes across as a gentle request that will benefit the caller. It should not come across as a demand. You continue after obtaining the information requested:

You: Mr. Smith, we're creating a customer profile for our database. That's what we're doing right now. It will help us to serve you most efficiently in the future. So if I may just get some more information from you . . .

After obtaining permission to ask more questions, you gather the database information that you need. Note that it is always most effective to explain what you are doing and to put it in terms that show how what you ask the customer to do will benefit the customer. Be sure to make any choices clear. Choice empowers the customer:

You: We usually ship via United Shipping Service, with a three- to five-day turnaround time. Do you have any other shipping preference?

After recording any responses to the "choice" questions, you continue:

You: Okay, the order. You want (quantity) widgets, correct?

Caller: That's right.

You: Those are available in white or black. Which do you prefer?

Be careful how you ask these kinds of questions concerning choice. Use words like *prefer* rather than *want*. *Prefer* emphasizes the customer's power of choice, whereas *want* suggests that you are impatient to have the customer make up his mind.

Caller: White—for all of them.

You: I've got that. We are shipping to you at (you repeat the shipping address you have been given) a dozen white widgets. Is that correct?

Caller: Right.

You: The total price, with shipping, is $XXX if you use a major credit card. For an added charge of $X, we will ship C.O.D. Which would you prefer?

Caller: I'll use my credit card.

You: Okay. I'm ready for the number.

Caller: (Gives the number.)

You: And that card expires . . . ?

Note that even here it is possible to do some of the work for the caller. Instead of demanding "Expiration date?" you start the caller's response for him.

Caller: (Provides expiration date.)

You: We are almost finished. Just let me read that credit card number back to you. (Does so.) Have I got it right?

Note that it is useful to keep the caller informed of the progress of the transaction: *We are almost finished.*

Caller: Correct.

You: We're finished. You'll have your dozen white widgets by Tuesday. Mr. Smith, may I help you with anything else today?

End the call with an offer of more help. Make it clear that you are *offering* a service, not demanding that the caller tell you if there is anything else he wants.

Caller: That's about all.

You: It's a pleasure doing business with you. Please call me, Jim Roberts, at 555-5555, if you have any questions. Have a good day.

A key to building a productive relationship with your customers is to make them feel comfortable with the order-taking process. Customers who place orders by telephone fear three things:

1. They will be tied up on the phone for a long time.
2. Errors will be made.
3. They will be assaulted by a sales pitch.

Here is a scenario showing how you might address these fears from the start of the call:

Caller: I am calling to order a dozen widgets.

You: I can help you with that. This should take us about five minutes. That will give us plenty of time to ensure accuracy. May I have your name? . . .

From here the order process continues. Anxiety is produced by the unknown, and giving the caller a time estimate reduces the unknown. Just be certain that you give a realistic estimate. Here the time estimate is combined with an assurance that errors will be avoided.

Occasionally, a customer may express her fears to you:

Caller: You're not going to waste my time with a lot of sales hype, are you?

You: Your time is valuable, and you know what you want. Let's get right to the order.

> **TIP**
>
> There is nothing wrong with informing the caller about additional merchandise. You must ensure, however, that the information is presented as *information*, something useful to the caller rather than a sales pitch, which the customer perceives as useful only to you.

Ask the caller's permission before providing more information. The best time to do this is after the order has been taken and while you are repeating back the essential items of the order: "We are shipping 40 standard widgets to you at 1234 Mockingbird Lane, Pine Barren, New Jersey, 09876. Have you considered purchasing an adjusting kit for the widgets? It makes installation much simpler. Would you like any information on the kit?"

Only if the caller expresses interest should you continue. If not, conclude the transaction and book the order as is.

Avoiding Errors with Customer Orders

How do you know when you've "put yourself across" successfully? How is the effectiveness of business communication measured? One objective and accurate measure is the absence of errors. Few things are more damaging to customer satisfaction than shipping the wrong order or an order that contains errors.

Take these steps to failure-proof all orders:

STEP 1: Repeat information the customer gives you.

STEP 2: If some part of the order doesn't seem right, question it. Don't cast yourself in the role of passive order taker. Guide the customer to satisfaction.

> **TIP**
>
> In questioning any part of the customer's order avoid injecting a line of challenge. "Are you *sure* you want that?" may sound to the caller more like "You *are* stupid, aren't you?" Keep it neutral and gentle: "I just want to confirm that you want such-and-such. Usually, so-and-so is better suited to the application you intend."

STEP 3: If you are certain that the caller is making a mistake, intervene: "Mr. Thomas, that accessory will not work with the widget you ordered. The compatible accessory is . . ."

TIP

How do you know when the customer is making a mistake? There is no substitute for knowing your merchandise.

STEP 4: Even if you know your merchandise, you may sometimes need to obtain additional information in order to help a caller order the correct item. Don't guess. Do what you have to do to obtain the information. If you must look something up, ask permission to put the caller on hold. Explain to the caller what you are doing and that you are doing it to *help him*. Give the caller an estimate of how long he will be on hold.

TIP

Never correct an error without advising the customer that you are doing so. Always confirm any corrections with the caller.

Informing Customers about Price Increases

Informing customers of price increases is both very important and quite delicate. In general, the preferable approach is proactive; that is, regular customers should receive mailings or even phone calls in advance of significant price increases. This serves three purposes:

1. It will avoid the sticker-shock factor at the time of an order.
2. It may make the customer feel that you are dealing decently and straightforwardly with him and giving him personal attention.
3. It may motivate preincrease sales.

TIP

Catalog and price list materials should always include disclaimers about price—that they are subject to change without notice.

Your script: telling customers about a price hike

Here's an example of a proactive call made to a regular customer, informing her of an impending price increase:

> **You:** Hello, Jane. This is Max Morris at XYZ Company. In reviewing my customer profiles, I see that you currently use a Type B widget. Tell me, Jane, have you given any thought to upgrading to a Type H widget?
>
> **Jane:** I've thought about it—and might do it some time in the future.
>
> **You:** Well, the reason I'm calling is that in 60 days, prices will be going up across the board on widgets, including the Type H.
>
> **Jane:** Oh, really . . .
>
> **You:** We're talking about a XX percent increase, from $XX to $XXX. There is a 60-day window to purchase at the current price, so if you are thinking about upgrading any time soon, now would be the time to do it.
>
> **Jane:** Are you *really* raising the price?
>
> **You:** Yes. This call is intended as a service to you. The Type H widgets are very popular. We don't need any gimmick to move them. But the fact is that our cost of material has risen sharply, and we just don't have any choice in the price increase.
>
> **Jane:** Do I have to place my order now?
>
> **You:** Jane, I'm ready to take your order now, and, if you like, I can discuss with you financing terms and our trade-in policy on your current unit. Or we can set up another time to talk. The point is that after November 3 the Type H widgets will be priced at $XXX.

Potentially stickier is informing the customer of an increase at the time of the order. Here is a customer who is ordering from an outdated catalog:

> **Caller** (having been informed of the higher price): Well, my catalog says $XX.

You: We have issued a new catalog, which includes certain price increases. Our cost of materials has risen sharply, and, unfortunately, we had no choice but to increase the price of the widget.

Caller: When did the prices go up?

You: About three months ago, on January 30.

Caller: It's only three months. Can't I get it at the old prices?

You: That wouldn't be fair to the others who have paid the announced price. Mr. Smith, if we didn't adjust the price, we would not be able to offer the widget. It was necessary.

Caller: Well, okay. It just doesn't seem fair.

You: It was necessary, given the increases in costs we incurred.

Informing Customers About Price Decreases

Obviously, price reductions will come to your customers as better news than an increase. Make the most of it.

- Do not announce a price reduction in advance.
- Consider promoting price reductions to move merchandise.
- Be prepared to cope with suspicions: "What's wrong with the widget? Why did you have to bring the price down?"
- Promote price reductions as evidence of your concern for and commitment to value.

YOUR SCRIPT: TELLING CUSTOMERS ABOUT A PRICE REDUCTION

A customer calls to order at the old price and gets the good news:

You: Are you aware of the new low price for the widget?

Caller: New low price?

You: That's right, $XX, down from $XXX.

Caller: Terrific! What's the problem?

You: No problem at all. This widget has been so successful that we have increased production and lowered our costs. We want to pass that savings on to you. That's the way we do business. We don't just make sales, we create customers.

WANT TO BUILD A RELATIONSHIP? ASK A FAVOR OF THE CUSTOMER

Most people hate asking for a favor. And they're right to feel this way—if they define *favor* as most of us do: asking for something in return for nothing.

Want to feel better about asking for favors? Then redefine the word. Think of the favor not as a bid to get something for nothing, but as providing your customer with an opportunity to help you.

Your Customers Love *Helping You*

Here's a revelation: most people enjoy helping others. Being asked to help empowers the helper. It is a flattering vote of confidence. It provides an occasion to feel good about oneself. Moreover, in the business world, many people rightly believe in a kind of commercial brand of karma: What goes around comes around. Doing a favor creates goodwill, which will ultimately benefit both the doer and the receiver of the favor.

There are four steps to asking a customer for a favor:

STEP 1: Establish the basis for the request. Usually, this is the fact of the business relationship itself: "We've worked together for so long that I feel comfortable asking you for a favor."

STEP 2: Be explicit and clear about what you want.

STEP 3: Explain how the favor will benefit you. This shows your customer just how much he will be able to help.

STEP 4: Express gratitude and thanks.

Getting Referrals and Recommendations

It's no secret that the best advertising for your business money cannot buy. And that, of course, is why it's the best. We're talking about word-of-mouth. Nothing is more convincing and compelling.

TIP

The value of word-of-mouth advertising is one reason why you should regard your current customers as your best customers. They are not only sources of additional sales, they can spread to others the good word about you.

Establish a mutually productive and profitable relationship with a customer and, chances are, she will be happy to recommend and refer your products and services to others. After all, she has positive motives for helping you:

- Doing so is an opportunity to do you a good turn, which makes the customer feel good and is good business.
- Doing so is an opportunity for the customer to build goodwill with one of her business associates by turning the associate on to a good thing.

Your script: asking a favor of a customer

Here is a typical favor-requesting scenario. You call a favorite customer:

You: Bill, I'm calling to ask you for a favor. Now, we've had such a great working relationship that I've actually looked forward to making this request. Here's what I need: a brief letter of recommendation to the ABC Company to help us secure a major contract with them. Let me tell you what's going on for us.

Customer: Okay.

You: We've been asked to bid on supplying ABC with widgets and installation and maintenance services. I'm sure you realize that this represents very substantial business for us.

A recommendation from you would be absolute dynamite. Really, really valuable.

Customer: I'll be happy to do what I can—but I don't have a lot of time . . .

You: You don't need to devote any special time to this. I will ask ABC to call *you*. When they do, I'd appreciate whatever sell job you can do for us. The points I'd really like to get across to them are these three:

> First, we give high value.
>
> Second, we provide a very high level of first-rate client support.
>
> And, third, we promise and deliver three-hour emergency response.
>
> That's it. Would you like me to fax over those points?

- *Help* the customer to help you. He will not be offended if you supply him with a script. It takes the burden of spontaneity off him.

Getting More Time—Extending a Deadline with a Customer

Nothing in business is responsible for the creation of more excuses than missing a deadline. Face it:

- Telling your customer that you are going to miss a deadline will *probably* make her anxious and angry.
- Excuses about missing the deadline will *certainly* make the customer angry and will *probably* contribute to anxiety as well ("I'm working with somebody who can do nothing but make excuses . . .").

In view of this three steps are appropriate:

STEP 1: Do whatever you can to avoid being late.

STEP 2: When you know you are going to be late on completion or delivery of a project or product, inform the customer as soon as possible. Provide *timely* information when you cannot make *timely* delivery.

Advance warning of an impending schedule problem will give both you and your customer time to work out suitable alternatives. This should reduce panic and hysteria, thereby making the loss of the deadline seem less urgent and less serious. Advance word of deadline problems will give the customer the message that, despite the slip, you remain in control and "on top of things." It will also give the customer a sense of maintaining control as well.

STEP 3:   Avoid excuses.

Let's talk about Step 3. Instead of offering excuses for deadline slippage, realize that time is a commodity. You can buy more of it, and, as in any other sale, the purchase of time is negotiable. What do *you* have to offer in exchange for more time? What will you buy that time with?

- A better product
- A more successful result

Moving proactively, well in advance of the crisis, enhances the atmosphere of negotiation. In addition, avoid using crisis-creating language, words like:

cannot	neglected
crisis	no
delay	problem
due	slipped
forgot	trouble
impossible	unaware
late	unreasonable

Choose instead the vocabulary of negotiation, words that suggest choice and control:

alter	investigate
aware	manage
better	methodical
can	modify
care	possible
careful	priorities
caution	reschedule
expedite	resources
if	will

Your script: asking a customer to extend a deadline

Here is a request for more time put in the form of a verbal progress report. No facts are withheld, but the tone of the request is matter-of-fact, conveying control, routine, nothing out of the ordinary. This is a phone call:

You: John, I'm calling with a progress report on the Delta project. We have completed the first two phases as originally scheduled, but we are finding that the research for phase 3 is consuming more time than we had scheduled. I think you'll agree that this is *not* the stage for cutting corners, so we will need to alter the schedule, adjusting the completion date for the entire project from June 12 to September 1.

Customer: That's a pretty big delay . . .

You: I am confident that the results—and the resulting peace of mind you'll derive more than justify the extra time we are asking for. If we take the time to do it right now, you'll experience fewer start-up glitches, and you'll be up and running to full capacity sooner.

Objections to overcome when asking for more time

Depending on *many* variables—the nature of the project, costs, lost revenue, the personalities involved, and on and on—asking for more time may be met with stiff resistance. Let's anticipate some of that here:

1. This is bad, bad for us. I was serious about that deadline. Now, look, you'd better just kick butt and get this thing in on time!

Reply with:

Mr. Perkins, I am very serious about the deadline, and that's why I'm talking to you about it now. This is the situation: I can give you a job you'll be 75 percent happy with if I deliver on deadline. Give me another week, and I can promise 100—percent satisfaction. The successful completion of the project is just as serious a matter as the deadline.

2. Look, what *do* you people do out there? I just can't understand it!

Reply with:

Ms. Garrison, we are moving ahead on the project. And one of the things we've just completed doing is an evaluation of the project in terms of how best to use our resources. We could cut corners, but that will only cost us time later. We'll have this conversation when the timeline's become a genuine crisis. We have control now. We have choices. That's why I want to modify the schedule—to build a better foundation now, so we'll avoid time-eating trouble later.

3. You have *got* to move faster than this!

Reply with:

Well, maybe we could. But neither of us would be comfortable with the results. And if we're not comfortable, how can we be confident?

4. Can you absolutely guarantee this will be the only delay?

Reply with:

I can guarantee that I will do everything possible to make certain that the schedule won't have to be altered again.

TIP

Answer with what you *can* do, not what you *cannot.*

Getting a Job Interview for a Friend or Relative

This is a frequently asked favor, but we conclude with it because it is also typical of the many miscellaneous favors you may ask a customer. With this favor request, as with all others, exercise thought before you call.

STEP 1: Evaluate what you are asking. Can you and your customer live happily with the consequences of the favor? In this case, will your friend or relative be a credit to you?

TIP

Don't ask for favors casually. Remember, you have a relationship riding not so much on the request, but on the consequences of acting on that request.

STEP 2:   Acknowledge the magnitude of the favor. Doing the favor will require effort from the customer. Acknowledge this.

STEP 3:   Avoid *telling* the customer how he should feel about doing the favor: "Look, I know this is a real pain . . ." If it's a "real pain," why are you inflicting it? Let the customer decide.

STEP 4:   Do not falsely build up the job candidate, but do vouch for him. If you cannot recommend him for the job, you should not be asking for this favor.

STEP 5:   Express your appreciation, but do not emphasize how this favor benefits you. The customer should feel that, yes, he's doing you a service by interviewing your friend or relative, but also that you are doing *him* a favor by recommending a good employee.

YOUR SCRIPT: ASKING A CUSTOMER TO SET UP A JOB INTERVIEW

This scenario adds another element to the formal steps in requesting a job interview for a friend or relative: humor—a light, informal touch.

You: Kelly, I made a promise to myself years ago that I would *never* do what I'm about to do. I know you've been looking for an assistant, and I'd like to recommend and ask you to interview my nephew.

Customer: Ohhh . . . I don't know . . .

You: Now, come on, Kelly, you can stop groaning. The pleasant surprise in all this is that Jim, my nephew, is very bright, very eager, and a self-starter. He is just about to graduate from Midwestern University with a major in business, and he has a 3.4 grade-point average. He's also spent the summer interning at Smith and Company. They will furnish references.

But, Kelly, there's another thing. Jim's like me. You can't help but love him. He's just a great guy!

And, look, Kelly, you're too good a friend and customer for me to send you somebody I'm not proud of. Of course, you are under no obligations of any kind. You know that. But I would appreciate your talking with Jim.

Customer: Okay. Have him call me.

You: Kelly, I really appreciate it. I know you'll both enjoy the meeting.

HOW TO TURN DOWN A REQUEST WITHOUT TURNING OFF A CUSTOMER

It would make life easier if you could always say yes. Yes is easier than no. For about three minutes.

The fact is that, without no, life would be impossible. Difficult and risky as it may be to decline a request, especially from a customer, doing so is sometimes absolutely necessary.

Five Secrets of Declining a Request for a Favor

1. Be certain that you should or must decline. If it is possible to say yes, do so. There is great relationship-building value in agreeing to perform a favor. Avoid knee-jerk nos.
2. If you must say no, begin by expressing regret.
3. Explain why you cannot perform the favor.
4. Apologize—but not profusely. Above all, do not waste the customer's time with a long apology. This comes across as a "punishment" for having asked a favor. It will discourage communication between you and the customer.
5. Offer something positive: the future. If it is possible and appropriate, suggest future circumstances and conditions that will enable you to perform the favor—the next time it is asked.

Avoiding a Flat-Out No

Saying no to a request doesn't necessarily mean having to say no to the *requester*. If possible, avoid an outright no and try to provide a no, but. This is nothing more than substituting a positive for a negative, emphasizing what you *can* do instead of what you *cannot*. Do this by providing alternatives to the customer's request.

- Be as specific as possible: "I can't deliver by Thursday, but I can deliver by the following Monday *and* expedite installation, which should save you three days on the back end."

> **TIP**
> Don't be vague about your alternative: "I can't. Maybe we can figure out something else." This is almost as frustrating as an outright no.

- If possible and appropriate, offer more than one *specific* and *helpful* alternative: "I can't deliver the entire order by Tuesday, but I can offer you a choice of alternatives. I can deliver a partial order by Tuesday, with the balance to come Friday, or I can prepare the complete shipment here for you to pick it up on Tuesday." Such choices empower the customer, making her feel less like someone who didn't get what she wanted and more in control.

> **TIP**
> Avoid overwhelming your customer with a laundry list of alternatives. If there really are multiple alternatives, provide guidance. Don't leave the customer to sink or swim on her own.

- No is a dead end. If you can't offer alternatives, perhaps you can offer a degree of no—which is, after all, also a degree of yes—rather than a final negative: "We can't extend to you the $70,000 line of credit you request, but we can offer an $18,000 line right now. As we do more business together, we can certainly revisit, and, I hope, revise this limit."
- Provide reasons for no. This is preferable to an arbitrary denial.
- If possible, state the conditions under which a yes would be possible: "We can't extend credit to you at this time, because of your history of slow payment. I would like to take another look at your credit picture in six months, which should give you time to catch up your open accounts. At that time, we'll reconsider the application."

Telling a Customer You Can't Change the Price

People who make their living by negotiating—salespeople, attorneys, professional mediators, and the like—insist that "everything is negotiable."

This is an example of hyperbole. While it is true that *more* is negotiable than most of us may believe, there are certain terms, amounts, and conditions that cannot be bargained. What happens when you have one of these absolutes and a customer approaches who is a believer in the everything-is-negotiable maxim? What happens when your price really is "carved in stone," but your customer insists on negotiating?

- The customer may yield and purchase the product.
- The customer may yield—grudgingly—and purchase the product. This time.
- You may lose the sale.
- You may lose the sale *and* the customer.

The preferable outcome, obviously, is the first. The strategy for arriving at it is to hold firm to what you cannot change and do one of the following:

- Offer alternatives in the case of items you can change.

or

- Explain why the price cannot change (and hope the customer accepts the justness of the explanation).

YOUR SCRIPT: CONVINCING A CUSTOMER YOUR PRICE IS FIRM

This is a face-to-face encounter.

Customer: Okay, that's your *list* price. Now, what can you do for me?

You: We are not authorized to alter the price. We formulate a price we can live with—the most attractive price we can create for you. The margins are sliced thin, because we're interested in selling these in quantity. The advantage to you is that we come out with our best shot. The disadvantage of coming *out* with your best shot is that you don't have room to negotiate.

Customer: Come on. Everything's negotiable.

You: I can work with you to reduce installation charges, by giving you our preferred customer rate. I can offer an extended warranty at cost. I can give you our preferred customer rate on freight. These things do mean significant savings—$XX amount, if you took advantage of all of them. But the base price is our best price.

Watch your body language. Use open handed gestures and plenty of eye contact. Avoid gestures that signal defiance or closedness. Avoid gestures that suggest apology, particularly failure to maintain eye contact.

Customer: I might just try elsewhere.

Resist the temptation to "dare" the customer to do just this. The customer understands that the most persuasive negotiating tool he has is his feet. He can walk away. You have to be *willing* to let him do this, while keeping the offer open to him.

You: I am confident that you won't find a better price. But if you want to look, we'll be here to serve you when you come back. You won't find a better deal. Please remember that the deals I'm offering on extended warranty and freight, as well as installation amounts to $XX. I mean, that's money saved that would otherwise be coming out of your pocket.

Customer: Okay. I don't have the time to go elsewhere. Let's go with your price . . .

Explaining Why You Can't Extend Payment Terms

It is certainly not uncommon to renegotiate payment terms. Sometimes doing so is a matter of convenience for both parties involved. Sometimes the only alternative to such renegotiation is default and failure to collect anything. Again, therefore, the first step in responding to a request to extend payment terms is to avoid a knee-jerk no in favor of renegotiating terms. If, however, renegotiating is not an option, the no must be accompanied by sound reasoning that will seem fair to the customer.

TIP

It is a bad idea to appeal to such "authority" as "company policy" as a reason for not negotiating extended terms. Appeals to such abstractions frustrate the customer and make your firm appear rigid and without regard for customers and their needs.

YOUR SCRIPT: TELLING A CUSTOMER YOU CAN'T EXTEND PAYMENT TERMS

Here is an example of a no that relies on reasoned motives of fairness:

You: Mr. Thomas, this is Ellen James at XYZ Company. We spoke yesterday about renegotiating payment terms for your widgets. After reviewing the whole deal, Mr. Thomas, I find that I am unable to alter the terms. The prices you were given for the widgets were based on the terms to which you agreed. Changing that now would unfairly change the deal for us. We were able to offer you the widgets at the price you negotiated because of the terms to which you agreed. As part of the deal, I need you to adhere to those terms.

Denying a Customer's Request for Information

Information is usually easy to provide, and providing it on request goes a long way toward building an effective relationship with your customers. But if you find that you cannot provide requested information, you must take steps to ensure that failing or declining to satisfy the customer's request does not damage the relationship with that customer.

STEP 1:   Make clear the reason for not being able to furnish the requested information.

Acceptable reasons for not furnishing requested information include:

- You don't have the information.
- The information is proprietary.
- You have access to the information, but it is not in your control. (For example, another customer or client controls the information.)
- The information is confidential.

STEP 2: Apologize.

STEP 3: Thank the customer for his understanding.

YOUR SCRIPT: TURNING DOWN A REQUEST FOR INFORMATION

Here is a response to a request for information you do not have:

You: I'm sorry, we don't have that information here. My suggestion is that you contact . . .

> **TIP**
>
> If possible, suggest alternate likely sources for information that you do not have.

> **TIP**
>
> Avoid sending customers or callers from your department to another in order to obtain information you don't have at your fingertips. If there is any way for you to obtain the information, do so. You—not the customer—should do the work.

Here is a scenario in which proprietary information was requested:

You: That information is proprietary.

Customer: Well, I don't want your corporate secrets. I just want to get those addresses.

You: The information is considered company property, and it is restricted to internal access only. I cannot transmit it outside of the company.

Customer: Is there someone else I could speak to?

You: For reasons of our security and the security of our customers, we do not share this information. I don't have any alternative suggestion.

You may be able to access information, but it is controlled by another customer or other third party.

You: That information belongs to our customer. I couldn't share it with you.

Customer: You have access to that information. What harm would it do to give me the information?

You: It would harm the property rights of our customer. We must respect and protect those, as we respect and protect yours. The information simply is not mine to give.

Keep your reply to requests for confidential information brief.

You: That information is confidential.

Customer: Oh, really . . . what harm can I do with it?

You: We must respect the confidentiality. We've promised to.

Explaining to a Customer That You Can't Lend Equipment

Lending equipment, when feasible, can be useful in building stronger relationships with your customers; however, it is not always possible or desirable to lend equipment, especially vital equipment, which you need to have on hand for your own purposes. Most customers will understand this, and there is no need to be overly apologetic. It is important, though, to explain why the equipment cannot be loaned. Don't let this decision come across as arbitrary. Above all, do not make mindless reference to "company policy." Give a current, pressing, immediate reason rather than a reference to a standing rule. As with other situations in which you find that you have to say no, try to offer alternatives.

TIP

Avoid complaining about your company's rules or saying something like "the boss won't let us." Such remarks are unprofessional and reflect well neither on you nor on your organization.

Your script: telling a customer you can't lend equipment

You've been asked to lend equipment to a customer, who is willing to rent the equipment from you; however, the equipment is needed for your own current production.

You: John, I'm sorry, but that equipment is 100 percent in use on our own production.

Customer: I'm really in a bind.

You: I appreciate that. And that is exactly where my company would be if I took any of our equipment out of production right now. But maybe I can help in another way. I can give you some contact numbers to call. Some of these may have equipment available.

Turning Down a Request for Rush Order/Service

If you can embrace an opportunity to "go the extra mile" for a customer, do so. Nothing creates satisfaction more efficiently and effectively than a demonstration of extra effort. But, of course, resources are finite, and you can't stretch for every customer all of the time.

STEP 1: Express regret that you cannot provide the rush service requested.

STEP 2: Explain why you cannot.

STEP 3: Offer what you can.

STEP 4: Emphasize that you are being realistic, that you do not want to mislead the customer with empty, feel-good promises.

STEP 5: Thank the customer for her understanding.

Your script: denying a request for rush service

A sample reply to a request for rush service:

You: Ms. Maxwell, XYZ is known for going the extra mile for its customers. I've tried to make arrangements to expedite shipment of your order for delivery before Thursday, but I have not succeeded.

This is our busiest season, and, making the situation even more difficult, we have been left temporarily shorthanded due to the illness of a number of our employees. This is just not a very promising time to try to expedite a shipment. Right now, we are working on an over-time schedule as it is.

Now, Ms. Maxwell, I am doing everything possible to shave some time off your shipping date, but I do not want to make you promises I cannot keep. Misleading you will do neither of us any good. I can promise you that we *will* do better than the original delivery date, but we will not make Thursday. I'll know by the end of the day just when your shipment will leave here, and I'll give you a call with that information.

Ms. Maxwell, I appreciate your understanding in this matter.

Explaining Why You Can't Provide an Odd Lot

In wholesale situations, it is often impractical to fill orders for odd lots. Company order forms should make this clear, and whoever is responsible for taking the customer's order should also be aware of odd lot policies. If, despite instructions, the customer insists on ordering an odd lot, you will need to be firm but neutral. Give the customer choices.

YOUR SCRIPT: TURNING DOWN AN ODD-LOT REQUEST

You: Mr. Wilson, I'm calling in regard to your order. As stated on our order form, the smallest order we can fill is for 12 dozen widgets. You've ordered half that number.

Customer: Why can't I order the quantity I want?

You: Our prices are based on wholesale orders in large lots. If we break them down, our prices go up. The prices we quoted you were based on our minimum wholesale order. It would be unfair to us and to other customers to make an exception. We just can't do business that way.

Now, I do have some options for you to consider. You can go ahead and put in the minimum order of 12 dozen. That's the easiest. Or you can put that order in, and we'd be willing to divide payment for a nominal carrying charge. How would you like to proceed?

- There is, of course, another alternative. The customer may cancel the order. You must assume that he is aware of that. Don't "dare" the customer to cancel, however, by pointing this out as one of his alternatives. *Assume* he wants to take delivery of the merchandise.

Telling a Customer You Can't Perform Requested Modification

Look for a way to satisfy the customer. If you cannot satisfy her on precisely her terms, look for the next closest thing. An example follows.

YOUR SCRIPT: DISCUSSING MODIFICATIONS WITH A CUSTOMER.

You: Brenda, I've looked over the list of modifications you want made to the Model 3 widget. Economically, we can't afford to tool up to make the modifications you requested on an order of fewer than a hundred units. The numbers just won't work.

I've discussed this with our design and engineering people, and we've come up with two alternatives: You could, of course, up the quantity of your order. At a hundred units, we can make the modifications at a price we all can live with. But, Brenda, have you given consideration to the Model 5 widget? It incorporates most of the features the modified Model 3 would offer. May I take a few minutes to go over them?

WHEN A CUSTOMER ASKS YOU TO "BEND" SAFETY RULES OR REGULATIONS

One type of customer "favor" is particularly unwelcome. It is the request that you shortcut or circumvent some safety procedure or regulation. Of course, this is one request you cannot grant.

- Exposing your customer to a safety hazard is no favor; in addition, you expose yourself and your firm to legal liability.

Enforcing safety regulations can be a thankless job. Your customers may or may not react well to it. You need to navigate a middle course that makes no compromise on issues of safety, but that does not alienate customers, either.

Your script: refusing to compromise on safety rules

You: I noticed as we walked by the widget we installed last year that the safety device had been disconnected. I would like to reconnect it for you before I leave.

Don't accuse anyone of anything. Eliminate pronouns (*"You* disconnected the safety device."). Just report neutral facts.

Customer: That's the way we want it. The safety device slows the machine down too much. We're all grown-ups here. We're careful.

You: That's right. *Careful.* We're both concerned with safety. That interlock can't be left unconnected.

Use *we* to create a community of interest and avoid an *I* versus *you* conflict.

Customer: Look, do me a favor. Just forget it. It's our machine. We'll take the responsibility for it.

You: Well, it's true that you bought the machine, but it does carry our brand name, and I did notice the safety device disconnected. I do need to reconnect the interlock. I must protect myself and my company from unnecessary liability exposure. I'll note in my service report that the safety device is disconnected and that you and I discussed the issue. I must explain that I offered to reconnect the device and that my offer was refused. We keep all communications in our files and send copies to our attorneys. If in the future—and we certainly hope this never occurs—someone is involved in an accident and our company is named as a party in a negligence case, we will use the letters to demonstrate that we were operating in good faith and made you aware of the risks you were incurring.

Customer: Aren't you taking things a bit too far here? You're threatening me with your lawyers!

You: No, not at all. I'm just telling you what I have to do. I am trying to keep you informed. You are my customer. You have a right to know what we must do.

CHAPTER 9

Putting Yourself Across . . . When Handling Credit, Collection, and Customer Complaints

SELF-TEST YOUR SAVVY IN COMMUNICATING ABOUT CREDIT, COLLECTION, AND COMPLAINTS

The following is a simple diagnostic test. A smaller and more selective version of the self-test in Chapter 1, its purpose is not to test your knowledge of communication theory or techniques, but to help you gauge how effectively you communicate about credit, collection, and customer complaints in a day-to-day business context. For the most part, you will find it easy to guess the "right" answer. But getting the "right" answer is not the point of the test. Respond honestly, even if you feel that your response is not the best one possible. This is *not* a contest. The object is solely self-inventory.

1. Ideally, a collection call is an effort to *help* the customer pay. T/F _____

2. I believe in giving my customers *positive* incentives for paying on time. T/F _____

3. I can honestly say that I *learn* from my mistakes. T/F _____

4. I can't always give the customer all the credit he wants. T/F _____

5. I avoid collection calls by riding herd on cash flow from the beginning. T/F _____

6. My company stands behind its products/services. T/F _____

7. Our credit process is self-explanatory. T/F _____

8. The customer is always right. T/F _____

9. Mature customers are not unduly upset by a credit rejection. T/F _____

10. I deal sensitively with my customer's money issues.   T/F ____

11. By definition, a collection call cannot be pleasant.   T/F ____

12. A delinquent customer is a *delinquent* and should be punished.   T/F ____

13. I don't have time for collections. I call an agency—or our attorneys.   T/F ____

14. You don't have to *sell* credit. It sells itself.   T/F ____

15. I emphasize what I *can* do, not what I *can't*.   T/F ____

16. I get angry when I'm owed money.   T/F ____

17. You have to be a hard-nosed negotiator.   T/F ____

18. Credit is something I give selected customers.   T/F ____

19. Sometimes it's cheaper just to give the customer what she wants—even if she's wrong.   T/F ____

20. I make collection calls at reasonable hours.   T/F ____

21. Cash-flow management involves continually communicating with customers.   T/F ____

22. I may decline credit, but I never reject a customer.   T/F ____

23. Credit means *investing* in your customers.   T/F ____

24. I never threaten my customers.   T/F ____

25. I promote the benefits of my company's credit programs.   T/F ____

26. I sell credit as I sell other merchandise. It's a product.   T/F ____

27. When something goes wrong, I apologize profusely.   T/F ____

28. I try always to offer my customers options and choices.   T/F ____

29. I walk customers through the credit-application process.   T/F ____

TOTAL T/F   ____

Score 1 point for each "True" response and 0 for each "False" response, EXCEPT for questions 7, 8, 9, 11, 12, 13, 14, 16, 17, 18, and 27. For *these questions only*, SUBTRACT 1 point for each "True" response. Record your total. A score below +16 indicates that you would benefit from practicing the communication techniques discussed in this chapter. (Note: It is possible to have a negative score.)

WORDS TO USE FOR CREDIT, COLLECTION, AND COMPLAINTS

able	compelled	experience
accommodate	competitive	explain
active	confident	extending
advantage	confidential	fair
advise	configuration	features
agree	confirmation	force
agreeable	convenience	forced
allow	convince	frank
alternative	convinced	friendly
apologize	cooperate	frustration
appreciate	cooperation	glitch
appropriate	creating	grateful
assist	current	guaranteed
assistance	custom	happy
assume	delighted	help
assure	delinquent	immediate
assured	dependable	important
attention	disappointed	information
benefit	discount	inquiry
budget	doublecheck	investment
choice	easier	invite
choose	encouraging	invited
communicate	expect	issue
communication	expedite	latest
compel	expedited	maintain

WORDS TO USE FOR CREDIT, COLLECTION, AND COMPLAINTS *cont'd*

majority	prompt	serious
mistake	promptly	service
modify	proposal	significant
mutual	proud	solve
necessary	quality	sorry
opportunity	reason	special
optimal	reasonable	specified
optimum	refund	standard
option	reimburse	substantial
owe	reliable	support
patience	reminder	talked
payment	replace	today
performance	replacement	together
personal	resolve	unavoidable
pleased	respond	understand
pleasure	response	understanding
possible	responsive	unpaid
privilege	satisfaction	value
problem	satisfy	vital
program	save	waive
promise	savings	willing
promised	scheduled	

PHRASES TO USE FOR CREDIT, COLLECTION, AND COMPLAINTS

account back on track

added value

alternative-payment options

answers will help me determine

PHRASES TO USE FOR CREDIT, COLLECTION, AND COMPLAINTS *cont'd*

apologize for the inconvenience

apologize personally

appreciate your understanding

appreciate your business

as promised

avoid these charges

bear in mind

best case/worst case

best value possible

bottom line

continue providing

continue serving you

credit privileges

direct line

discount program

do everything possible

Do you happen to have your order number handy?

either/or

establish a pattern of prompt payment

expedite shipment

finance charge

formulate a payment plan we both can live with

good afternoon

good morning

grateful for your understanding

great customer

happy to hear from you

help us avoid

highest level

How may I help you?

PHRASES TO USE FOR CREDIT, COLLECTION, AND COMPLAINTS *cont'd*

I fully understand

I am calling to check

I estimate

I want to thank you

I'm sorry to hear

if you like

in business together

in good standing

is that agreeable

Is there anything else I can help you with today?

it will take

it's your call

leave the choice to you

legal counsel advises

let's work together

letter of agreement

making it possible

mutual satisfaction

my error

my mistake

necessary steps

no additional costs

no hidden charges

not too late

not carved in stone

offer will be good

on behalf of

packed with terrific features

partial payment

PHRASES TO USE FOR CREDIT, COLLECTION, AND COMPLAINTS *cont'd*

payment cycle

payment plan

payment schedule

personal attention

please help

prompt payment

prompt response

remains unpaid

resolve the problem

save yourself money

send your payment today

seriously delinquent

seriously past due

service and value

service charges

settle this account

settling the outstanding balance

shared your letter

small-company service

sorry you had a problem

sound to you reasonable

special offer

subject to an additional charge

substantial savings

suffer a blemish on your credit record

suspend your credit

take comments like yours very seriously

take advantage

thank you for paying promptly

PHRASES TO USE FOR CREDIT, COLLECTION, AND COMPLAINTS *cont'd*

thanks for your order

that information will speed things up

up to you

up and running

we make every effort

we work hard

we'll proceed accordingly

whatever is necessary

Which option would you prefer?

Which would you prefer?

within my power

without delay

you can help us

you can be certain

you may reduce

your satisfaction is our primary concern

WORDS TO AVOID IN CREDIT, COLLECTION, AND HANDLING COMPLAINTS

avoid	no
blame	poor
can't	sue
dumb	tough
fail	turf
fault	unfair
immediately	unreasonable
inadequate	won't
incompetent	wrong

PHRASES TO AVOID IN CREDIT, COLLECTION, AND HANDLING COMPLAINTS

accidents happen

can't be done

carved in stone

do something about it

get off my case

give me a break

I can't

I forgot

I'm only human

no can do

nothing we can do about it

out of luck

tough luck

What do you expect?

won't even try it

won't work that way

wrong way

you are insulting us

you have to

you have no choice

you're on your own

CREDIT, COLLECTION, AND HANDLING COMPLAINTS: BODY-LANGUAGE STRATEGY AND BODY LANGUAGE TO AVOID

The most effective body-language strategy is essentially the same as that discussed in Chapter 7. Be aware, however, that intense money issues can do some strange things to body language—both yours and your customer's.

- Eye contact becomes a problem. You may find in yourself a natural tendency to avoid eye contact when discussing money, especially the sometimes delicate issues of credit. More usually, you may find that your customer avoids eye contact. You should not read this as a sign of dishonesty or distrust, but as a natural gesture in these situations. Respond with reassurance. Smile. Adopt a pleasant tone.

- Smile. Making credit decisions is always a two-handed process. On the one hand, you are eager to make the credit arrangements that will allow this customer to do business—or more business—with you. On the other hand, you must be skeptical and cautious. These latter qualities do not usually express themselves in a smile. Nevertheless, it is a smile that is called for in this situation.

The key to body-language strategy during the credit process is to make your customer feel accepted, welcome. There is nothing to be gained by giving nonverbal expression to your skepticism or reserve. Obviously, however, you should make no *verbal* promises you cannot keep.

- Watch the customer's hands. Hands that stray near the face or mouth while the customer answers critical questions *may* signal that the customer is being less than thoroughly honest. Don't challenge, but do beware.

- Keep watching. A customer who runs his hands through his hair or who rubs the back of his neck with his hand is probably frustrated. This is an opportunity to provide reassurance or explanation.

- A customer who folds her arms across her chest is probably expressing resistance. This would be a good time for gentle leading questions: "Is there anything I can clarify for you? Anything we should discuss at this point?"

- Similarly, you should avoid such gestures as folding arms across the chest or standing with hands on your hips. These are gestures of exclusion.

CREDIT: INVESTING IN YOUR CUSTOMERS

This is not the time and place for an elementary lecture on credit. You know what it is. Just make sure that you *think* about what it is before you enter into a credit negotiation with a customer.

- Credit is an investment in a customer.

You make investments in people, companies, and things of value—people, companies, and things that you believe will return to you greater value than your original investment. Credit is not something you *give*. It is an investment. It represents value *to you*. Let these thoughts put you in the right frame of mind for the discussion.

Selling Your Credit Package to Customers

So approach the customer with a certain humility and gratitude; however, approach her also in the knowledge that you are offering additional value. The credit package is something of value and use to the customer. It is, in effect, an additional product benefit. Your most effective verbal strategy is to promote it as such.

Before you present the credit package to a customer, consider what a product *benefit* is. It is *not* the same thing as a product *feature*, which is merely an attribute of the product. For example, nonbreakable material is a *feature* of a certain coffee mug. A *benefit* is what good things the customer will derive from purchasing and using the product. Often, product benefits have a significant emotional content. Let's return to our cup. One of its chief features is that it is nonbreakable. The *benefit* this particular feature provides is security: You can enjoy your piping-hot coffee without worrying about the cup breaking.

- Explain the *features* of your credit program, but *promote* the *benefits*.

  Benefits might include:

- Increased purchasing power
- Enhanced cash-flow management
- More control
- More flexibility

YOUR SCRIPT: PRESENTING YOUR CREDIT PACKAGE.

Keep the selling tone light.

You: The credit package we offer will not only give you increased purchasing power, but will help you manage your cash flow. Our terms are flexible enough to put you in charge.

TIP

If you offer a choice of packages, present the choices clearly and present the idea of choice as yet another product benefit. Nothing enhances the customer's feeling of control—and, therefore, well-being—more effectively than a sense of having choices.

Asking Credit Applicants the Right Questions

Credit information must be recorded in written form, of course, but you may find that it speeds up the application process if you *verbally* request certain items of information.

- Never *demand* information.
- Filling out a credit application requires labor; acknowledge this and express your appreciation for your customer's efforts.
- Emphasize the fact that the customer may speed the application process along by furnishing requested information fully, correctly, and promptly.

YOUR SCRIPT: ASKING FOR CREDIT INFORMATION

Here are some approaches to getting the credit information you need:

1. **You:** I need you to do me a favor. Please send me copies of your financial statements for the last three quarters, so that I can expedite your application and set up a line of credit right away.

2. **You:** Phil, I've got all the basic information I need to get your credit line set up—except for a copy of your latest financial statement. As soon as you send that to me, I'll be able to complete your application. Can you get that out by tomorrow?

3. **You:** Mary, to get your credit line set up I'm going to need financial statements for the past three quarters. You'll see on the credit application a request for two credit references. If you want to give those to me now—or call me with them tomorrow—I can really expedite this process and get you set up right away.

Reporting on the Progress of a Credit Application

If the credit-application process consumes more than a few days, expect to be peppered with calls asking for progress reports. Why not enhance your relationship with your customers by taking the initiative and calling *them* with a report first.

> **TIP**
>
> The actual substance of the report matters less than the mere fact that you are taking the time to make the call and give the report. Do not make or imply promises you may not be able to keep.

YOUR SCRIPT: REPORTING ON THE PROGRESS OF A CREDIT APPLICATION

Here is an example of a progress-report call:

You: Peter! This is (your name) from XYZ Company. I was calling just to let you know that we're in the home stretch along the way to setting up the line of credit you asked for. I don't see any problems at this point, so I *expect* the line to be established before the end of the week. I'll call you back then—sooner if we hit any snags.

Another:

You: Sarah, this is (your name). I'm just calling with a progress report on the line of credit you asked for. Our financial partners are looking over your paperwork now, and I expect to be calling you back by Thursday.

> **TIP**
>
> The progress report doesn't have to be detailed. Its principal purpose is to reassure the customer that his application *is* being processed and that you *are* working for him.

What to Say When You Can Honor the Credit Application

The tone to establish is one of welcome. Avoid sounding overly congratulatory, as this will come across as inflated and perhaps even offensive—as if you hadn't expected this customer to qualify. If you deliver the good news in person, a warm, hearty handshake is called for.

Your script: honoring the credit application

You greet the customer who has walked into your office:

You (with a handshake): Welcome aboard! I'm delighted to sign you up for a line of credit of $XXXX. It's subject to the terms discussed on the application form. Do you have any questions about these? Would you like to review them together?

After answering any questions and reviewing terms, close with:

You: We look forward to working together. This line of credit will give you a lot of flexibility and cash-flow control.

TIP

Of course, *all* credit terms should be spelled out in formal letter of agreement or, preferably, a printed contract. It is critically important that nothing said verbally should differ from terms specified in writing.

Specifying Credit Limits and Conditions to a Customer

The limits, conditions, and terms of a credit agreement with a customer should be fully specified in writing. Normally, you should not have to cover these details verbally when you welcome the customer into your "credit family"; however, there may be cases where you want to point out special conditions or limitations or, most important, where you have granted credit amounts or terms that differ from what the customer had requested. In such cases, verbally preparing your customer can be quite useful.

As usual, the most effective strategy is to emphasize the positive—what you *are doing* for the customer—rather than stress what you cannot do. Keep the conversation as upbeat as possible.

Your script: explaining credit limits and conditions

While emphasizing the positive, provide reasons for giving the customer less than she asked for:

1. **You:** Ms. Young, we are prepared to extend to you a line of credit of $XXX at this time. The credit agreement I'm about to hand you explains the terms, which are those we discussed previously.

   Now, I know that $XXX is less of a credit line than you asked for, so let me explain what we've done. Your financial statements indicate a healthy business with a very promising future, but we have to weigh this against the fact that you have been in operation only 18 months. Ms. Young, as soon as you've crossed the two-year mark, we'd like to review your updated financials with an eye toward increasing your line.

2. **You:** Joe, I am setting up a credit line of $XXX for you at this time. That should give you some maneuvering room and purchasing power—even though it's not all that you had been looking for. I wish I could oblige with the full amount you requested. However, your financial statements suggest that, right now, you are just too heavily obligated for us to add to that burden beyond $XXX.

   Customer: Oh, man. This is a real problem for us. We really need a line of $XXXX.

   You: I understand. We can review your financials again next quarter and see where you are in paying down some of your open accounts. We certainly want to extend to you all the credit that we can.

3. **You:** Hank, welcome to our "credit family." I'm sure you'll find that this credit line will make it more convenient to do business with us.

   Hank, I know that the line is somewhat smaller than you had requested. So let's look at your next quarter's financial statement, and review your credit line with an eye toward increasing it.

What to Say When You Cannot Honor the Credit Application

There's no denying that it's much easier to welcome a customer to your "credit family" than it is to tell him that you must decline credit. There is no magic formula that will ensure that your action will not drive this customer away. It *is* possible that the customer will become angry and alienated. He may even find a vendor whose credit policies are more liberal than yours. Nevertheless, you can take verbal measures to minimize damage to your relationship:

STEP 1:   Do not begin with an apology. Begin with thanks for the application.

STEP 2:   Tell the customer that your company "is unable to extend the requested credit at this time."

STEP 3:   If possible, offer hope for reconsideration.

STEP 4:   Be specific about the conditions that must be met to make successful reconsideration possible.

STEP 5:   Be specific about when the customer should reapply.

STEP 6:   Make it clear that the customer is valuable to you, and that you value his business.

STEP 7:   Assure the customer of continued top-notch service on a cash-with-order (or other) basis.

STEP 8:   Thank the customer for his understanding.

TIP

Declining the customer's credit application must be done in writing. Be careful to say nothing that adds to, modifies, or differs from the information contained in any written communication.

YOUR SCRIPT: DENYING THE CREDIT APPLICATION

You telephone the customer to deliver the bad news. It *is* a good idea for you to move proactively and make the call rather than wait for the customer to call in to check on the status of his credit application. Making the call conveys that you do value the customer, even if you could not oblige him in this instance.

1. **You:** Mr. Roberts, this is (your name) at XYZ Company. I wanted to thank you for applying for credit with us, but I must tell you that, at this time, your credit record shows a history of slow payment, and,

given your current obligations, we feel that it is appropriate to postpone acting on your request for three months in order to give you the time required to catch up on your open accounts.

We'll be pleased to look at your financials next quarter and reevaluate the application. For the immediate future, of course, we remain eager to serve you on a payment-with-order basis.

2. **You**: Ms. Thomas, this is (your name) at XYZ Company. I'm calling about your credit application. Thank you for your interest in us, but because you have only recently established your business, and in view of our own limited resources, we need some more experience with you as a "pay-as-you-go" customer before we can set up a line of credit.

What I'd like to suggest is that you reapply in six months, after we've worked together for a while on a cash basis. And do be assured that, during this period, we will continue to give you the very best prices and service in the industry. We appreciate your business, Ms. Thomas, and we look forward to working with you and to helping you establish yourself in our community.

The following script takes a situation that could be stated negatively—"You need someone to guarantee your credit"—and turns it into a positive statement of an alternative to an out-and-out no:

3. **You**: Pete, we'd very much like to work with you to set up a line of credit; however, the financial statements you sent indicated that you are undercapitalized at present, and we think this would make it difficult for you to meet payments on our terms. Now, my suggestion is that you find a person or firm to guarantee your open account with us. That would allow us to serve your credit needs as you become increasingly well established.

Of course, alternatively, we hope that you'll continue working with us on a cash basis and reapply for credit within, say, six months.

COLLECTING MONEY THAT'S OVERDUE

Maybe it's time to start thinking about the money you *don't* have. I don't mean the sales you haven't made yet, the customers you haven't called yet, the killer widget you haven't invented yet. I'm not talking about *making* money. That's what business used to be mostly about—*making* money. You sold something, you developed something, and you turned it all into cash. But among the many trends trendspotters spot in today's business environment, one stands out, even if it's seldom talked about. Business has been moving deeper and deeper into a twilight zone in which solid cash has dissolved into a vaporous ether called "accounts receivable." The business world used to be divided into

1. Customers who paid on time
2. Delinquent accounts
3. Out-and-out deadbeats

Nowadays, even your better accounts routinely let invoices go beyond 30 days before they pay. Worse, 60-, 90-, and 120-day remittances have come to seem as inevitable as the seasons themselves.

- Your customers and clients do not think it is permissible to wait one, two, three, or four months before they pay you, they think it is *normal*, practically a law of nature.

Now, one way to try to get the money that is due you is to make collection calls and write collection letters. Both of these can be tough assignments. After all, you don't want to alienate a customer—even a delinquent customer.

More effective is a communicative approach to your customers that seeks to avoid delinquency problems in the first place. This approach revolves around a single secret:

- *The people who owe you money actually want to pay you.*

Make no mistake: few people *like* to pay. But *everyone* enjoys being in a position to do so. Few people like to pay. But *nobody* relishes owing.

Some Verbal Secrets for Preventing Payment Problems

At its simplest, any business is a dynamic system that generates and expends cash. The concept of cash *flow* is useful, at least to a point. Cash flows into the business, where it is directed into the pipelines that run to the various mechanisms enabling the business to draw in more cash. To a certain extent, cash flow is similar to the operation of an automobile. In a car, fuel, a raw commodity, is taken in, processed, and converted into various specific actions aimed at keeping the vehicle going. If the fuel line gets clogged or suffers from vapor lock, or the fuel pump breaks down, or the carburetor malfunctions (in an older car), or the fuel injector gums up (in more recent models), or other mechanical systems break down, the car coughs, sputters, and rolls to a dead stop.

Now, there are two kinds of car owners: those who practice regular preventive maintenance and those who stare by the side of the road with blank incomprehension into the inert mass beneath the raised hood of the vehicle that has suddenly quit on them.

Managing cash flow is not unlike maintaining an automobile. There are those who

- Integrate cash flow into the daily management of their business, continually keeping in touch with customers, vendors, and lenders before, during, and after money changes hands

And those who

- Cut in some collection agency for a big chunk of what should have been profits because an account was allowed to break down

Talk to your customers. Get on top of *their* payment problems before they become *your* cash-flow problems.

- Old-style managers stress response to circumstances.
- New-style managers emphasize anticipation.
- Be a new-style manager.

Anticipate trends and needs in order to take advantage of potential opportunities for profit *and* to avoid or prepare for approaching liabilities. Address cash flow from the beginning of a business transaction. Don't wait for a problem.

'Tis Better to Help than to Extort

Think about how you felt the last time you were owed money by an unresponsive customer. Whatever your exact feelings, it is a safe bet that they were anything but friendly. In fact, the delinquent customer soon comes to seem a silent enemy, an adversary against whom you are willing to level the "big guns" of a collection agency or lawyer, though it cost you dearly.

Almost always, there is a more effective alternative than the adversarial, warlike approach.

STEP 1: Begin by assuming that your customer wants to pay you (that is, doesn't want to *owe* you).

STEP 2: Realize that you want to be paid.

STEP 3: Conclude, therefore, that you and the customer share a common interest.

STEP 4: Conclude further that people with interests in common should communicate with each other.

STEP 5: Call the customer with an offer of help: You want to help her do what you both want—pay you.

TIP

Collection agencies and lawyers are a last resort. Be aware that once you bring them into the picture, you sever *helpful* communication with the customer.

Talking with the New Customer

Begin the conversation *before* any money is due, let alone overdue. In fact, you can begin talking even before a deal is concluded:

1. **You:** Hello, Mr. Garrison. This is (your name) at XYZ Company. I know how eager you are to get prices on the widget project, so I thought I'd give you a call to let you know that we'll have the bid prepared early this afternoon and fax it to you. We are cutting the numbers as close to the bone as we can—but I might point out to you that you can take an additional 3 percent off the top if you pay the invoice total within ten days of our invoice date. It'll give us both a break: You save a few dollars, and we keep our cash flowing. Keep that extra discount in mind when you review the figures, and do give me a call if you have any questions.

2. **You:** Hello, Ms. Jones. This is (your name) at XYZ Company. I'm calling to let you know that the proposal for the widget project will be faxed this afternoon. I know you're eager to get started, and I think you'll be pleased with the figures. We've built in an extra incentive discount for ten-day turnaround on our invoice, which is something you might want to think about when you're comparing our bid to others. We like to make it simple to cooperate—lower costs on your side and better ease cash flow on ours. I look forward to your call after you receive the proposal.

3. **You:** Hello, Bill. This is (your name) at XYZ Company. I thought I'd call to let you know that our proposal for the widget project was sent out to you this morning. I think you'll be pleased with the numbers— and you might want to bear in mind that, good as the prices are, they're based on payment within 30 days. We'll knock off an additional 3 percent for payment made within ten days of our invoice date. Do give me a call if you have any questions about the proposal or the incentive discount program.

The incentive discount for quick payment should be repeated in writing in such items as:

- Statements of bids
- Cover letters accompanying proposals
- Cover letters with payment schedules
- Inserts accompanying shipment
- Invoices or invoice fliers

COUNTERING A NEGATIVE RESPONSE TO YOUR DISCOUNT INCENTIVE

The discount incentive is a *positive* and *proactive* collections measure. Nevertheless, you may, from time to time, encounter a negative response from the cynical customer who sees the proverbial half-filled water glass as half empty:

You: You'll notice that we've invited you to take an additional 3 percent off the total for making payment within ten days.

Customer: What you really mean is that you tack on 3 percent for bills past ten days.

You: Not at all. Our standard terms are 30 days net. Beyond 30 days we do charge 1.5 percent per month, up to 90 days. After that, we consider the account delinquent. The 3 percent discount for prompt payment is a genuine discount off our best net price. It's not a hidden charge. It is, quite frankly, an incentive. We're a small company, and it's worth 3 percent to us keep as much cash coming in just as quickly as we can get it in here. That's the unvarnished truth. But don't feel pressured. We're just as happy to do business on the basis of 30 days net.

Pushing the incentive discount

If you are serious about cash flow, you have to make a serious commitment to communication. Let's say you have a customer who doesn't take advantage of your incentive discount for a ten-day payment turnaround. You can hardly make a collection call at this point. The payment terms are, after all, 30 days. But you can make a *helpful* call. Just be certain to keep it helpful and friendly. Here's a bid for the future:

You: Hi, this is (your name) from XYZ Company. I was just looking over our customer list and noticed that your September 1 order is the first order you've placed with us. Were you aware of our 3 percent discount offer for accounts paid within ten days of our invoice date?

Customer: Yes, but I'm afraid I just haven't been able to get around to that invoice yet.

You: Well, it's no problem, of course. You account is on 30-day net terms. But I did want to alert you to our offer, just in case it had slipped by you. Maybe you'll want to take advantage of it on the next order.

As the account nears the 30-day mark, make another friendly call:

1. **You**: Hello, this is (your name) from XYZ Company. I thought I'd give you a friendly call to remind you that your account is approaching the 30-day mark, which means that we'll be tacking on a 1.5 percent finance charge beginning October 15. There's no problem with the account, of course, but it seemed to me that you might want to avoid paying even a few dollars extra. If you can get payment to us by October 20, we'll bill the account at net.

2. **You:** Hello, Bill. This is (your name) calling from XYZ Company. I had written a note to myself to give you a call before your account with us went beyond 30 days. Now there's absolutely no problem with the account, but I did want to remind you that a 1.5 percent finance charge kicks in after September 1. I thought you might want to be reminded in order to save yourself a few dollars.

You have received payment from a new customer. It is a week late on 30-day terms. Most companies would let this pass without comment. Certainly, this is not an occasion for a scolding telephone call. However, a timely, helpful, and friendly communication might expedite cash flow in the future:

You: Hello, Mary. This is (your name) from XYZ Company. I've just received your August payment on your account. Thanks. There's no problem as far as we're concerned, but are you aware that, since we received the payment after the due date, it's subject to a $20 service charge? I thought I'd call because the payment was only ten days behind the due date, and it seems a shame to incur service charges unnecessarily. If you can get us your next payment by September 15, you'll avoid a service charge on that one.

Once the new account has decidedly slipped past the 30-day net period, you might find a special new-customer incentive persuasive:

1. **You:** Hello, Ms. Reynolds. This is (your name) of XYZ Company. I was just going over some accounts and noticed that yours has passed the 30-day mark, which means that we're about to send you a new invoice with a $25 service charge tacked on. To tell you the truth, it's easier for me to make this phone call than to process and mail a new invoice. If you can settle your account now—get the check into the mail today— I won't have to do up another invoice and you'll save $25. You're a new customer, and I hate to hit you up with an extra charge.

2. **You:** Hello, Mr. Smith. This is (your name) of XYZ Company. I'm calling to save you some money. Your account with us has just gone past 30 days, which means that it is subject to a service charge of $25. To be frank, I'd much rather have that account paid in full at the present time than collect an additional $25 on it later. If you can get payment to me

by Monday, I will waive the service charge. I don't like having to charge extra—especially in the case of a brand-new customer like you.

3. **You:** Hello, Ms. Nelson. This is (your name) of XYZ Company. In looking over our accounts, I noticed that yours has passed the 30-day mark. Normally, we'd assess a service charge at this point, but since you are a brand-new customer, I'm willing to waive the service charge if you can get a check into the mail today.

   Customer: I'd love to, but our cash-flow position isn't the greatest just now. I'm going to have to let the bill go for another couple of weeks and pay the service charge.

   You: Well, that's not the end of the world, of course. And I certainly know what it's like to try to manage cash flow these days. Before we leave the matter, is there anything I can do to help? What I'm thinking is that, if you can send me a check for half of the current invoice now and pay the balance by the middle of the month, I'm still willing to waive the service charge. I like to make things as flexible as possible for my customers, especially the new ones.

Talking with the Established Customer

The most effective strategy for collection-related communication with an established customer is to think of the customer as a business partner. You have a relationship. You are in business together. You have interests in common. The key is to keep lines of communication open.

> **TIP**
> If a payment problem develops, communicate first and foremost your *concern* for the customer.

INSTALLMENT PAYMENT PROBLEM

One of the most frequently encountered payment problems with established customers involve missed installment payments. Emphasize the positive. Demonstrate that you are calling precisely because this glitch is exceptional:

You: Hello, John. This is (your name) from XYZ Company. Your payment of $XXX, which was due on Friday, hasn't arrived in our office. You're always so punctual with these payments, I was concerned. When did you send that out?

Customer: Well, I was planning on sending it out later in the week.

You: It was due on Friday. Can you get it into the mail today?

Customer: I'm not sure.

You: Well, I'll look for it by the first of the week. Does that sound all right with you?

Customer: Yes. Sorry about it. You'll have it then.

You: Great. If there is anything I can help you with, please give me a call.

Bounced checks

Bounced checks are another financial hazard, even in established customer relationships. It is best to approach the issue matter of factly, without alarm or emotion. If the customer apologizes, accept the apology gracefully.

You: Hello, Jill. This is (your name) from XYZ Company. We had an unwelcome surprise in the mail this morning. Your check, number 1234, was returned by the bank. I can go ahead and redeposit it, if everything's all clear on your end. I do need a check for an additional $25 to cover what the bank charges us and our own handling costs.

More serious payment lapses

Once an unpaid account approaches 60 days, it is time to get serious about helping your customer pay.

- Continue to use positive and negative incentives.
- Maintain communication in order to create the emotional as well as the business climate in which the errant account will positively entertain thoughts about paying you.

How do you convince someone to pay?

One strategy is to bully and threaten. This may work—once. After that, you will almost certainly have lost a customer. A much better approach is to *help* your customer make the decision to pay by demonstrating how it will benefit him.

STEP 1: If you have a schedule of service/finance charges in place, you can make a phone call, reminding him how much is owed now and how much more will be due after a given date.

STEP 2: Build on your relationship with the customer. Explain that prompt, personal service at the best prices requires the cooperation of the customer in the form of prompt payment, which keeps costs down.

STEP 3: Point out that prices originally quoted and agreed to were based on net terms. In ordering from you, not only did your customer promise to pay promptly, but he also received in return for that promise the added value of the best possible prices.

TIP

An appeal to fairness can be quite effective, if it is handled with a light hand.

The most common resistance you are likely to encounter is vagueness and evasiveness.

- Ask questions that can be answered, questions that relate to dates and amounts.
- If the customer tells you that now is a bad time to talk, remind him that *we* are running short of time and ask when it would be a good time to call back. Get a definite time.
- If the customer is vague about when she can pay, ask her to think the matter over, and tell her that you will call back at a specific time to get her response.
- If the customer passes the buck to his "accounting people," ask him if you should be talking to his accounting person yourself.
- If the customer is willing to negotiate, do so.

> **TIP**
> Once you have reached an agreement in principle, send the customer a memo summarizing your new understanding.

With accounts that have gone beyond the sixty-day mark, the primary task is definition and direction.

- Remind the customer of his obligation.
- Define the dates and the amounts involved in satisfying it.

In the case of payment due for commodity goods or services that are delivered or performed on an ongoing basis, discuss with the customer the following:

- There is the inevitable fact that the commodity or service delivery will be stopped unless payment is received by a certain date.
- There are the costs of discontinuing and restarting delivery or service.
- The fact that, in most cases, payment is made immediately after the service or commodity delivery is discontinued. Then extra costs are incurred. Why not avoid this by paying now?

Your scripts: handling serious payment lapses

1. **You:** Hello, Dick. This is (your name) from XYZ Company. I'm calling to talk to you about your account with us. It's approaching 60 days, and I'd like to ask you when we can expect payment. As you know, the prices we originally quoted you were based on 30-day net terms. Now that we're closing in on 60 days, you're looking at a $300 carrying charge on this account. Frankly, I'd rather have the account settled now than collect that charge. Can you get us a check by Friday?

   Customer: I'll have to talk to my accounting people.

   You: Is there someone in your accounting department that *I* should be talking to? I'll give him or her an opportunity to save you some money.

2. **You:** Hello, Jane. This is (your name) from XYZ Company. I'm calling to talk to you about your account with us. The prices we gave you were based on 30-day net terms, and we're now getting close to the 60-day point. We're a small company, and it's really very difficult for us to carry open accounts for any length of time. It would help us a great deal if you could pay the account in full.

   Customer: I'll look into it.

   You: May I call you at this time tomorrow to get a status report from you and, if necessary, to work out a payment plan together?

   Customer: Tomorrow is a bad time.

   You: Well, we are running short on time. After Tuesday, the account is subject to a $150 carrying charge, and I'd much rather work with you on a payment strategy that will save you that fee. When is a good time to call?

3. **You:** Hello, Carl. This is (your name) from XYZ Company. I'm calling to talk to you about your account with us. As you know, the prices we originally quoted you were based on 30-day net terms. We're approaching 60 days, which means that you will be paying us a $200 carrying charge on the account. Frankly, I'd rather have the account settled now than collect that fee. Can you get us a check by Friday?

   Customer: I'm in a real cash-flow bind just now. You know how it is.

   You: Unfortunately, I do. That's why I'd like to work with you on this. To help us both out. We need to come up with a plan that we can both live with. The balance due is $1,750. If I can get $650 by Friday, I'd be in a position to waive the carrying charges on the entire balance due—provided the account is completely settled by October 4. How does that sound?

   Customer: I just can't manage it at this time. I'll have to pay you later and just absorb the finance charges.

   You: Well, before we give up, can you tell me if I'm in the ballpark?

   Customer: You really want to get some money, don't you?

You: I told you that I know what it's like to have to manage cash flow carefully. Yeah, I can use all the cash I can get. What if we set up four payments and spread them out?

Talking with the Seriously Delinquent Customer

Even when an unpaid account remains open approaching 90 days, there is still room for such positive incentives as renegotiation of original cost incentives. This is also a good time to introduce such negative incentives as timely reminders of mounting service charges. Additionally, letters and telephone conversations at this point should direct the customer to ask himself why the bill has gone unpaid and what further delay will cost him, in terms of service charges as well as impact on credit history.

It may not seem so at the time, but at the 90-day point, the creditor is in a strong position.

- If a program of finance or service charges is in place, the creditor has more negotiating power at her command.
- Even if no external incentives are available, the delinquent account is usually more anxious to settle now than he was earlier.

> **TIP**
>
> Remember: the delinquent account can settle *only* if you keep the lines of communication open.

> **TIP**
>
> As the open account approaches 90 days, it is important not to issue threats or to give in to panic or anger. Now is the time for sound reasoning. This is your account's final opportunity to remain in good standing, and it is you who are giving him that opportunity.

As an account hovers near serious delinquency, your most effective collection strategy is to begin to separate yourself from such entities as *company policy, our accountants, our attorneys,* and the passage of time itself. It works like this: You would like to grant infinite extensions, but company policy (or our accountants or our attorneys) won't let you because time is running out.

> **TIP**
>
> Ordinarily, references to *company policy* are a bad customer-service idea; however, as a scapegoat in collections situations, company policy may come in handy.

This rhetorical strategy is intended to strengthen the cooperative bond between two people who have to work within certain rules. The subtle separation of the voice now on the phone—you—and "the company," "the rules," or "our policy" suggests that you and your customer are in control of the situation *now*, but soon, if positive action is not taken, other forces will take over. Credit will be suspended. Lawyers will take action. Things will get ugly. Choices will be few.

Note carefully that this approach is not a threat, and it should not be expressed as a threat. But unresolved debt is a serious matter, and it is time to let your customer become aware of this fact.

YOUR SCRIPTS: TALKING WITH SERIOUSLY DELINQUENT CUSTOMERS

Here are some scenarios using positive incentives:

1. **You:** Hello, Mike. This is (your name) at XYZ Company. I want to alert you to the next invoice you'll be getting from us. By the time you receive the statement, your account with us will have gone past 90 days, which means that you'll be assessed $175 in service charges. To be frank, I'm interested in getting your payment as soon as possible, and I'm willing to waive not only the 90-day charge, but the 60-day charge, which you, at this point, owe. That means that if you get a check into the mail today, you'll save $175. If you wait for the invoice, the $175 charge *will* apply.

2. **You:** Hello, Ms. Dinkler. This is (your name) at XYZ Company. I just put into the mail a statement of your account with us. You already have two statements from us, sent at 30 and at 60 days. I've sent this one a little early, because I wanted to give you the opportunity to beat the 90-day deadline and avoid paying a service charge of $150. Are you interested in saving some more money?

   Customer: I guess I am.

You: It's strictly your option, but if you can get a check into the mail today, you'll not only beat the 90-day service charge, I'll also waive the 60-day charge. You'll save a total of $150. How does that sound to you?

Customer: It sounds reasonable enough..

You: Then I should be looking for your check in the next day or two?

Customer: Yes.

3. **You:** Hello, Mr. Peterson. This is (your name) at XYZ Company. I just put a statement of your account with us in the mail. You already have two statements from us, sent at 30 and at 60 days. I've sent this one a little early, because I wanted to give you the opportunity to beat the 90-day deadline and avoid paying a service charge of $225. Are you interested in saving some more money?

Customer: I guess I am.

You: It's your decision, of course. But if you can get a check into the mail today, you'll save $225.

Customer: Look, it sounds fair enough, but I'm short on cash just now. I know you want to get paid, but with my cash flow, I'm afraid it will be another couple of weeks.

You: You're certainly right that I'd like to collect on this invoice. And I'd like to save you some money as well—without sending you to the poorhouse in the process. If you could manage to pay half now and the balance by the end of the month, which will put you beyond 90 days, I'd still be willing to waive the service charges.

Here are two ideas for using negative incentives:

1. **You:** Hello, Ms. Wallace. This is (your name) at XYZ Company. I was just going over some accounts here, and I noticed that yours is about to go past 90 days. Now that's not disaster, and I'm not calling to dun you, but I did want to alert you to the fact that the account is about to slip through another month unpaid. And what that means to you is a service charge of $150. If you want to avoid that charge, might I sug-

gest that you send out a check today? Once you slip past the fifteenth, I *must* assess the service charge.

Customer: I just don't have the cash on hand right now. Can you give me a grace period on that service charge?

You: When would you be paying?

Customer: In about two to three weeks.

You: Well, that's going to start getting close to 120 days, after which the account is delinquent. I'd like to accommodate you, but, you know, we're a small company, and we can't afford to carry an account that long without a service charge. If you can get me $1,200 by the twelfth, we can at least avoid letting the account slip into delinquency. Then we can work out together a schedule for the balance. How does that sound?

Is there a point at which you should give up hope? Once an unpaid account has passed 120 days, you have some important choices to make.

- Should you suspend the customer's credit? (The answer is, almost without reservation, yes.)
- Should you turn the account over to a collection agency or an attorney? (That depends on the amount involved and your relationship with the client or customer.)

Even more important are these questions:

- What more do I have to give?
- And what do I have left to gain?

You can still give your help, your offer to work with your customer to resolve his debt to you. This may seem difficult or impossible as you drift toward what neither of you can avoid perceiving as an adversarial relationship, perhaps even legal action. But this is where the tone and rhetoric of your communications play so important a role. At the 90-day mark, you began to separate yourself from the force of the inevitable and unmovable—company policy, our attorney, and the like. Now that separation should be made more dramatic. Hold yourself apart from the necessary steps that are impending. Remain available for discussion and negotiation.

> **TIP**
>
> Often, the first issue to address is lack of response. Accounts that have drifted this far tend not to reply to letters or take phone calls. Try to establish—or reestablish—contact.

STEP 1:   Open the lines of communication.

STEP 2:   Outline your customer's choices at this point.

STEP 3:   Make it clear that the choices are the customer's. You are running out of choices. In *X* number of days you will "have no choice" but to suspend the customer's credit unless he "chooses" to pay *X* amount by such-and-such a date.

Be aware that your customer feels that he has little power and that you are holding all the cards. It is true that you can take away his credit, and you can take him to court. The problem is that these will not help you resolve the situation quickly. Your strategy now should be to communicate in such a way as to empower your customer. Let him know that

- He can choose to settle.
- He can choose to help himself.
- He can choose to preserve his credit—with you as well as his credit record generally.

But to do all of these things, he has to work with you—*now.*

MORE SCRIPTS: TALKING WITH SERIOUSLY DELINQUENT CUSTOMERS

1. **You:** Hello, Ms. Thomas. This is (your name) at XYZ Company. I'm calling about your account with us. It has gone past 120 days for the second time this year. Ms. Thomas, I'm being pressured here to put your credit on hold and even turn the account over to a collection agency. Now, I'd rather not do that. I'd rather work with you to settle the account. Can you get me a check right away?

    Customer: I've been meaning to call you guys. I've got some real cash-flow problems that I'm trying to get out from under. Can I call you in a week or so to work this out?

You: The account is already 120 days past due, and, as I said, this isn't the first time. I know it's not going to help either one of us to press you for a snap answer now, but I can't really afford to put off the discussion for a "week or so," either. What if I give you a day to review your situation and then call back the day after tomorrow at about this time? My concern is to get this account settled, to work with you in settling it—to help you settle it—and to keep doing business with you in the future. So, may I call you Wednesday?

2. **You:** Hello, Mr. Samuels. This is (your name) calling from XYZ Company. I'm calling now to save us both a lot of trouble in the days and weeks to come. Your account with us has been outstanding now for more than 120 days. We've tried repeatedly to contact you about this, but we've received no reply. I'd like to avoid turning this over to our attorney for collection. Do you think we can work out payment on this account?

3. **You:** Hello, Ms. Ernst. This is (your name) calling from XYZ Company. I'm calling about your account with us. It's passed 120 days due, and I'm getting pressured here to turn it over to our lawyers. I was hoping that a simple phone call might make that unnecessary. The amount due is $1,800. Can you get a check to us today?

   Customer: Frankly, no. I've been meaning to call you. We've had some—uh—problems here, and I'm afraid I've had to let some accounts go longer than they should.

   You: Maybe I can help. The total due, as I said, is $1,800. What portion of this could you manage to pay *now*? I really want to hold off having to turn this over to collections—especially if you're in a crunch.

COLLECTION TALK VERSUS COLLECTION LETTERS

Talk, according to the cliché, is cheap. Should you spend time on the phone? Or would you be better off putting everything in writing?

The answer is not either/or, but both.

- Combine collection calls with letters.

- Confirm all verbal agreements in writing.
- Back up any verbal advisories or warnings with the same in writing.
- Take care not to contradict a written statement with a verbal one or vice versa.

A combination of verbal and written collection messages is more effective than either a verbal or written program alone.

CRITICAL ISSUE: AVOIDING THREATS AND HARASSMENT

The efforts you make to collect debts are subject to federal and state regulations. Doing any of the following is not only bad business, it may be illegal.

- Calling at unreasonable hours—early in the morning or late at night
- Attempting to pressure or embarrass the customer by discussing his indebtedness with anyone other than the customer himself
- Threatening the customer
- Using abusive language

Collection calls should be polite and businesslike. Their purpose should be to help the customer settle the debt, not punish him for his indebtedness or negligence.

HANDLING CUSTOMER COMPLAINTS

Nobody wants things to go wrong. But that doesn't mean you need to live in fear of mistakes, mishaps, and disasters. They will happen. Learn to make the best of them.

Seriously. The *best*.

How you respond to an error or mishap provides an opportunity to give your customer exceptional "extra-mile" service. From the disaster *can* come a satisfied customer.

If the widget your company sold to Ms. Smith fizzles, she *will* be more than a little annoyed. But what will happen if she calls your company and finds no help? Outrage, anger, fear, frustration, and feelings of abandonment. You will have lost a customer, whose negative word of mouth may lose you many more.

The answer? Be there for her.

- Responding to complaints is damage control.
- But it's more than damage control.
- Responding to complaints is satisfying warranty obligations and the like.
- But it is more than simply this.
- Responding to complaints demonstrates your company's willingness to stand behind its product or service.
- Responding to complaints should be a pledge to make things right again.

Effectively handled, your response to mistakes, mishaps, and disasters will not only redeem your company in the customer's estimation, it will actually build or strengthen a bond between your firm and the customer. Sure, Ms. Smith still won't like the fact that her widget blew up. But she will feel a whole lot better about your company. She may tell her friends about the widget problem, true enough, but she will devote most of her story to how the company mobilized its forces to *help her out*.

> **TIP**
>
> Responding to complaints is an opportunity to build and strengthen a positive relationship with your customer. It is an opportunity to turn a negative into a positive.

Reaping the Rewards of Utter Disaster: Ten Secrets Revealed

1. *Understand that your customer is anxious, frustrated, and angry.* These are intense feelings calling not for condescending assurances that "everything will be all right," but for a pair of urgent responses:

   - You are committed to help
   - You are able—competent—to help

2. *Begin by listening to the complaint, gathering as much information as you can.* You are trying to get facts. You want the customer to talk. Part of that talking may be more like venting. You will be tempted to react defensively. Resist that temptation. Let the customer reveal as much as possible.

3. *Acknowledge the complaint.* This does not mean admitting wrongdoing. Simply acknowledge that the product or service is not satisfying the customer.

4. *Express empathy, understanding, and concern:* "We're sorry that this has happened." Or: "We're sorry that the product is not performing to your satisfaction." Again, this is not the time to take on blame. Acknowledge the customer's feelings and respond—humanly and humanely—to them.

5. *If you know you can fix the problem, tell the caller what you propose to do.* The good news is that most problems can be fixed. Few require extensive investigation or creativity. Most have ready-made solutions available. If you can find and apply one of these, be certain to *explain* what you propose to do.

6. *Explain to the customer what she must do.* This includes whatever steps she needs to take to make the repair, replacement, or adjustment possible (for example, take the product to the nearest authorized dealer).

7. *Explain all necessary procedures*—not only what you are asking the customer to do, but what you (and your company) will do. How will the steps you propose to take fix the problem?

8. *Provide all of the information the customer needs*—such as a list of authorized repair facilities in his area. Follow up by mailing this list.

9. *Provide closure to the call by apologizing.* This does not mean making abject protestations of guilt. Do not dwell on the negatives, and certainly do not underscore your company's culpability. Instead, use your apology as a springboard to ending the call on an upbeat note.

10. *Emphasize your gratitude for the customer's patience and understanding.* Saying "I sure am sorry this has occurred" is not the same as saying "This is our fault, and we're terrible."

But what do you do in those relatively few cases where there is no quick fix?

- Do not abandon the caller: "There's really nothing I can do."
- Provide a plan of further action.

- Propose a set of alternatives.
- Suggest a temporary fix.

Dealing with a Variety of Customer-Complaint Scenarios

Here are some typical phone scenarios:

1. **Customer:** My name is John Smith. I purchased a widget from you, and I am not happy with it.

   You: I am sorry to hear that the widget isn't performing to your satisfaction, Mr. Smith. Can you describe the problem?

   Customer: (Describes the problem.)

   You: We can certainly fix that. Now, there are two ways we can work to resolve the problem and get you up and running as quickly and painlessly as possible. From what you describe, I'm pretty certain that the problem is with a bad converter. I can either send you a replacement converter, with full instructions for installing it. Or, if you prefer, you may return the entire unit to us, and we will replace the defective part. The first alternative is the quickest way to resolve the problem, but you may feel more comfortable having us perform the work. It's up to you.

   Customer: I'm all thumbs. You guys better do the work.

   You: I understand. Let me give you a few directions: First, please be careful to pack the unit in its original carton with all of the original shipping material. The carton and the shipping material are specifically designed to prevent damage. Send the unit to (give address) and mark on the carton the following return authorization number: 123456. Ship via (specify carrier). We will reimburse you for shipping costs.

   Customer: Okay, I got that. But what's your turnaround time?

You: Right now, I'd say ten days is a good bet. We might be able to better that a bit.

Customer: Okay.

You: Mr. Smith, I apologize for the inconvenience you have been caused, and I thank you for your patience and understanding. We'll resolve the problem as quickly as possible.

2. **Customer:** Yes, hello. My name is Mary Clark, and I'm really steamed about the Deluxe Widget, which I just bought. Your advertisements said that it would do (lists functions). Well, I can't get it do any of these things very well. I want my money back!

   You: I'm sorry to hear that you are disappointed with the Widget. Ms. Clark, the last thing we want to do is to mislead any of our customers. That's a terrible way to do business, and it certainly is not the way *we* do business. Ms. Clark, based on what you're telling me, I believe that you misread our advertisement. The product functions you are describing apply to our model 234, a significantly more feature-rich—and, therefore, more expensive—model. You've purchased the base model, 123.

   Customer: Ohhh . . . Then I guess I'm just stuck . . .

   You: Not at all. Here are two alternatives: First, if you like, I will authorize a full cash refund. Just repack the Widget in its original carton, including all accessories, and take it to the dealer from whom you purchased it. But, look, there was a reason you bought the Widget. You wanted to take advantage of all of its features. I can tell you more about model number 234, which does offer the features you describe— and more. You know, Ms. Clark, there are also some intermediate-range models you might want to know about. If you like, you may exchange your current unit for one of the more advanced models. You'll be given full credit for your purchase price. You'll just pay the difference. How would you like to proceed?

3. **Customer:** My name is Max Reger. The widget you sold me last month is nothing but trouble. I've brought it in for repair *twice*—in *one* month! I'm so unhappy with it that I not only want my money back, but intend never to do business with you again!

You: I can understand and appreciate your anger. The fact is that the widget failed you and, what's even worse, it failed you repeatedly. I'm sure that my telling you how rare such a failure is—let alone repeated failure—isn't much help to you. The point is that our product failed *you*.

Now, Mr. Reger, there's no problem with refunding the purchase price to you. If that's what you want, I will authorize it immediately. The refund will be sent out as soon as we receive your unit. But might I suggest another alternative?

Customer: I don't know. I'm not really interested . . .

You: Let me just *suggest* that you try a replacement unit. Don't give up on us just yet. If you like, I will send, without charge, a service representative to your site to supervise installation and to ensure that the unit is operating in an optimal environment.

What to Say When Your Customer Is Wrong

The customer, goes the old, old saying, *is always right.*

Like any number of "old sayings," this one isn't true. Yet there is something valuable to be learned from it:

- Never let the customer feel that he was wrong in having chosen to do business with your company.

And there is more:

- The customer may not be right, but you have to work with him.

When most customers complain, they have good reason. The complaints are usually valid. Sometimes the customer's lack of satisfaction arises from a problem with the product or service, sometimes from unrealistic expectations, sometimes from misunderstanding how the product operates or just what it is supposed to do. Sometimes, though, customer complaints are *unfounded.* The customer is just plain wrong.

Your objective in handling such calls is not to argue the customer into admitting that he is wrong, but to educate him:

1. To *demonstrate* that the complaint is without basis
2. To do this without alienating the customer

TIP

The most desirable outcome of these scenarios is for the customer to complete the call, having been pleased that what he thought was a problem has been solved.

Once you determine that a caller's complaint is unfounded, do the following:

STEP 1: Listen. Gather all the facts.

STEP 2: Tell the customer that you appreciate his concern.

STEP 3: Explain why the complaint is not valid.

TIP

Be careful with Step 3. Do not raise subjective issues such as taste or judgment. Keep the focus sharply on the product or service issue at hand.

STEP 4: Don't abandon the customer. Offer appropriate alternatives, including (for example), advice on using the product more effectively, sources of additional information, alternative products or accessories designed to make the product perform more nearly as the customer may wish.

STEP 5: Do not apologize. Neither you nor your product is at fault here. Moreover, apologizing in this circumstance is offensive, as if you are telling the customer, "I'm sorry I'm right and you're wrong."

STEP 6: Provide effective, positive closure by expressing your regret that the customer was less than fully satisfied.

STEP 7: Express your hope that the alternative(s) you propose will be of help to the caller.

ALTERNATIVE STRATEGY WHEN THE CUSTOMER IS WRONG

No law says that you must insist that you are right just because you are right. Many firms routinely take products back and refund the customer's money, even when the customer is absolutely wrong. Why? Such firms would rather let the customer abuse them now than bad-mouth them to others later. It may be cheaper and easier to give away a product or refund a sale than to counteract the consequences of negative word-of-mouth advertising.

YOUR SCRIPTS: HANDLING COMPLAINTS WHEN THE CUSTOMER IS WRONG

Here are some scenarios in which the customer is decidedly *not* right:

1. **Customer:** This is Peter Barnes calling. I bought a widget from your company, which I'm just not happy with. I want to get a full cash refund.

   You: I'm looking up your order on my computer now. It's just coming up onto the screen. Mr. Barnes, you purchased the widget on terms that specify no cash refund.

   Customer: I know. That's true. But I'm *really* unhappy. I just won't settle for anything less than a full refund. I don't intend to be a victim of your company's policy.

   You: Mr. Barnes, I understand your feelings, but these terms are not simply a matter of "company policy." They are part of the reason that we were able to offer the widget to you at such a low cost. The non-refund terms are part of the bargain you made with us when you purchased the widget.

   Customer: Well, I guess I see your point . . .

   You: However, sir, you still have options. You might exchange the widget for a different model or you can return it and accept a store credit, which has no time limit whatsoever. You can use it like cash here at the store. I think you'll agree that you still have quite a bit of flexibility, certainly enough to make a purchase decision you will be happy with.

2. **Customer:** This is Charlie Gobel. I recently purchased a Model 123 widget from you, plugged it into the power supply on my Acme AC, and the widget promptly burned out! I want a replacement unit.

   You: I'm very sorry this happened, but my company cannot take responsibility for the damage in this case. The Model 123 is designed for direct current only. By hooking it up to your Acme AC, you ran AC through it. Our spec sheet and warning labels clearly caution against doing this, explaining that alternating current will destroy the coils. That voids the warranty.

   Customer: What!? I can't believe it . . .

   You: Mr. Gobel, you do have some options here. Now, while I cannot make a warranty replacement in this case, I can offer to repair the motor. Most likely, the only damage is to the coil. That repair will run $50 plus $5 for shipping. If you prefer, you can take the unit directly to one of our authorized repair shops. The good news is that once the repair is made your original warranty will be reactivated.

3. **Customer:** What is the matter with your shipping department? I ordered model 12345 and received 34567 instead! I need to make an exchange as quickly as possible.

   You: Let me access your record. May I have your name?

   Customer: (Gives name and other information requested.)

   You: Okay. I'm calling up your record on my computer right now. It should come up on the monitor in just a second or two. Yes. There we are. Mr. Gaines, we clearly have an order here for model 34567.

   Customer: Yes. Well, if you do, that just means *you* took the order down wrong!

   You: That is not likely, Mr. Gaines, but, if you like, I can retrieve the paperwork. I can get your original purchase order. This will take about three minutes. May I put you on hold for that long?

Customer: Yes, go ahead. Let's get to the bottom of this.

You (returning): I have the purchase order here, signed by you, and it does specify model 34567. If you like, I'll fax you the document . . .

Customer: No. That won't be necessary. I guess I made a mistake.

You: Well, unfortunately, the model you ordered and received is a custom design, which means that I cannot simply exchange it for 12345. But I can offer you partial credit—$150—on your 34567 toward purchase of a 12345.

However, Mr. Gaines, have you considered just keeping what you have? You know, the 34567 should deliver satisfaction. Is there anything you don't like about it?

Customer: Well, not really. It's just not what I thought I'd ordered.

You: My suggestion is that you try the unit for a while. See if it does the job for you. If you're still unhappy with it in two weeks, give me a call, and I'll arrange the return for credit I just mentioned. How does that sound to you?

CHAPTER 10

Putting Yourself Across . . .
to Vendors and Suppliers

SELF-TEST YOUR SAVVY IN COMMUNICATING WITH VENDORS AND SUPPLIERS

The following is a simple diagnostic test. A smaller and more selective version of the self-test in Chapter 1, its purpose is not to test your knowledge of communication theory or techniques, but to help you gauge how effectively you communicate with vendors and suppliers in a day-to-day business context. For the most part, you will find it easy to guess the "right" answer. But getting the "right" answer is not the point of the test. Respond honestly, even if you feel that your response is not the best one possible. This is *not* a contest. The object is solely self-inventory.

1. When a collection call comes, I just promise 'em anything.   T/F _____

2. I'm an impulse buyer.   T/F _____

3. Vendors are cheats.   T/F _____

4. I consider my creditor an ally, not an adversary.   T/F _____

5. I feel that, as far as overdue payables go, "Let sleeping dogs lie."   T/F _____

6. I give vendors verbal orders backed up by written orders.   T/F _____

7. A good vendor should feel like your partner.   T/F _____

8. When I have money trouble, I do what I can to avoid my creditors.   T/F _____

9. Service is important to me.   T/F _____

10. When I'm caught in a cash crunch, I get on the phone
    to the people I owe.   T/F ____

11. I like to talk to vendors.   T/F ____

12. I listen to what vendors tell me.   T/F ____

13. I make credit terms part of any negotiation.   T/F ____

14. My motto regarding vendors: "Give 'em hell!"   T/F ____

15. I negotiate for value rather than price.   T/F ____

16. I negotiate with vendors as I negotiate with customers. T/F ____

17. I never get the best deal.   T/F ____

18. Vendors often cheat me.   T/F ____

19. I put my heart and soul into a deal. I get emotional. T/F ____

20. I think it is important to create strong relationships
    with vendors.   T/F ____

21. I try to research the market before I settle on any
    one vendor.   T/F ____

22. I try to make vendors feel *good* about serving me.   T/F ____

TOTAL T/F   ____

Score 1 point for each "True" response and 0 for each "False" response, EXCEPT for questions 1, 2, 3, 5, 8, 14, 17, 18, and 19. For *these questions only*, SUBTRACT 1 point for each "True" response. Record your total. A score below +11 indicates that you would benefit from practicing the communication techniques discussed in this chapter. (Note: It is possible to have a negative score.)

WORDS TO USE WITH VENDORS AND SUPPLIERS

alternatives	careful
ballpark	comparison
best	deal

dependable

discuss

expect

expectation

lowest

negotiate

options

quality

reliable

responsive

select

service

specifications

value

PHRASES TO USE WITH VENDORS AND SUPPLIERS

Do you want to make the deal?

How firm is that price?

I have been looking

I'm listening

not an adequate value

not good enough

quite a bit more than I can spend/invest

real price

tell me what you can offer

Where can we go from here?

WORDS TO AVOID WITH VENDORS AND SUPPLIERS

absolute

bargain

cheap

excited

fair

good

great

immediately

now

terrific

wonderful

PHRASES TO AVOID WITH VENDORS AND SUPPLIERS

can't wait

give me the works

I don't know anything about this stuff

it's urgent

I'm in your hands

I'm desperate

money is no object

right away

will pay anything

BODY-LANGUAGE STRATEGY FOR VENDORS AND SUPPLIERS

The appropriate strategies are those of any sales situation. Use the strategies discussed in Chapter 7.

BODY LANGUAGE TO AVOID WITH VENDORS AND SUPPLIERS

Consult Chapter 7 for body language to avoid.

GETTING VENDORS TO GIVE YOU THEIR BEST

Businesses don't only sell goods and services to others, they also buy, and a good "buy" negotiation is really a good "sales" negotiation. When you make a business purchase, you need to *sell* your supplier on the notion of giving you super service, giving you the best deal possible, and supplying the highest-quality product. Let's face it, it you'll have a better shot at getting all of this if you are buying a lot of stuff or a lot of services from the vendor in question. Talk about communication? *Money* talks.

But making a big deal does not guarantee a good deal or great service, nor do you *have* to make a huge purchase to expect (or get) first-class treatment. The secret is communication.

STARTING OFF ON THE RIGHT FOOT WITH A VENDOR

Your "sales" pitch should commence when you solicit information from a vendor.

STEP 1: Begin by describing your business, emphasizing your reputation and special needs, and so on.

STEP 2: In a polite but straightforward way, *challenge* the supplier to measure up to the requirements of your business.

TIP

Don't be obnoxious about it. Pose the challenge in positive terms: "I've heard a lot of good things about you. I'm expecting to be dazzled."

STEP 3: Be as specific as possible about the kind of information you require from the vendor. You may want to submit a list of requirements.

If you take the next step with a vendor and solicit a bid, it is often helpful to back up your verbal requests with a letter or memo itemizing those specifications and requirements. In the case of complex specs, written documentation is absolutely necessary. This is also the case when you are soliciting competitive bids from more than one vendor.

- Even when you send a full spec sheet, consider augmenting this with a phone call.
- Begin the call by complimenting the vendor on his product and presentation.
- Let him know that *he* has persuaded you to expect great things from him.
- Use the call to highlight any points you may wish to emphasize in your spec sheet, or to ask for information that may have been omitted from the spec sheet (for example, "What is your customer-support policy?").
- Let the supplier know that you have solicited bids from other *excellent* companies.
- Close by inviting questions and establishing a firm deadline for submission of the bid.

YOUR SCRIPTS: APPROACHING VENDORS.

You might telephone a vendor with a message that runs something like one of these:

You: . . . We are a small maker of custom communication circuitry, known for the high quality of our work and the efficiency with which we carry out assignments. Let me lay it on the table: What we need is a supplier who can live up to our reputation. We've heard some very impressive things about you . . .

or:

You: . . . We are a small specialist marketing service with approximately 30 clients, for whom we drop about 200,000 national mailing pieces per month. We are currently looking to upgrade our list-maintenance software, which we run on a XYZ computer, using ABC Software. We want to replace the ABC software with something off the shelf. We've heard very good things about your pricing as well as your customer-support and training programs. What I'd like to see are spec sheets for all your relevant products, together with prices both for single and multiple users. Give us a detailed description of your customer support policy as well. One last thing: we need fast turnaround on this information. We plan to make the purchase as soon as possible.

Here is an idea for a call initiating a bid:

You: . . . We were all highly impressed by your presentation Friday, and we are confident that you can furnish the products and service we require. So, I'm going to put on the fax machine a formal request for a bid on the project. Now, I want you to know that we have solicited bids from a number of excellent suppliers. We intend to review them all intensively, so I must ask that you submit your bid no later than Wednesday. I can't give you any more time than this. You may call me directly at 555-5555 if you have any questions concerning the specifications. We look forward to receiving your bid.

TIP

Avoid hinting at the vendor's standing vis à vis the other bidders. It is sufficient to alert him to the fact that there *are* others.

SECRETS OF NEGOTIATING PRICE AND TERMS WITH VENDORS

Who doesn't know someone who *always* seems to get the best prices? A haggler. A real wheeler dealer. And, knowing such a person, who doesn't envy her? How does she do it? What's her secret?

Doubtless, there are many "secrets" to negotiating the most favorable price, but there are only three that will *never* fail you:

- Know the competitive field. Know what others charge for the same or similar products or services. Do your research.
- Remember always that the object of negotiating is to buy the product or service you want at the best price you can get. Focus on the product or service, not on the personality of the individual from whom you are buying it.
- Go into a negotiation prepared to walk away, if necessary.

STEP 1: Step 1, then, is straightforward and begins before you open the negotiation. Do whatever research is required to become familiar with the competitive field. This may be as simple as consulting a few catalogues and price lists. Or it may involve more legwork, with numerous conversations with suppliers.

STEP 2: The more you know about the product or service you are buying, the less you need to rely on your ability to assess the honesty, integrity, and negotiating skills of the stranger with whom you have to deal. Know the competitive field and you can focus on value, not on the personality of the salesperson or vendor.

TIP

It is all too easy for a buyer to lose focus, turning the negotiation into a personality contest between buyer and seller. Such a contest may feel like real work. It is, after all, intense. But, if it *is* work, what's the point? To defeat another human being? The point *should* be to buy whatever needs to be bought and to buy it at the best price.

Everyone is familiar with the chief peril of buying an automobile: Cars appeal simultaneously to childlike fantasies and to an adult sense of self-indulgence. People really do "fall in love" with cars. The smell of the new vehicles, the bright lights of the showroom—these are seductive indeed, and the impulse is to buy and buy now.

In varying degrees, similar impulses can affect even business purchases. If you want to communicate and negotiate effectively, recognize and fight such impulses.

STEP 3: Avoid impulse buying.

When dealing with high-ticket items—items that, for one reason or another, you covet—a good way to ensure that you do not yield to impulse is to enter into your initial conversation with a vendor determined *not* to buy, but to talk. Consider this part of the research stage. Teach yourself that a deal need not be consummated quickly.

> **TIP**
> _____
> *Impulsive* is not a synonym for *decisive*.

STEP 4: After you have gathered sufficient data, open negotiations with the vendor who seems to offer the best value.

Let's pause to discuss a key term. Too many purchasers focus on the *price* of the merchandise or service they want to buy. Now, price is an important element of the negotiation, but it is *only* an element, a component—a component of *value*. Value is a kind of equation:

Value = price/benefits

Value is an expression of price in proportion to benefits derived from the product or service. A cheap product—a product with a low price—may or may not be a good value. A "cheap" product that offers few benefits is a poorer value than a pricier product that offers many benefits—provided that these are benefits you want and can use. Targeting value will help you negotiate far more effectively.

STEP 5: Use the best price you were quoted during your research phase as a starting point for getting an even better price.

Now, the hard part. If you and the vendor are far apart, it is time to use your most powerful nonverbal weapon: your feet (or just end the telephone conversation, if you are not negotiating in person).

STEP 6: If necessary, walk away from the deal.

Unless the price gap is hopelessly wide, chances are that the vendor will follow you. If not, and you don't find a better deal elsewhere, call back. Recap what happened:

> **You:** Hi, this is (your name). We were talking about a price on three dozen widgets. You were at \$XXX, and I offered \$XX. Have you given any further thought to price?

> See what happens. You may be able to meet somewhere in the middle.

There is one more alternative to walking away from the deal. Often, price is less of an obstacle than payment terms. Even if the price of goods or services remains steep, you may be able to negotiate sufficiently liberal terms to make the deal work. Generally, the best strategy is to settle on a price, then proceed to terms. If the vendor has been able to secure a price advantageous to him, he will be strongly motivated to arrive at terms that will make it possible for you to conclude the deal.

TALKING TO VENDORS ABOUT CREDIT

Talking to a vendor about credit is similar to talking to a bank or other financial institution about a loan in that your objective is to sell the vendor on the notion that she should have confidence in you. However, when applying to a vendor for credit, you have two advantages you do not enjoy when dealing with a bank:

1. Whether the bank wishes to believe it or not, the decision to lend you money is a decision to go into partnership with you. That is a fact, though a bank may choose not to think of it this way. A vendor, faced with the same fact, has no choice but to think of it this way. In order to make it possible for you to do business with him, the vendor knows that he must *find* a way to extend credit, to make you, in effect, his partner.

2. Vendors are not subject to anything like the restrictive regulations that govern banks. A vendor knows that he has to take risks in order to sell his product. The vendor *needs* to let you buy from him.

YOUR SCRIPTS: NEGOTIATING CREDIT TERMS

Here are some ideas for negotiating favorable credit terms. Seize on the positive—what you've been given—and work up from there. Do not emphasize what you lack.

1. **You:** Hello, Gary. This is (your name) from XYZ Company. I'm reviewing your bid for the widgets. Look, I think we're just about there, and I'm eager to sign, but I need either a break on the finance charge—down to X percent would work for us—or more space on the payment schedule. We need at least XX payments over XX months, not X payments over X months. We just don't have the cash flow for that.

   Basically, work with us on either of these options, and we're ready to sign.

2. **You:** Hello, Meg. This is (your name) from XYZ Company. I've just been looking over your bid on the widget project. Meg, I like what I see. Prices are good. Delivery schedule is fine. What I need to work on with you is the payment schedule. X payments over X months is going to hurt our cash flow. What would you say to XX payments over XX months? If you can live with that, I'm ready to make the buy.

3. **You:** Hello, Bob. This is (your name) from XYZ Company. I've had a chance to review your prices on the widget project. You've made the first cut. Now, what we need more flexibility on is your payment terms. We can do XX payments over XX months, but not the short-term schedule you propose.

   Vendor: Oh, I really don't know if we can stretch it out that far.

   The pessimist would take this response as a no. The optimist seizes on the "really don't know" and the generally roundabout structure of the sentence as a plea for a little more convincing. Proceed positively:

   You: Well, if you find that you can stretch that little bit, I'm inclined to sign right now. So, would you give it some thought and call me back later on today? We're ready to get moving.

Vendor: I'll try to get back to you today.

You: That would be good, because we've got to get started here with somebody. So I'd appreciate your pushing on it.

3. **You:** Hello, Sam. This is (your name) from XYZ Company. I've got your bid on the merchandise . We've enjoyed doing business with you in the past, and your prices look pretty fair this time around. The only serious problem I've got is with the payment schedule you've proposed.

Vendor: It's pretty standard. I mean, it's what we set up before.

You: I understand that, but, you know, one of the things we've liked about working with you is that we've never felt you were nailing us to a boilerplate. You've been willing to accommodate. And what I'm asking for is nothing radical in any case. Instead of X payments over X months, we need to spread XX payments over XX months. Sam, we can live with the finance charge, but I can't be tying up $XXX every month. Can you meet me halfway on this? I want to move forward with this project.

HOW TO GET SPECIAL TREATMENT FROM A VENDOR

Everyone wants special treatment. You don't go to a vendor and ask to be treated like a number. But how do you persuade a vendor to treat you well?

The most effective strategy is the same strategy to use whenever you want something for yourself. Appeal to the *other* person's self-interest.

STEP 1: Be pleasant and professional.

Coming on like a hard-nosed, impossible-to-please, fiercely demanding individual will tend to alienate rather than ingratiate.

STEP 2: Be specific about what you want.

Clear objectives and goals reduce anxiety, which makes the vendor feel good about working with you.

STEP 3: Make it clear that you want to establish a working relationship.

You already know that a key to success in a sales-oriented business is *not* making *a* sale, but in *creating a satisfied customer* who will generate repeat business and positive word of mouth. Appeal to the vendor's self-interest by letting her know that you want to be just such a customer for her. You are interested in finding a business "partner," not just someone to supply a single piece of merchandise or do a single job.

TIP

Do not make false or empty promises. Don't "guarantee" loads of business "if you treat us right." Just make it clear that you want to establish a stable, dependable, mutually productive working relationship.

YOUR SCRIPT: GETTING SPECIAL TREATMENT

Here's a bit of face-to-face conversation with a vendor:

You: We buy about a hundred widgets each quarter. That's a good chunk of business. Price is important, of course, and I do like your prices. But we also need a supplier who will *be there* for us, who will go the extra mile when we need him to. That means expediting delivery and being available for quick-turnaround odd-lot orders from time to time. That also means accuracy in filling our orders. I just don't have a lot of time to waste.

    If we can establish a stable, solid working relationship, well, as long as that's true, you've got my business.

REJECTING A VENDOR'S PROPOSAL—WITHOUT REJECTING THE VENDOR

Perhaps the single greatest lesson one can learn about putting oneself across in business—communicating effectively in the context of commerce—is *convincingly* to separate issues from personalities. Almost every difficult, unpleasant, or sensitive business communication is made easier or more effective by such a separation. In no case is this more true than when you must say no to a vendor.

Now, you may think: *This guy is in business. If his feelings are going to be hurt by rejection, that's* his *problem.* And you'd be right. Business is all about deals made and deals *not* made, and the businessperson who takes it all personally does, indeed, have a problem. However, if feelings are hurt, it's not just the other person's problem: it's yours as well.

- You may want or need to call on the rejected vendor again, at another time. You want him to have positive feelings about you and your firm.
- Rejection can serve a positive purpose. It can deliver a strong message to a vendor, telling him what he *must* do to get your business. But this message will be heard only if the relationship between you and the vendor continues. If rejection ends the relationship, the value of rejection is lost.

TIP

No law says that you have to explain to a vendor why you're turning him down; however, you will probably benefit from taking the time to do just that. Giving a concise reason for choosing one proposal over another is not only polite and decent—both essential to creating or preserving a positive relationship with a potential future supplier—it also helps to educate the supplier as to how he might serve you better in months or years to come. This will benefit both of you.

Your scripts: rejecting vendors' proposals

Here are some scenarios in which proposals and bids are rejected, but relationships preserved.

1. Remember: Say no to the proposal, not to the vendor.

    You: Your proposal for our project was very impressive, Bill, and it has triggered a lot of thought here. However, the approach outlined is just too costly, and we are going to go with a scaled-back version. But I want to thank you for a terrific effort, and I will certainly be calling on you in the future. I'm glad to have met you and to have seen what your company can do.

2. If possible, offer hope, not misleading encouragement. Your object is to get the vendor to perform for you.

You: We've finished reviewing your proposal for supplying the equipment, but unfortunately what you propose is not up to spec. Obviously, we're looking at other suppliers, but there is still a month before we close out on bids. Maybe you would like to take another look at our spec sheet and submit a revised proposal by the twelfth of next month?

3. A vendor has replied to your RFP (request for proposal) with a bid that was so far outside of the ballpark that you've not even *responded* to it. The danger of not responding is that you'll be caught short by a surprise phone call. He's on the line now. Your feelings in the matter? Based on the response to your RFP, you don't anticipate wanting or needing to do business with her in the future. Nevertheless, you are well aware that, in the business world, what goes around comes around. How do you say no firmly, but decently?

You: Charlotte, your proposal came in *40 percent* over our target cost figures. That's a gap I couldn't see even *asking* you to close. I went with a proposal that was much closer to the target.

TIP

Focus on your quantifiable, objective target versus the proposal. Avoid judgmental statements relating to capability, talent, or personality.

COMPLAINING PRODUCTIVELY TO A SUPPLIER

"Give 'em hell!" says your boss. She's referring to that shipment of widgets from the new supplier. Wrong colors. Wrong quantities. Wrong everything. "Give 'em hell!"

And *then* what?

What is your objective here? To vent your rage? Your boss's rage? Or is it to correct a problem?

If, on sober reflection, you decide in favor of the latter, try this approach:

- Rather than get angry, express disappointment. You want to send a message that you expected better things from such a fine vendor.

Sticking with this strategy may not be easy. At the least, it probably does not come naturally. After all, the emotion that motivates a complaint is not disappointment, but anger—or, at least, irritation. Giving vent to anger may make you feel better for a while, but then what are you left with? The original problem *and* an alienated and resentful vendor, who may no longer be particularly inclined to remedy the problem.

Complaining effectively is easier if you take these steps:

STEP 1: Clearly state the problem. As TV's Sergeant Joe Friday used to say, "Just the facts, ma'am." Make no accusations. Don't guess at motives or motivations. Just enumerate such details as the duration or frequency of the problem or error, as well as the *material* (not emotional) effect of the problem or error.

TIP

Whenever possible, quantify the consequences of the problem: "Late shipments this month have cost us upwards of $3,300."

STEP 2: Either propose a solution or ask for one.

STEP 3: Conclude by converting *I* and *you* into *we*. Affirm that you want to work *with*—not in opposition to—the vendor.

Shipment or Service Overdue

The most common complaints against vendors are related to time. Deadlines are missed. Schedules fall apart.

Your scripts: complaining about overdue shipments

1. Begin gently, if you can. Secure cooperation. A shipment arrived late enough to have an impact on manufacturing. You call the vendor, who offers some explanations and excuses. How do you say no to the excuses without cutting loose a vendor who has offers you favorable prices?

You: I understand the problems you are facing, but *we*—you and I—are facing a problem, too. We need to work out a reliable schedule. This can't happen again. We can't absorb a delay again. Let's work together on the problem and agree on a new shipping plan to prevent late deliveries in the future.

TIP
_____

Translate the *I*-versus-*you* situation into a *we*.

Here's a simpler situation:

You: Hello, Tom. This is (your name) at XYZ Company. We ordered a gross of widgets from you on April 3 and paid with the order a deposit of $XX. A month has gone by, and we have yet to receive the merchandise. I know you received the order, and you folks deposited our check. We were promised a three-week turnaround. What's happening?

Vendor: I'll look into it and get back to you.

You: Tom, when will I hear from you? Because, look, we're up against it here. Unless we get delivery by the 14th, we will cancel the order and recall our deposit.

Vendor: Well, I'll get back to you as soon as I can.

You: Tom, I don't *want* to have to cancel this order. We want the merchandise. And I'm sure you don't want to lose the order. Please work with us now to avoid something neither of us wants. Please give me a definite time when you will get back to me.

Vendor: You'll have the information this afternoon before five.

You: That would be great. Thanks.

2. Sometimes late is just *too* late. If you must cancel an order, make certain the vendor knows why. The call *must* be followed up with a written cancellation and repudiation of the order.

You: Tom, this is (your name) over at XYZ Company. You know that old saying, "Better late than never"? Well, unfortunately, it doesn't apply this time. Tom, we ordered a gross of widgets from you on March 15. At that time, we paid in full. You've deposited the check. Now, when we failed to receive the goods by April 15, I called you, asking for immediate delivery or return of our money. You promised immediate delivery. We're still waiting—and we can't wait any longer. Tom, I just sent you a fax canceling the order because of nondelivery, and I expect our money returned within the week.

Vendor: I think you're being unreasonable. I can look into it . . .

You: Tom, it's just too late, and there is nothing to be done now but cancel the order and return the money. When will you send out that check?

Repeated Errors by the Vendor

Repeated errors are, of course, especially frustrating. Calling to complain about such problems may involve two objectives:

1. To make it clear that the situation is unacceptable and cannot continue

2. To offer help, advice, or suggestions in an effort to improve the vendor's system problems

Again, address issues, not personalities or character.

YOUR SCRIPTS: COMPLAINING ABOUT REPEATED ERRORS

The following are two approaches to opening up discussion of repeated errors.

1. **You**: . . . We've been doing business with you for a long time now, and I feel I can speak frankly with you. The performance of your shipping department over the past three months has been unacceptable from our point of view. It's just this simple: Of 25 shipments we received since date, five have been late by at least three days; eight

have been incomplete; and three have included items we did not order. Bill, your shipping department's errors have cost us time and effort, and they have often inconvenienced our customers. These errors have to stop.

   I am very interested to hear your take on this situation. It might be productive for us to speak further about it. Maybe I can even make some suggestions you would find helpful.

2. **You:** . . . Edwina, as you know, I've been installing your product for some five years now. Most of the time, I've had no reason to be anything less than delighted. My customers were happy. I made money. Installations went smoothly. But since April, I have received 15 complaints from my customers, and I've had to replace eight units.

   I don't think either of us can avoid the conclusion that too many faulty units are being shipped. I have to think that you have a problem in your quality-control procedures.

   Vendor: I'm not aware of any problem. I mean, this is the first I've heard of this.

   You: I can't keep making my customers unhappy. Are you willing to review your quality-control procedures?

   Vendor: Sure . . . we'll review them.

   You: We do a lot of business together. I would like to meet with you after you've made your review and go over what steps you are taking to ensure that I'm not shipped an unacceptably high number of defective units.

WHAT TO SAY TO THE VENDOR IF YOU HAVE PAYMENT PROBLEMS

What are the hardest apologies to make? Other than incidents culminating in physical injury, the most difficult mishaps to apologize for concern money. And, in business, most apologies concern just that: late payments, missed payments, neglected bills, errors of addition or subtraction, even bounced checks.

Difficult? Yes. But, surprisingly, a straightforward, honest admission of financial error or problem gives you a certain strength to exploit.

- The admission and apology are often received with respect. It takes character to admit being wrong or to accept responsibility for dealing with a situation resulting from your financial error or difficulty.
- Admitting a problem and asking for assistance or patient indulgence empowers the creditor-vendor, giving him an opportunity to be gracious, understanding, and human—in short, giving him a chance to strengthen his partnership with you.

TIP

There is certainly no guarantee that the vendor will seize the opportunity to be decent. But if he responds with anger, good communication is even more important.

The old saw "Let sleeping dogs lie" is extremely destructive in business. If you want to ensure that your creditor will go ballistic, just give her the impression that you're blowing her off. Don't communicate. Don't answer phone calls. Throw those frantic letters in the wastebasket.

If, however, you want to avert a full-blown crisis and resolve financial problems to your advantage, go out of your way to communicate and to keep the lines of communication open. As soon as you anticipate a payment problem:

STEP 1: Advise your lender, vendor, or supplier.

STEP 2: Explain to the vendor the nature of the problem.

STEP 3: Explain how your problem will affect payment to the vendor.

STEP 4: Explain how you propose to deal with the problem.

STEP 5: Tell the vendor what you would like her to do to help *both* of you.

Let's face it, it is not always possible to anticipate cash-flow problems. On these occasions of unforeseen crisis, your only available option is an after-the-fact apology. This should not be a simple "I'm sorry," but

- Should explain the nature of the problem

- Should explain how you propose to deal with it
- Should outline how the vendor can help

TIP

If at all possible, the after-the-fact apology should be accompanied by some proposal for a solution. Even better, it should be accompanied by some *step toward* a solution. If, for example, the problem is a late payment, send the apology with a check for whatever portion of the money due you can pay.

Advising a Vendor of a Payment Problem

Telling a vendor about an impending payment problem can be emotionally difficult, but the occasion is an opportunity to take charge of a problematic situation and to demonstrate that you *have* taken charge and that the problem will not spin out of control.

The most effective strategy to formulate is one that incorporates an element of apology, but that conveys even more dominantly a tone of calm control rather than anguished contrition. If you cry *mea culpa* too loudly and too long, the vendor will believe you, conclude that you really are *terribly* at fault, and may therefore decline not only to forgive you but, more important, may choose not to take the necessary actions that will benefit you both.

TIP

Don't take the opposite tack, backing the vendor into a corner by self-righteously daring her to grant 30 days' grace on a receivable. Just don't put yourself across as a guilt-tormented sinner, either.

STEP 1: Strike the even-handed, middle tone by refraining from emotion-charged language. Avoid such words as *terrible, awful, dreadful, unfortunate, disaster, crisis,* and the like.

STEP 2: Present the facts straightforwardly.

STEP 3: If you have a specific request to make, do so directly after explaining the situation.

STEP 4: While you may conclude with an apology, do not apologize for the request or requests you make.

TIP

Avoid emotional words that tell your correspondent how to feel. Also take care to avoid telling your correspondent how he should judge your request. If you say something like, "I know this is a lot to ask," the vendor is likely, either consciously or unconsciously, to agree with you: *He is asking a lot!* Don't sandbag yourself. Make the request, and let the vendor decide just how big a favor you are asking.

STEP 5: Do not shift the focus to yourself by telling the vendor how bad you feel about the problem. Of course you feel bad. Why should your creditor be made to feel bad, too? Isn't it enough that she's not getting her money on time?

Your scripts: renegotiating payment terms

Here are two phone scripts for renegotiating terms—*before* payment problems actually develop:

1. **You:** . . . I don't usually quote the presidents, Jane, but Abe Lincoln, you know, advised against changing *horses* in midstream. Now, as far as I know, he had nothing against changing *payment terms* to make your customer's life easier. So I hope you'll hear me out.

   We want to extend payments on our account an additional three months, reducing our monthly payment from $XXX to $XX, *but* retaining our present rate of interest. Jane, I really would like to clear this debt as quickly as possible, but our operating costs have increased faster than our client list, and we have embarked on a program designed to reduce our overhead.

   That's what *we* get out of the deal. For you, you collect another three months interest—and our undying gratitude and good will.

   There is nothing wrong with a light touch—a bit of humor—just don't drown content in an attempt to get laughs at the vendor's expense.

2. **You:** Hello, Ken. This is (your name) at XYZ Company. I'm very pleased that you can take us on as a credit customer, and I've just been looking over the final forms. Everything is fine—except for the payment due date. I'm hoping you can be flexible on that. Instead of the

first of the month, we'd like to pay on the fifteenth. This works out much more smoothly with our payment-and-collection cycle. I won't have to hassle my clients each month, and, more important, it will keep the money flowing into your operation without any problems.

Here are some ideas for advising vendors of impending problems:

1. **You:** Hello, John. This is (your name) at XYZ Company. I'm calling in reference to our account with you—that's account number 12345. I am hoping you can help us over what looks to be a rough patch. We've just had some equipment breakdowns and, consequently, a number of heavy and unanticipated expenses. It would be a great help in managing cash flow if we could reschedule our payment due dates for the next six months. We currently pay on the first of each month. I would like to push that back to the twentieth. The rescheduling will help us out of a tight spot.

2: **You:** . . . We are digging out from under a number of emergency expenses that have been heaped on us this month, and I'm calling to advise you that we will be ten days late in getting a check to you for the widgets you shipped on March 5. Is this delay going to pose any serious problem for you? You *will* have the check by the twenty-fourth.

3. **You:** . . . I need to ask for your help—or, at least, for your patience. We're navigating some ticklish cash-flow situations here, and it would help me a great deal if I could defer paying off your account for 20 days. Is that going to present you with a serious problem? If not, it would sure help me out.

4. **You:** . . . I'm calling to let you know that we're going to be 20 days late getting a check to you. I'm hoping this doesn't present a problem for you.

    Vendor: Normally, it wouldn't. We usually have some flexibility. But, this month, it's not news I wanted to hear.

    You: We are talking about 20 days, but would it help if I could get you $XX by the 1st and the balance on the twentieth?

5. **You:** . . . I'm calling to let you know that we're going to be 20 days late getting a check to you. I'm hoping this doesn't present a problem for you.

Vendor: Unfortunately, it *does* present a problem.

You: I wish I didn't have to put you in this position. Given our situation, however, I don't see any way to avoid a late payment. I can come up with $XX now, if that would make it easier for you to accommodate us.

6. **You:** . . . I'm calling about our account with you, Jack. It looks as if we're going to be late with this month's payment. We've had some emergency expenses. I can hand-deliver a check on the twelfth, which will put us less than two weeks past due. I hope you can help us out with some flexibility this month. It's an unusual circumstance, which I don't anticipate happening again.

7. **You:** . . . I'm calling in reference to our account. I am anticipating a delay in paying next month's installment, and I'd like to work out an arrangement to defer that payment for 20 days.

Vendor: That's something I just can't do. I suggest you try to defer another of your expenses.

You: This is a unique circumstance, which will not be repeated. I suppose I could have just skipped the payment and taken the consequences, but I want to maintain a good working relationship with you. What would make it possible for you to assist me?

Vendor: I could speak to my credit manager . . .

You: I would really appreciate that. I don't believe in evading responsibility. I'd like us to reach an understanding that will get us both through next month. Will you call me after you've spoken to your credit manager, or should I call you?

Here are a pair of phone calls advising the vendor of a partial payment. It is not a good idea to send partial payment without advising the vendor of this.

1. **You:** . . . I just put into the mail for you a $XXX check. Before you congratulate me, let me point out that your invoice is for $XXXX, and it's about due. I've run into some cash-flow problems here, and I

thought you'd rather have a portion of the payment now than wait another 20 days or so for the whole thing. I will be sending you the balance by the twenty-fifth. Is this going to work out for you?

2. **You:** . . . You're about to get less than you deserve—and I wanted to be the first to tell you. I just sent off to you a check for $XX, which is one third of the total we owe on your last invoice. I just got hit with some unexpected emergency repair costs, which have thrown my cash position way off. I'm hoping you can see your way clear to help me out by giving me a little breathing space on this invoice. $XX is on the way to you. Another $XX will go out on the fifteenth, and the balance will go out at the end of the month. Unless my whole office goes up in smoke, I can guarantee those dates. Can you live with them?

Apologizing for Late Payment or Other Financial Glitches

If you can't advise of upcoming problems, you can apologize for problems that have already occurred.

STEP 1: Begin by realizing that the mere fact of formally apologizing for a late payment or a missed payment or other financial glitch goes a long way toward defusing a potentially destructive situation.

STEP 2: Make it clear that you *are* apologizing. Use such phrases as "I hope you will accept my apology," "I'm sorry," and the like.

STEP 3: Include with the apology some positive steps toward remedying the error. Enclose a check, if appropriate and possible, either for the full amount or a partial amount. At the least, propose a definite plan for settling your account or rectifying the error.

STEP 4: Include a brief and direct explanation of whatever has caused the problem.

STEP 5: Include the vendor in the solution. Ask what *she* would like you to do. Use phrases like, "How do you want to proceed?" "What would be best for you?" "What would be least inconvenient?" "I suggest doing such and such, but how do you want to move on this?"

TIP

Depending on your relationship with your correspondent, don't be afraid to keep the tone lighthearted, even humorous—especially at your own expense. Honesty is disarming. If you tell your correspondent that you made a "dumb" mistake, she will respect your hard-nosed self-assessment and admire your willingness to cut through any pretense of corporate bureaucracy by taking responsibility for your actions.

Your scripts: apologizing for late payment

Simple is often the best:

1. **You:** Hello, Frank. This is (your name) at XYZ Company. I've just put into the mail a check for $XX, which, I'm afraid, is overdue. I wanted to let you know that the money is on the way, and I wanted to apologize for being late with it. It won't happen again.

2. **You:** . . . You know, you really ought to print your invoices on bigger paper—maybe the size of a poster—for confused folks like me who shuffle sheets on their desks until something gets lost. Your invoice, which I see is dated March 10, got buried on my desk, and now, I'm embarrassed to say, is overdue. I've made the check out and I'm putting it into the mail now. I'm very sorry for the slip-up, and I appreciate your not hollering at me, which you have every right to do.

Sometimes a little more explanation is required:

3. **You:** . . . Things got a little hectic here, and I've been hustling to get my payables out the door. I just sent you a check for $XX, which, I know, is late.

    Vendor: Yes, it *is* late. I was about to call you.

    You: Well, as the saying goes, the check is in the mail.

    Vendor: I've heard *that* one before.

    You: I bet you have. But I wanted you to hear it from me—personally. And I wanted to apologize for the delay. It will not happen again.

4. **You:** . . . It has been a very rough couple of weeks—very hectic and a lot of pressure. The good news is that I've just sent you a check for $XX. The bad news is that it's two weeks late. I thought I'd call to let you know that it's on its way and to beg—on bended knee, no less—your forgiveness.

Vendor: Oh, really, it's no problem. These things happen.

You: Not to me, they don't. I don't make it a practice to pay late. I really do appreciate your understanding.

Responding to Collection Calls

Despite your best intentions, a bill can go unpaid, and a vendor—or a collection agency—can make a collection call. Depending on the tone of the caller, such a call can rattle even the most experienced business person. In responding, try these tactics:

- You will be asked for immediate answers. Don't feel compelled to give them. If you need time to review a billing situation, say so—but give your caller an exact time when you will get back to him, and do not fail to do as you promised.
- Apologize directly, but not abjectly.
- Negotiate. If, for example, your caller demands payment in full and you are not in a position to make it, suggest a partial payment, using a phrase such as, "Would X amount help now?"
- Express appreciation for the caller's patience, understanding, and willingness to cooperate.
- Ask your caller how she would like to proceed, what would be best for her, and so on.

TIP

If your caller is really steamed—and, even among professionals, this can happen—resist the temptation either to cave in, just saying what the caller wants to hear, or to respond with anger yourself. Use the caller's name; make sure he knows he is dealing with a person to whom courtesy is due.

Do not be in too great a hurry to agree with collectors.

- Determine the facts.
- Compare balances due, dates, and so on.
- If you conclude you are in the wrong, admit it, apologize, and (if possible) negotiate an *immediate* interim action such as a partial payment.

TIP

If the situation is really hot, it may be best to cool things off by playing for time. Tell your caller that you recognize the problem and that you will take care of it, but you have to review the matter with your bookkeeper *immediately*. Give your caller an exact time when *you* will call him back.

YOUR SCRIPTS: RESPONDING TO COLLECTION CALLS

Here are some collection response scenarios:

1. **Vendor:** I'm calling about your account with us. We're showing that $XX was due on the fifteenth.

   You: You're right. I should have called. We've had some emergency expenses here, and I delayed sending out some of my payables. I can get payment in full to you by the twentieth of next month. Will that work for you?

   Vendor: I really don't like to wait that long.

   You: Would it help if I got $X out to you now, and the balance by the twentieth? I can manage that.

   Vendor: That's better for us.

   You: I appreciate your understanding, and I'm sorry—both for being late and for neglecting to give you a call earlier.

2. **Vendor:** I'm calling about your account with us. We're showing that $XXX was due on May 13.

   You: Let me look at my book. My ledger shows that a check for that amount was mailed to you on May 4. It's our check number 12345. You should have gotten it by now.

Vendor: No, it's not here.

You: I see. How would you like to proceed? I can put a stop on the check we sent and send you out a new one today. Or we can wait until the end of the week.

Vendor: I think it would be best to get a new check.

You: Okay. Let me confirm your address. I'll get that right out to you, and I'm sorry the check went astray.

3. **Vendor:** I'm calling about your account with us. Do you intend to pay it?

You: Am I speaking to Pete Williams (name of usual contact)?

Vendor: Yes, this is Pete.

You: Pete, of course we intend to pay the amount due. I am showing a balance due of $XXX. Is that what you've got?

Vendor: Yes.

You: And you're right. We're late. I am very sorry. I am not prepared at this time to pay the full balance due. I can send you $XX now, and the balance by the end of February.

Vendor: I wish you had called me earlier, if there was a problem.

You: Pete, I agree with you. I should have asked for your help on this to begin with. It would have made the situation easier for you and, certainly, for me. I apologize. And I hope we can work together on the basis I suggested: $XX now, and the balance by February 28.

THANKING A VENDOR AND GIVING REFERRALS

Saying Thanks to a Vendor

When a vendor goes the extra mile for you, expressing thanks not only acknowledges that fact and makes the vendor feel good, it makes you feel good, too. But thanks is not only an act of courtesy. It is also a means of *reinforcing* positive action and building a relationship in which extra-mile service can become the norm. Behavioral psychologists have long known that positive reinforcement is much more effective than negative reinforcement (threats and the like) in creating desired behavior or action. But what makes the difference between a perfunctory, formal thank you and a truly meaningful expression of thanks?

Specificity. Facts. Details.

The strategy for making an effective thank you call is to stick to the facts.

STEP 1: State exactly what you are thanking the vendor for.

STEP 2: Say something about the positive effect of the vendor's extra-mile action.

STEP 3: Close with an expression of appreciation.

> **TIP**
>
> The key to an effective thank-you call is to be specific, expressing thanks and then explaining how valuable the service, favor, whatever is. You don't need to exaggerate the good consequences of the act. Just be as specific as possible.

Being specific about the effect of the extra-mile action satisfies the human urge to see, to realize, the results of effort. It is a strong means of reinforcing positive behavior. Remember to

- Keep the thanks straightforward
- Use verbs and nouns—specifics—instead of adjectives
- Let the warmth of your voice come through in your message

YOUR SCRIPTS: EXPRESSING THANKS TO VENDORS

Here are some spontaneous thank-you calls to vendors.

1. **You:** Frank, your guidance in upgrading our software saved us at least $XXX in direct software and training costs. That means a lot to us. We're very grateful for the time and care you took with us.

2. **You**: Betty, you saved the day when you managed to expedite shipment of the Johnson order. You don't know how close we came to losing a major customer, but, thanks to your extra-mile effort, we delivered on time and ended up strengthening that relationship. We're very grateful to you for your hard work and commitment to us.

Giving Vendor Referrals

Referral calls should be a pleasure to make. They not only present an opportunity to help a deserving vendor, they also directly benefit your interests.

- It is worthwhile to extend your influence and judgment throughout the business community.

- Sending a good vendor to a colleague builds a positive relationship with that colleague as well as with the vendor.

- A good referral is a favor to two people: the vendor and the colleague.

As with thanking a vendor for extra-mile service, the key to making effective referrals is to be as specific as possible.

- Avoid vague adjectives.

- Mention specific events, projects, and accomplishments relating to the vendor you are recommending.

TIP

Do not make the referral unless you can do so without reservation. If you have any doubts about the vendor, decline the vendor's request for a recommendation.

TIP

If a vendor asks you to call a colleague with a recommendation, you can make the call easier by asking the vendor to tell you what he'd like you to mention.

YOUR SCRIPT: GIVING VENDOR REFERRALS

Here's an example of a vendor referral:

You: Norma, Sarah Coates at WXY Widgets asked me to give you a call to tell you something about her and her company. We've been doing business with WXY for three years, and I wouldn't think of going to any other supplier. Not only are WXY's prices fair—I think unbeatable—the service is personal, direct, and responsive. Just a few days ago, I need an odd-lot assortment of widgets for a rush job. I called Sarah. She had an up-to-the-minute inventory on everything, and the *single* time she didn't have on one hand, she got it for me that same day. And this isn't an isolated case. This is the kind of responsiveness I expect from WXY. So, I'm very happy to recommend her company to you.

CHAPTER 11

Putting Yourself Across . . . to Lenders and Investors

SELF-TEST YOUR SAVVY IN COMMUNICATING WITH LENDERS AND INVESTORS

The following is a simple diagnostic test. A smaller and more selective version of the self-test in Chapter 1, its purpose is not to test your knowledge of communication theory or techniques, but to help you gauge how effectively you communicate with lenders and investors in a day-to-day business context. For the most part, you will find it easy to guess the "right" answer. But getting the "right" answer is not the point of the test. Respond honestly, even if you feel that your response is not the best one possible. This is *not* a contest. The object is solely self-inventory.

1. If a prospect fails to return my calls, I try, try again.   T/F ____

2. I always use a soft-sell strategy.   T/F ____

3. I am willing—personally—to explain and defend my credit history.   T/F ____

4. I am confident that I have the expertise to get the job done.   T/F ____

5. Investors and lenders generally have confidence in me.   T/F ____

6. Going back to an original investor for more money is easier than finding new sources.   T/F ____

7. No business plan should exceed five or six pages.   T/F ____

8. I don't ask for more without offering more.   T/F ____

9. I don't say anything. I put it all in writing.   T/F ____

10. I highlight my written business plan with a verbal send-off.   T/F ____

11. There is nothing wrong with hiring a consultant to help with the business plan.   T/F ____

12. It is better to renegotiate terms before your account becomes delinquent.   T/F ____

13. Everyone lies on loan applications.   T/F ____

14. Banks loan you money only if you can prove you don't need it.   T/F ____

15. I make follow-up calls to ensure that the prospect has all the information he needs.   T/F ____

16. Loan officers are busy. I don't annoy them with follow-up calls.   T/F ____

17. I often follow up with prospects who have turned me down—just in case.   T/F ____

18. Business plans should be extremely detailed.   T/F ____

19. I present investment as an opportunity.   T/F ____

20. Investment prospects are annoyed by follow-up calls. I try not to make them.   T/F ____

21. I see the business plan as a *real* plan, not just a sales tool.   T/F ____

22. I sell the future.   T/F ____

23. I want prospective investors to ask a lot of questions.   T/F ____

TOTAL T/F   ____

Score 1 point for each "True" response and 0 for each "False" response, EXCEPT for questions 2, 7, 9, 13, 14, 16, 18, and 20. For *these questions only,* SUBTRACT 1 point for each "True" response. Record your total. A score below +13 indicates that you would benefit from practicing the communication techniques discussed in this chapter. (Note: It is possible to have a negative score.)

WORDS TO USE WITH LENDERS AND INVESTORS

advice

advise

aggressive

alternatives

caution

checklist

evaluate

expertise

explain

growth

issues

negotiate

opportunity

options

outline

plan

potential

precise

precisely

present

problem

proceed

quantity

safe

safety

satisfaction

strategy

PHRASES TO USE WITH LENDERS AND INVESTORS

best guess

best-case scenario

give me the percentages

how confident are you

issues to address

lay out for you

make a list

next move

pin down

pros and cons

what are the odds

what's the probability

worst-case scenario

WORDS TO AVOID WITH LENDERS AND INVESTORS

basically	generally
broke	must
desperate	shyster
desperation	urgent

PHRASES TO AVOID WITH LENDERS AND INVESTORS

get on the stick

hurry up

in general

let me talk to you

now or never

once in a lifetime

take all the time you need

take it or leave it

tell me what I should do

What's my next move?

BODY-LANGUAGE STRATEGY FOR COMMUNICATING WITH LENDERS AND INVESTORS

Review Chapter 7 for a discussion of body-language strategy that is appropriate for working with clients and customers as well as lenders and investors. In addition, keep uppermost in mind two objectives of nonverbal communication with lenders and investors:

1. To communicate honesty and trustworthiness—"character"
2. To communicate confidence

Accordingly, review in particular comments in the "Body-Language Strategy" section of Chapter 7 covering the handshake and posture. Communicating with lenders and investors benefits from a firm, warm handshake and from an upright posture. Use open gestures. Establish and maintain eye contact.

People tend to associate a lower-pitched voice with authority and honesty. If you can cultivate the lower registers of your voice, do so. This advice applies to men and women alike. Deliberately pitching your voice a bit lower than normal should also help slow your speech and improve your enunciation. The more clearly you speak, the more confident you seem, and the more confidence you inspire in others.

BODY LANGUAGE TO AVOID WITH LENDERS AND INVESTORS

Avoid gestures that express

- Evasiveness
- Timidity
- Uncertainty
- Vagueness
- General nervousness

The following body language may kill a deal:

- Avoidance of eye contact
- Bringing the hands to the mouth
- Rubbing the face
- Shielding the eyes
- Running hands through hair or manipulating your hair
- Rubbing the back of the neck
- Rubbing the eyes
- Scratching yourself—anywhere
- Licking the lips
- Biting the lips
- Slouching
- Shifting weight from side to side (standing)

- Leg movement (sitting)
- Shaking the head *no*

SECRETS OF SELLING YOUR FUTURE TO LENDERS AND INVESTORS

Why doesn't everybody with at least a little money to invest clean up on the stock market?

There are undoubtedly many plausible answers to this question, but the most meaningful answer is simple:

- *Few people understand what it means to invest in the future.*

Putting money in a *relatively* mature company is *relatively* safe but also *relatively* unprofitable. The future of a mature company will probably be little different from its present; therefore, investments will probably enjoy only modest growth.

Your strategic objective in communicating with investors and lenders is to educate them about your future and, once they are sufficiently educated, to *sell* them a share of that future.

Selling. That is what communicating to investors and lenders is. As in most other sales situations, there are two broad approaches:

1. *The soft sell.* This approach appeals to reason and intellect. Usually, the soft sell appeals to the more sophisticated investor, the person accustomed to making up his or her own mind.
2. *The hard sell.* This approach makes its case more directly, often bypassing the intellect in order to appeal to the emotions. If a soft sell is a word to the wise, a hard sell is an impassioned plea.

Both soft-sell and hard-sell strategies can be effective. Choosing between them depends on the nature of your business and on the kind of investor you are after.

- The soft sell is an attempt to open the door to further discussion.
- At its most extreme, the hard sell tries to open the door, enter the room, make the sale, and leave with the cash.

> **TIP**
>
> Be careful. In most jurisdictions, soliciting investment money requires a full-disclosure prospectus. Make certain that you are thoroughly familiar with all applicable laws governing the solicitation of investments. The laws vary from business to business and jurisdiction to jurisdiction.

- The hard sell will often provoke a more definite response from the prospect, which, depending on the type of investment and the type of investor, may be a more definitely *positive* or a more definitely *negative* response.
- The soft sell is less definite, but also less risky. Knock politely on a door, and you may be refused admittance, but at least you won't get *kicked* out.

For all their differences, the soft-sell and the hard-sell approaches typically must achieve seven objectives to be successful:

1. Give the prospective investor or lender a good reason for your having approached him.

> **TIP**
>
> When approaching investors, you may want to identify the prospect as a member of an elite group—one of a group of historically successful investors, for example.

2. Make a case for the investment opportunity; that is, identify a hitherto unmet need for which there is a lucrative market.
3. Explain how your project or company will meet this need.
4. Persuade the investor of your personal ability to meet the need, that you are qualified to run the company or project.
5. Enumerate the benefits—to the investor or lender—of the investment or loan.
6. Outline a course of action.

In a hard sell, outlining a course of action may involve prodding the prospect with provocative questions (which you always answer for him) and announcing that you will follow up personally to solicit a response. The soft sell, in contrast, merely lays the groundwork for a follow-up, then asks for an invitation to follow up.

7. Invite questions.

Never be afraid of questions. Not only is it up to you to demonstrate that you have nothing to hide, but questions in and of themselves represent an investment in your company or project. The more interactive the prospect is willing to be, the better your chances of making the sale.

YOUR SCRIPTS: COMMUNICATING WITH LENDERS AND INVESTORS

Here are some ideas for conversations with potential investors or lenders. We begin with a soft-sell approach:

1. **You:** . . . Mr. Perkins, I've always believed that when I needed help, it's best to go right to the top. That's why I'm calling you, a leader of this city's business and cultural community.

    Last year, some 650 small presses in the United States and Canada published some 3,500 books intended to appeal to the general reader. Unfortunately, few of these presses had access to a decent distribution service, and, therefore, the "general reader" never saw the majority of these books, let alone had the opportunity to buy them.

    I have a plan to change this situation with a company I call Bookserve, Inc., a distribution-and-warehouse service for independent and small presses. The publishers are crying out for such a service.

    But, Mr. Perkins, the small presses are not the only ones who will profit from the enterprise. Bookstores will gain access to vast, enticing new stocks. And readers everywhere, of course, will benefit.

    And then there is you. Investors in Bookserve, Inc., should realize profits within three to four years after start-up. How do I know? I've been in book distribution for more than 20 years and am currently general manager of XYZ Company, one of the nation's most successful distributors.

    I know I can make Bookserve, Inc., a major success, and I would like to set up—at this time—an appointment to speak with you in person and present to you a detailed business plan.

2. **You:** . . . Ms. Deacon, we all like to win. Too often, however, one person's triumph comes at the cost of another's defeat.

    But not this time.

    I'd like the opportunity to talk with you about an investment opportunity in which everyone involved will win.

    Last year, some 650 small presses in the United States and Canada published some 3,500 books intended to appeal to the general reader. Unfortunately, few of these presses had access to a decent distribution service, and, therefore, the "general reader" never saw the majority of these books, let alone had the opportunity to buy them.

    My plan is to change all this with a company called Bookserve, Inc., a distribution-and-warehouse service for small presses. After working more than 20 years in book distribution (I'm currently general manager of XYZ Company, one of the nation's most successful book distributors), I know I can make this company a winner.

    I know, too, that it will make winners of small presses, bookstores, and readers. And it will make winners of those who invest in Bookserve, Inc.

    I want very much to introduce myself to you in person and to present a detailed business plan. I will be in your city on . . .

3. **You:** . . . When Bill Johnson at EFG Company told me that you are an avid reader *and* a shrewd investor, that was all I needed to hear. I knew that I had to call you.

    Mr. Nelson, last year, some 650 small presses in the United States and Canada published some 3,500 books intended to appeal to the general reader. Unfortunately, few of these presses had access to a decent distribution service, and, therefore, the "general reader" never saw the majority of these books, let alone had the opportunity to buy them.

    My plan is to change all this with a company called Bookserve, Inc., a distribution-and-warehouse service for small presses. After working more than 20 years in book distribution (I'm currently general manager of XYZ Company, one of the nation's most successful distributors), I know I can make Bookserve, Inc., work—for small presses, for book dealers, for the reading public, and for you, the investor.

    I'm going to be in your town from May tenth through the twelfth, and I am eager to set up an appointment to introduce myself in person and to present you with a detailed business plan, which you can study at your leisure.

4. **You**: Ms. Kelly, your name appears in some of the best places, especially the annual reports of numerous small innovative entrepreneurial firms. That's why I am calling you right now.

   I've started a company called Bookserve, Inc., a distribution-and-warehouse service for small presses. Last year, some 650 such presses in the United States and Canada published about 3,500 books intended to appeal to the general reader. Unfortunately, few small presses have access to a decent distribution service and, therefore, the "general reader" never sees the majority of these books, let alone has the opportunity to buy them.

   With the help of investors like you, Bookserve, Inc., will change all that. The small presses will profit, bookstores will profit, readers will profit, and, of course, investors will profit.

   I look forward to speaking with you, meeting you in person, telling you more about myself, and presenting a detailed business plan for Bookserve, Inc.

And now, for comparison, some hard-sell approaches:

1. **You**: . . . Mr. Williams, I know of 650 companies that need your help and that are willing to give you a fair share of their profits for helping them.

   Let me explain.

   Last year, some 650 small presses in the United States and Canada published over 3,500 books they intended for the general reader. Because few of these presses had access to a decent distribution service, the "general reader" never saw the majority of these books, let alone had the opportunity to buy them.

   My plan is to change all this with a company called Bookserve, Inc., a distribution-and-warehouse service for small presses. After working more 20 twenty years in book distribution (I'm currently general manager of XYZ Company, one of the nation's most successful distributors), I know I can make Bookserve, Inc., work—for small presses, for book dealers, for the reading public, and for you, the investor.

   Shall I go on?

Prospect: Sure. I'm listening.

You: I want to introduce myself in person and show you a detailed business plan, which explains how you can expect to realize a profit on your investment in just three to four years. I want to explain how, with your help, we will revolutionize an industry, perform a cultural service, and make money in the bargain. I will be in town . . .

2. **You:** . . .You've heard about the notion of doing well by doing good, haven't you?

   Prospect: Yes.

   You: Well, cynics say things just don't ever really work that way. But how many wealthy cynics do you know? Look, there are 650 small companies in this country and Canada that need your help—and that will share their profits with you to get it.
   Should I tell you more?

   Prospect: I'm interested in hearing your story.

   You: Then let me explain. Last year, some 650 small presses in the United States and Canada published approximately 3,500 books they intended for the general reader. Because few of these presses had access to a decent distribution service, the "general reader" never saw the majority of these books, let alone had the opportunity to buy them.
   My plan is to change all this with a company called Bookserve, Inc., a distribution-and-warehouse service for small presses. After working more than 20 years in book distribution (I'm currently general manager of XYZ Company, one of the nation's most successful distributors), I know I can make Bookserve, Inc., work—for small presses, for book dealers, for the reading public, and for you, the investor.
   Mr. Larson, I'd like an opportunity to introduce myself in person and to present a full business plan. I'll be in town . . .

3. **You:** . . . Everybody wants to make more money. That's not news. But let me get specific. I can name right now about 650 entrepreneurial CEOs who want to make more—and who are willing to share their profits with you in order to do so.
   There are just about 650 small presses in the United States and Canada turning out terrific books intended to appeal to the general

reader—some 3,500 titles last year alone. Unfortunately, the "general reader" rarely sees or even hears of these books (let alone buys them) because small presses have never been able to get the kind of distribution they desperately need.

I want to change that with a company called Bookserve, Inc., a warehouse-and-distribution service for small presses. And I want you to help me now so that you can share in the profits later—not *much* later, just three to four years.

Twenty years in book distribution (I'm currently general manager of XYZ Company, one of the nation's most successful distributors) makes me confident that Bookserve, Inc., will work spectacularly well.

I'm also confident that you, a literate investor accustomed to making the right decision, will want to see me when I will be in your area. I'll be armed with a detailed business plan.

4. **You:** I've got a question *and* an answer for you. What would you do if you had a terrific product you couldn't sell? Here's the answer: You'd pay somebody to sell it for you.

The fact is that there are about 650 fine companies out there who are looking for that somebody. And that somebody could be you.

I am creating a company called Bookserve, Inc., a warehouse-and-distribution service for small presses. Last year, some 650 of them in the United States and Canada published approximately 3,500 books they intended for the general reader. The trouble is that the "general reader" neither saw nor heard of most of these books (let alone bought them) because small presses have never been able to get the kind of distribution they desperately need.

Bookserve, Inc., is meant to change all that. It will help small presses sell books, open up a vast array of new suppliers to book retailers, provide readers with a treasure trove of unique and worthwhile books, and, for a few shrewd investors, generate revenue.

Twenty years in book distribution (I'm currently general manager of XYZ Company, one of the nation's most successful distributors) leaves no room for doubt in my mind that I will make Bookserve, Inc., work. I also have no doubt that you'll be interested enough in the project to allow me the opportunity to meet with you in person next week. I want to show you a detailed business plan. . . .

PRESENTING A PROSPECTUS OR BUSINESS PLAN

Once you have sufficiently interested a prospect in your company, project, or venture, it is time to follow up—and follow up quickly—with a detailed business plan. Now, *How to Say It at Work* is not a book devoted to creating a business plan. There are plenty of books—as well as software for the personal computer—to help you there. Two good general volumes to consult are

- James B. Arkebauer's *McGraw-Hill Guide to Writing a High-Impact Business Plan* (McGraw-Hill, 1994)
- Joseph Covello and Brian Hazelgran's *Your First Business Plan* (Small Business Source Books, 1993)

And if you prefer working with PC software, Tim Berry's *Business Plan Pro* (Palo Alto Software) is a good choice. Whatever books or computer programs you use, just remember that there is no one-size-fits-all prescription for writing a business plan. Suit the plan to:

- Your business, venture, or project
- The kind of investor you are going after

> **TIP**
>
> It is imperative that, once the investor's interest is piqued, the business plan is presented without delay. Momentum is one of the keys to unlocking capital.

Let's say you're an inventor or the developer of new products. Why not just call on your local venture capitalist with a prototype in hand? What could be more persuasive (provided the darn thing works, of course)?

The truth is that the savvy investor *will* look at the prototype—at some point. But what he'll want to see first is your business plan. The plan you present should serve four basic purposes:

1. It should be a tool to pry loose money.
2. It should be obviously and clearly usable as a guide to running the business once the funding is in place. That is, it *really* should be a business *plan*—not just something to show to investors.

3. It should serve as persuasive evidence of your ability to think, to organize, to plan, to anticipate, to create.

Finally, *for yourself:*

4. The business plan should turn up any problems and issues that need to be resolved. Review your plan carefully. Redraft and redraft it until the problems *are* solved.

However you decide to structure and pitch your business plan, observe the following:

- Don't skimp, but do strive to be concise. The plan should be readable in a single sitting—which means about 20 to 30 pages for most projects or ventures.

- Avoid vagueness and pie-in-the-sky, but do not smother the investor in details.

TIP

Detailed breakdowns, test-market results, focus-group numbers, and so on should be available in a backup document for the investor who asks to see these things.

In addition to a business plan, you should be prepared to furnish a more specifically detailed marketing plan, a document that will cover, at minimum, ten key issues.

1. The customer
2. The product or project
3. The market: size? growth potential?
4. A strategy for distribution of the product or service
5. A strategy for pricing
6. A strategy for promotion

7. How your company and product relate to the established industry

8. How you propose to compete—and win

9. The environment: political and regulatory, legal, cultural, economic

10. The technological context

TIP

Don't rule out hiring a consultant to help you prepare your business plan. If bringing an expert on board saves time and speeds your proposal to investors and lenders, it's worth it.

YOUR SCRIPTS: PRESENTING YOUR BUSINESS PLAN

If you don't present your business plan in person, a phone call alerting the prospect to its arrival is a valuable step to take:

1. **You:** . . . I am happy to tell you that the business plan for Bookserve, Inc., is on its way by overnight mail. Although it speaks for itself, you might want to look for these highlights: probable return on your investment within six months, profit on start-up capital within three to four years, a client base of 450 to 650 firms, and diversity within a focused, targeted market. It has been a pleasure speaking with you about this project, and I look forward to your response to the business plan. I will call you early next week to get your reaction to it.

2. **You:** . . . After our conversation yesterday, I'm not surprised you asked to see the business plan. You should have it later today. Once you've read through it, you will see why I'm so excited about the company. Now, it is true, as you pointed out, that small presses cannot afford to put much money behind promotion. As I mentioned to you, however, the key to selling books is not advertising but distribution. And that, of course, is what we are all about. You might also bear in mind a few other highlights as you read through the prospectus: probable return on investment within six months, profit on start-up capital in three to four years, client base of 450 to 650 firms, and diversity within a focused, targeted market. It's a winner—but you'll see that for yourself. I'll call you early next week to discuss.

PRESENTING AN ANNUAL REPORT: SECRETS
OF KEEPING THE IDEA ALOFT

Shouldn't an annual report speak for itself? The answer is *yes, but* . . .

Telephoning key investors in advance of sending the annual report can accomplish three things:

1. It personalizes the report, reinforcing the impression that you regard this investor as a key player and partner in your enterprise.

2. It draws attention to highlights and achievements of the year.

3. It explains—or puts into perspective—any disappointments.

YOUR SCRIPTS: ENHANCING THE ANNUAL REPORT

Examples of calls you might make just before the annual report is issued:

1. **You:** . . . I've just sent out to you the first annual report of Bookserve, Inc. You will find it both interesting and, I am happy to say, highly *enjoyable* reading. Like any good investor, you'll go right to the bottom line, of course, and I know you'll like what you see there. But I also respectfully direct your attention to the growth of our client list, which exceeds the prospectus numbers by 14 percent, and our retail penetration, which is right on target.

    George, I am grateful for your support during this past year and trust that you look forward to the next year as much as I do. Give me a call if you have questions about the report.

2. **You:** . . . Fay, I just sent our first annual report out to you. Now, you don't need that report to tell you that we have come through a rough start-up year. But take a good look at the numbers in that report. You'll see that the growth of our client list is right on target, and while our retail penetration has fallen 5 percent behind what we expected, it has picked up with each quarter. For now, in this rocky retail climate, the very good news is that we *have* come through. For the future, the numbers suggest a pattern of increasingly rapid growth.

    Fay, I'm proud of this report, and I greatly appreciate your support during a challenging period. Together, I am confident we can look forward to a brighter future. Call me if you have any questions.

FOLLOWING UP (GO EASY ON THE SPURS)

Following Up with Investor Prospects

Follow-up calls can be valuable in the following situations:

- In the interval between initial contact with a prospect and the next contact, a personal interview, or the transmission of a business plan
- When a prospect fails to return your calls
- If a prospect declines to invest

YOUR SCRIPTS: FOLLOWING UP WITH PROSPECTIVE INVESTORS

The following call would be useful to keep the level of the prospect's excitement high:

You: It was a pleasure speaking with you on the telephone yesterday, and I look forward to our meeting a week from Thursday.

Your questions were stimulating, challenging, shrewd, and entirely appropriate. I am confident that the business plan I will present when I see you answers them all.

What really excites me is that our conversation convinced me that you are the kind of investor Bookserve needs—one who does more than simply throw money at a project. See you Thursday next week.

Here is a follow-up aimed at encouraging the prospect to read a prospectus, business plan, or other material that was left with him:

You: Thanks for giving me the opportunity to present the business plan for Bookserve. It's apparent that you are a careful investor and that you will subject the material I left to a rigorous review. So much the better for Bookserve.

As you do work your way through the proposal, please keep the following points in mind: You can distribute your investment capital over eight quarters, with the option to pull out at any time; your voting privileges on the board of directors are proportional to your investment; you always retain the right to review the list of publishers and titles we will carry; and most important, you are contributing to a 100 percent win-win enterprise. Six hundred fifty deserving companies will profit from your investment. Book retailers will profit from your invest-ment. The book-buying public will profit from your investment. And, yes, *you* will profit from your investment.

Anyway, I'll call back next week, after you've had ample oppor-tunity to review the proposal in depth. In the meantime, of course, don't hesitate to call with questions.

The following scenario is useful when you are met with indifference. This is a message left on the prospect's voice mail:

You: . . . Hello, Carol. You're not one to dodge a call, so I assume you've been too swamped to get back to me on the Bookserve pro-posal. It's a winning proposition, and I'd hate to see us both lose just because we couldn't make contact. I'll call again early next week. In the meantime, I hope you'll have an opportunity to examine the busi-ness plan I left with you.

When you meet with a no, it may or may not be time to move on to another prospect. Follow up with a call if you aren't certain that you gave the initial pitch your best shot:

You: . . . I appreciate the time you gave me to present my proposal for Bookserve, Inc. Of course, I'm disappointed by your decision not to invest in the enterprise. I can't help thinking that, in my zeal to present a detailed plan, I caused you to lose sight of a few essential points that might other-wise have influenced your decision. Did I make the following clear?

First, that you can distribute your investment capital over eight quarters, with the option to pull out at any time. Second, that your vot-ing privileges on the board of directors are proportional to your invest-ment. And, third, that you always retain the right to review the list of publishers and titles we will carry. Are there any questions I left unan-swered? I appreciate the time you've given me. Of course, I'd appreciate even more any time you might devote to reconsidering the proposal.

Following Up with Lenders

In the case of loan applications, a follow-up call may be necessary to get the loan officer off the dime. It is unfortunate that banks are justly notorious for crawling just when you need them to sprint. A judicious follow-up call can help speed things up.

STEP 1:   Begin by letting the loan officer know that you realize how busy he is.

STEP 2:   Go on to explain (without the least trace of whining) why you need a prompt answer.

TIP

The loan officer should feel that you are asking for help not from a faceless bureaucrat, but from an individual who is about to become your de facto business partner. It is amazing, as well as gratifying, to discover that business people welcome opportunities to be helpful. Keeping this fact of human nature in mind makes the chore of follow-up calls much easier.

STEP 3:   Gently goad the loan officer into action by giving him an opportunity to be helpful.

YOUR SCRIPTS: FOLLOWING UP WITH LENDERS

Here are some approaches to sluggish bankers:

1. **You:** . . . It has been *X* days since I submitted my application for this loan. I faxed you on the fifteenth, but I received no reply. I realize that processing a business loan can be painstaking and time-consuming, but I am confident that you appreciate the impossibility of maintaining responsible financial management in the absence of financial information. Mr. Thomas, I need an update on the status of my loan application.

2. **You:** . . . In *X* days, Ms. Donaldson, I face the quarterly chore of advising my backers as to the financial state of my company. Right now there is a disturbingly large question mark looming over "funds available." You, Ms. Donaldson, have it in your power to remove that question mark. Please: Where are we on my loan application? Is there any additional information you need from me?

3. **You:** . . . Silence, they say, is golden, Mr. Kern, but this is taking the virtue a bit far. I first met with you on May tenth and filed my loan application on May fourteenth. Since that time, I have had no substantive word on the status of my application. Is there a problem? If there is, let me in on it, so that we can work together to resolve it. If there is no problem, I need an answer to this application.

HOW TO PUT THE PAST INTO PERSPECTIVE (CREDIT-HISTORY GAFFES AND GLITCHES)

Sorry, but no matter how well you put yourself across, you're not likely to convince any bank or conventional lending institution to give you cash unless you have a decent balance sheet, prospects for a bright future—*and* a reasonably clean credit history. The good news is that "reasonably clean" is a matter of some judgment and, as such, may be colored by the way you present that history.

Most banks and conventional lending institutions will request a formal letter explaining any questionable episodes in a loan applicant's credit history. But even before you put it in writing, you should be prepared with a calm, reasoned *verbal* explanation of credit gaffes and glitches.

STEP 1:   Don't be in *too* great a hurry to explain.

This is one time when it does not pay to be overly proactive. Unless the blemish on your credit history is very substantial and very obvious, let the lender decide whether it is worth discussing. Don't volunteer your opinion that an incident or incidents *require* explanation. Wait to be asked. In the case of "substantial and obvious" credit-history problems, such as the following, you *should* consider speaking with the lender when you discuss terms or at the time that you file your application.

- Bankruptcy
- Legal judgments against you
- Obviously heavy debt load
- Substantial losses

STEP 2:   If you are asked about specific episodes of your credit history, respond calmly. Adopt an even, businesslike tone.

TIP

Avoid defensiveness. Avoid a confessional tone. Avoid such telltale negative body language as failure to make eye contact, biting of the lips, bringing the hands to the face or mouth, and head shaking. Avoid nervous laughter.

STEP 3: Make no obvious attempt to minimize or dismiss the incident in question. The lender *believes* it may be important.

You'll have to *show* that the episode is not significant. If you merely assert that it is not, the lender will tend to assume the opposite, and you will likely be denied the loan.

STEP 4: Provide a concise explanation of the episode, including all mitigating circumstances.

TIP

Be careful that what you say verbally does not conflict with anything you have put in writing or plan to put in writing. Remember, even if you give a persuasive verbal explanation of credit-history gaffes and glitches, you will almost certainly be asked to provide a written explanation as well. You are speaking for the record.

STEP 5: Put the glitch into perspective. Picture it as a small blotch on the otherwise exemplary credit history of a prosperous company.

TIP

Putting a credit-history glitch in perspective—in context—may be the most persuasive tactic available to you. But you *must* work within the facts. You cannot lie. Doing so may, at the least, result in the loan being denied or, even worse, repudiated later. At its worst, giving false information on a loan application is criminal fraud.

STEP 6: End by announcing your availability to answer further questions.

How effective is a good verbal explanation of credit-history difficulties? The effectiveness depends on the gravity of the financial or credit problem in question. If you make it a habit not to pay your bills, no amount of explaining is likely to get you a loan.

YOUR SCRIPTS: HANDLING QUESTIONS ABOUT YOUR CREDIT HISTORY

Here are typical verbal responses to questions about irregularities in credit history. While the answers should never be vague or evasive, do not smother the loan officer in details. Keep the response concise. If the loan officer needs more information, she will ask you. Remember, too, that you will almost certainly be asked subsequently to embody the verbal explanation in a formal letter of explanation.

1. **Lender:** I see that you had a late payment on your corporate credit card last quarter.

   You: That's right. From May 10 to June 5, both principals of our company were out of the country. The explanation for this *single* tardy payment is that neither my partner nor I was present when the bill arrived, and in the backlog of work that had accumulated by the time of our return, this bill was shuffled to the bottom of the heap. That was careless, but it was an accident. I mean, you'll note that the payment was made only 10 days beyond the 30-day limit. We've held the credit card for X years, and this is the single instance of a late payment.

2. **Lender:** I am troubled by three late payments noted in the credit report we secured in processing your loan application.

   You: You will note that all of the late payments occurred during the March to May period. During that time, we lost two of our major clients: ABC Company failed to secure anticipated funding for a project contracted with us, and DEF Company petitioned for Chapter 11 bankruptcy at the end of March. Consequently, our available cash was unexpectedly low for the period. We contacted the credit officers at the three firms in question and arranged deferred payments. I can furnish, in writing, the details of these arrangements, as well as the names of the contact people we worked with. Most important, all of those accounts are now currently up to date.

The following is phone-call response to a query made earlier by the loan officer:

3. **You:** . . . I was surprised and distressed to hear that the SOL Credit Reporting Agency reported late payments to ABC Company. Mr. Larson, this report is in error. I have contacted SOL to advise them of their error and to demand that they correct it. I have also contacted Claire Peters at ABC Company, who has agreed to send you directly a letter confirming that the credit report is indeed in error and affirming our good payment record with them. She'll fax that to you, following it up in the mail with hard copy.

   Mr. Larson, I will call again early next week to confirm that you have received Ms. Peters's letter, and I trust that this credit reporter's error will not delay processing our application.

4. **You:** . . . We have made no secret of the financial problems we experienced last year. The delinquent accounts to which you refer, however, have been settled. I am faxing the relevant documents.

   Ms. Flint, I think you'll agree that our most recent financial statements amply demonstrate that our difficulties are well behind us, and we are in a period of growth and increased profitability. Since June, our credit record—with banks as well as with vendors—has been without blemish. We're not only a good risk, we're a good investment.

WHEN THINGS GO WRONG: RENEGOTIATING TERMS

Sometimes temporary cash-flow problems make it desirable or necessary to renegotiate the terms of a loan. This is a common situation, and it should be met with routine rationality. However, when *Homo sapiens* find it difficult to meet monthly obligations, the species' prime and primal instinct is to run and hide.

The *last* thing he wants to do is contact the lender.

This behavior, instinctive though it may be, is, in fact, very self-destructive.

- The most important time to maintain close communication with a lender is precisely when you are having difficulty paying him.

If you fail to communicate, the lender will naturally assume that you are evading her (because you are) and that you are trying to get away with something (which is exactly what you are trying to do). If, on the other hand, you communicate effectively, you are assuring the lender that, though you have problems and those problems are affecting her as well as yourself, you have no intention of dodging your responsibility. On the contrary, you are anxious to work things out together.

- It is even better to initiate this process of communication *before* your account becomes delinquent.
- If you know that you are going to be unable to meet a payment, advise the lender of this difficulty in advance, proposing, as you do so, a realistic alternative—usually deferred payment.

STEP 1:   Advise the loan officer of the problem.

STEP 2:   Explain the reason for the problem, stressing the (anticipated) temporary nature of the difficulty.

STEP 3:   Propose an alternative.

STEP 4:   Put the problem in perspective: This is a glitch in an otherwise profitable business relationship; it is the exception and most definitely not the rule.

STEP 5:   Apologize, fully acknowledging that your difficulty is creating an "inconvenience" for the lender, and thank the lender for her anticipated "understanding" and "cooperation."

TIP

Where more complex repayment solutions are called for, it is best to enclose a detailed plan with a cover letter, which thanks the lender for her willingness to consider renegotiating the terms of the loan and which also may point to highlights of the proposed plan that benefit the lender.

Your scripts: renegotiating payment terms

Here are some phone scripts for advising a lender of an *anticipated* payment problem:

1. **You:** . . . Because of cash-flow problems resulting from the sudden loss of a major client, we cannot make the May 15 payment before the end of the month. I anticipate that the current shortfall will have been made up by July, so subsequent payments should be on time.

    Because we've enjoyed such a good relationship, I feel comfortable asking you to bear with us for two weeks. I'm sorry for any inconvenience this may cause, but I am very grateful for your assistance.

2. **You:** . . . Payment of receivables due us from several clients by June 1 will be delayed until approximately August 1. This situation is beyond our control, and, unfortunately, it really impacts on our cash flow. I'm going to have to defer a payment due you on June 15. I will be able to make the payment by July 15. Can you live with this?

    Lender: It's not news I wanted to hear. We'll need the request in writing, and I will have to assess a service charge.

    You: I understand. I'll get a letter off to you immediately, and I'm sorry for the inconvenience to you. Thanks for your understanding.

3. **You:** . . . Jill, I have to tell you that, like many businesses in this community, we have been hit hard by the slump in the local economy. Orders this quarter have been off by 24 percent. We are expanding our sales efforts, but I don't see substantial improvement soon.

    We want above all to avoid bankruptcy and to maintain an excellent and equitable relationship with our creditors. To do this, I need to speak with you about renegotiating the terms of repayment of our loan. . . .

4. **You:** . . . You may have heard about the fire in our office, on Friday. The damage from flames and smoke was bad enough, but the water! It's done a number on our hard-copy as well as our computer files. Now, insurance pays for the physical damage, but not for the time lost and revenues deferred as we scramble here to sort out shipping orders, invoices, payments due, and the like. I would be very grateful if you would grant us a thirty-day extension on our payment due this month. This will give us the breathing space we need to clean up here and to collect receivables due us.

HOW TO GET MORE MONEY FROM INVESTORS AND LENDERS

When you return to original investors or lenders with a request for additional funds, you have two good reasons *not* to face your task with dread.

- Experienced salespeople know that their *best* customers are their *current* customers. Repeat business is generally easier to get than new business. The same principle applies to investors. Once an investment commitment is made, it is easier to obtain additional investments than it is to campaign among new prospects.
- Don't ask to be *given* more. Instead, *offer* more. Amplify and increase the opportunity.

The most effective strategies are based on the current investor's commitment and the offer of additional benefits.

Your scripts: getting more money from an investor

Here are some approaches to broaching the subject of additional investment:

1. **You:** . . . So you've had an opportunity to read our first quarterly report?

   Investor: Yes, I have.

   You: As you can see from the numbers, our initial client base is larger than anticipated. That, of course, is great news. But accommodating these added clients requires another $XXXX in start-up funding than we had originally projected. I am sending to you a detailed breakdown of what we need and how an additional investment is likely to increase your returns. We have an opportunity to acquire clients even more quickly than we had originally projected, and I need your help to take advantage of this opportunity for *your* company.

2. **You:** . . . Marsha, I'm very grateful for your offer to invest $XXX in the project. You know, my father used to tell me that, after you make a sale, it's time to shut your mouth. But I can't quite bring myself to do that. Before I go ahead and ask you to send us your check, I would

like you to think more about your investment and to think about value received.

The investment you propose entitles you to XXX shares in the project. An additional $XXX buys XXX more shares. That's an X percent stake in the enterprise.

Marsha, I am delighted to accept any investment you care to make, but I am also eager to ensure that you will be satisfied that you have made the best deal.

Index